HEADSTART IN HISTORY

COLONISATION AND
CONFLICT 1750-1990

SERIES EDITOR: ROSEMARY REES

MARTIN COLLIER

BILL MARRIOTT

Heinemann

Heinemann is an imprint of Pearson Education Limited,
a company incorporated in England and Wales, having
its registered office at Edinburgh Gate, Harlow, Essex,
CM20 2JE. Registered company number: 872828
Heinemann is a registered trademark of
Pearson Education Limited

© Martin Collier and Bill Marriott 2002

First published 2002

ISBN 978-0-435-32304-2

10
10

Produced by Gecko Ltd, Bicester, Oxon
Illustrated by Gecko Ltd, Geoff Ward
Original illustrations © Heinemann Educational Publishers 2002
Cover design by Hicksdesign
Picture research by Liz Moore
Printed and bound in China (CTPS/10)
Index compiled by Ian D. Crane

Photographic acknowledgements

The authors and publisher would like to thank the following for permission to reproduce photographs:

AKG London: 178B; Anti-Slavery International/James Harris: 81B; Bilderdienst Suddeutscher Verlag: 181I; Bridgeman Art Library: 22A, 40G, 55A, 62Q, 246A; Bridgeman Art Library/Imperial War Museum: 121A; Bridgeman Art Library/Manchester City Art Galleries: 87E; Bridgeman Art Library/National Library of Australia: 27A; Bridgeman Art Library/Royal Agricultural Society of England: 51E; Bridgeman Art Library/The Illustrated London News Picture Library: 93A; Bridgeman Art Library/Walker Art Gallery: 19A; Camera Press/Don McCullin: 231E; Corbis: 80A, 139A, 221H, 251C; Corbis/AFP: 253D; Corbis/Michael St. Maur Sheil: 134B; Corbis/Richard T. Nowitz: 202B, 224L; Eye Ubiquitous/Paul Thompson: 132E; Getty Images: 241B; Hulton Archive/H. Mille: 189G; Hulton Archive: 59J, 161A, 164H, 240A; Hulton Deutsche: 57F; Hulton Getty: 168Q; Imperial War Museum: 144C; John Webb: 85D; Mary Evans Picture Library: 9B, 29B, 90B, 141I; National Portrait Gallery: 69D; Peter Newark's Historical Pictures: 33A, 228B; Peter Newark's Military Pictures: 11A; Popperfoto: 170A, 185B; Popperfoto/Bob Thomas: 76D; Popperfoto/United Press International: 208A; Post Office: 64A; Punch: 78A, 104A, 133A, 180G; Rex Features: 213H; Robert Hunt Library: 115B, 162B; Sam Nzima: 211E; Science & Society Picture Library/National Railway Museum: 70F; Science & Society Picture Library/Science Museum: 57C, 59I, 68C, 96C, 97D; Topham Picturepoint: 38C, 101B, 136D, 172C, 187C, 195A, 222I; Topham Picturepoint/Press Association: 234F; USHMM Photo Archives: 197A; Wellcome Library: 43J

Cover photograph © Imperial War Museum

Written acknowledgements

The authors and publishers gratefully acknowledge the following publications from which written sources in the book are drawn. In some sources the wording or sentence structure has been simplified.

P. Addison *The War is Over* (BBC, London, 1985): 168P; Alan Brooks & Jeremy Brickhill *Whirlwind before the Storm* (International Defence & Aid Fund for Southern Africa, 1980): 211F; Angus Calder *The Myth of the Blitz* (J. Cape, London, 1991): 154F; John Charmley *Churchill: The End of Glory* (Hodder, 1993): 154E; Sebastian Faulks *Birdsong* (Vintage, London, 1993): 125C; Niall Ferguson *The Pity of War* (Allen Lane, London, 1998): 145B; Peter Fleming *Invasion 1940* (White Lion Publishers, 1958): 163D; Lucy Freeman & Alma Bond *America's First Woman Warrior: The Courage of Deborah Sampson* (Paragon House, 1992): 16E; Pauline Gregg A Social & Economic History of Britain, 1760–1980 (Harrap, 1969): 92E; Pheobe A. Hanaford *Daughters of America – The story of Deborah Samson* (B.B.Russell, Boston, 1982): 15D; Adam Hart-Davis *Science & Technology* (London National Portrait Gallery, 1995): 60K; Mark Hovell *The Chartist Movement* (Manchester University Press, 1917): 92E; Philip Ingram *Challenge & Change: A Modern World Study after 1900* (Hodder & Stoughton, 2000): 191H; Rudyard Kipling *The School History of England* (1911): 34E; Rudyard Kipling *The White Man's Burden* (1898): 26H; G. Kitson Clark *The Making of Victorian England* (1965): 78C; Norman Langmate *The Home Front: An Anthology of Personal Experience* 1938–45 (Chatto & Windus, 1981): 163F; Stuart Miller *Mastering Modern European History* (Macmillan Education, 1997): 191K; Christabel Pankhurst *Unshakled* (Morgan & Scott, 1959): 103H; B.N. Pandey *The Break-up of British India* (1969): 26G; Frank Richards *Old Soldiers Never Die* (1933): 145D; Dan Roberts *A Moment in Time* (University of Richmond, 1993): 23D; Siegfried Sassoon *The Complete Memoirs of George Sherston* (Faber and Faber, 1937): 145C; Jon Stallworthy (Ed.) *Wilfred Owen/The Complete Poems and Fragments* (Chatto & Windus, 1983): 143B; Ralph Stedman Jones *Language of Class* (1982): 92F; A.J.P. Taylor *English History 1914–1945* (Penguin, 1965): 162C

Websites

On pages where you are asked to go to www.heinemann.co.uk/hotlinks to complete a task or download information, please insert the code 3040P where prompted.

Contents

Expansion of trade and empire 1750–1900

In 1900 Britain had an empire that covered a quarter of the world's land surface. An empire is when one country, in this case Britain, gains control and has power over another country or countries. How was it that Britain, a relatively small north-west European island, was able to gain such power? The key to understanding this question is by looking at three important factors: trade, war and exploration.

There are two very clear stages to the development and growth of the British Empire:

- **The old colonial system**. From 1750 to the middle of the nineteenth century, the main reason for building an empire was to improve trade. The aim of the British was to set up colonies in the Americas and Asia in order to provide goods such as sugar and tobacco. The colonies also served as an important market for British goods. The British used their armed forces to set up colonies and to prevent Britain's rivals, especially France and Russia, from building up empires of the same size.

- **The 'new imperialism'**. It wasn't until towards the end of the nineteenth century that the empire was popular with the British people. Slavery, which had been such an important part of the British Empire in the eighteenth century (see pages 7–9) was abolished and colonies such as Canada wanted some kind of self-government. However, the empire continued to grow, especially in Africa. From the 1870s onwards this expansion was increasingly justified by the idea of what the poet, Rudyard Kipling, called 'the white man's burden'. Behind this view was the racist belief in the superiority of the white British and their ability to 'civilise' the world.

Trade remained the essential element of the empire. The empire lasted so long (until after the Second World War) because of the ability of the British to protect successfully their gains.

Trade and empire

From the mid-seventeenth century to the early nineteenth century, the builders of the empire were not governments but trading companies, such as the East India Company. This company was given a charter (which meant it was given permission) by Queen Elizabeth I in 1600 to trade with countries in the East. Trading companies attempted to gain land and seize control of raw materials in whichever area they were operating. Most importantly, the trading companies wanted to create a monopoly (complete control over trade in something) in the raw materials they were dealing in.

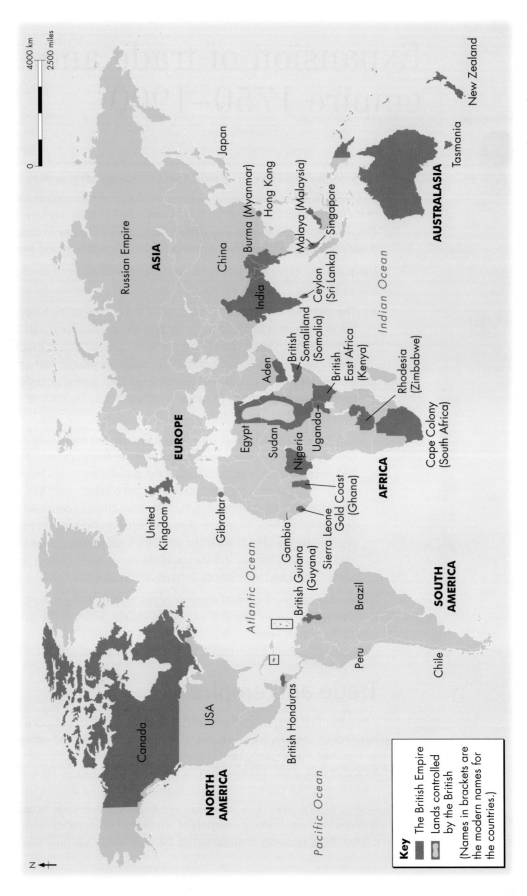

The British Empire in 1900.

Key
- The British Empire
- Lands controlled by the British

(Names in brackets are the modern names for the countries.)

NORTH AMERICA
- Canada
- USA
- British Honduras

SOUTH AMERICA
- British Guiana (Guyana)
- Peru
- Brazil
- Chile

EUROPE
- United Kingdom
- Gibraltar

AFRICA
- Gambia
- Sierra Leone
- Gold Coast (Ghana)
- Nigeria
- Egypt
- Sudan
- Uganda
- British East Africa (Kenya)
- British Somaliland (Somalia)
- Aden
- Rhodesia (Zimbabwe)
- Cape Colony (South Africa)

ASIA
- Russian Empire
- China
- Japan
- India
- Burma (Myanmar)
- Hong Kong
- Ceylon (Sri Lanka)
- Malaya (Malaysia)
- Singapore

AUSTRALASIA
- Tasmania
- New Zealand

Atlantic Ocean
Pacific Ocean
Indian Ocean

0 — 4000 km
0 — 2500 miles

N

When other European countries such as France, the Netherlands or Spain challenged a British company's trade in goods, the British government often stepped in to fight on their behalf (although some companies, such as the East India Company, had their own armies). The governments intervened because at the time most people believed in the ideas known as mercantilism. These ideas were:

- Wealth is created by trade.

- All nations want to sell more goods abroad (exports) than they buy from abroad (imports). Therefore trade has to be controlled.

- The best way to control trade is to create colonies. This means that a country can control what is imported and exported by their colonies. It also means that there is a market for exports.

- It is the role of the government to protect trade, both with armies and with tariffs (a tax imposed on goods imported into a country).

What was the slave trade?

In the seventeenth and eighteenth centuries, one of the most profitable trades was in slaves. As Portuguese, Spanish, French and British settlers in South America and the West Indies began to grow sugar cane, cotton and tobacco crops, so their demand for workers increased. It was the British, more than any other nation, that developed the Atlantic slave system known as the 'Triangular Trade' (see below). Each leg of the trade carried different items to trade.

The Triangular Trade.

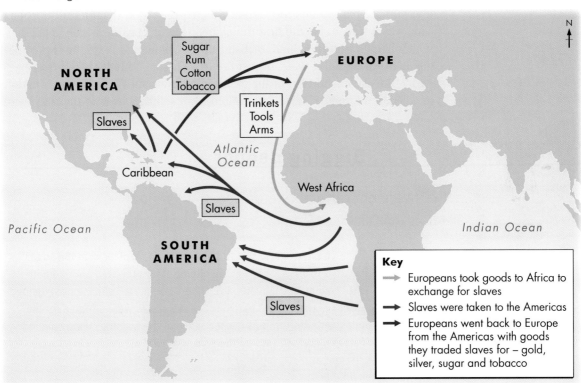

- Europe to Africa: manufactured and other goods were exchanged for slaves.

- Africa to the Americas: slaves were sold to plantation owners.

- The Americas to Europe: raw materials such as cotton and goods such as tobacco and sugar were traded.

European slave traders got slaves in a number of ways. Occasionally they mounted raids on the West African coast, capturing Africans whom they then enslaved. African and Arab slave traders brought slaves to slave markets on the West African coast. There they would be bought by European slave traders. These slave traders brought goods from Europe which they exchanged for the slaves. The slaves would then be transported to the Americas on a journey known as the 'Middle Passage'. Between 1700 and 1807 around 12 million Africans were transported across the Atlantic. Roughly fifteen per cent of those transported died on the journey. Investigations into the slave trade revealed that conditions on board the slave ships were horrific. In 1788 a committee of the House of Commons in London found that the slave ship *The Brookes* was carrying over 600 slaves from Africa to the Americas. This was despite the fact that the ship was designed to carry only 451 people.

The impact of the slave trade was considerable. Huge fortunes were created and ports such as Liverpool, Bristol and Glasgow were built on the profits of the trade in slaves. Between 1690 and 1807 around 11,000 ships left Britain, half of them from Liverpool, intending to trade in slaves. As a result of the slave trade and the work of slaves in the West Indian sugar, cotton and tobacco plantations the standard of living rose in Britain and Europe. This was because, for the first time, cheap sugar became widely available, which helped improve diets. British industry benefited from the export of its goods to Africa but it was not just the British who benefited from slavery. In Africa the slave trade led to the creation of powerful West African kingdoms as a small number of Africans profited from selling slaves to the Europeans.

Digging deeper

What were conditions like on the slave ships?

SOURCE A

Throughout the journey the slaves were chained together by their hands and feet. They had to eat, sleep and relieve themselves in the same place. Slaves were often kept below deck in the dark. Diseases such as smallpox and dysentery wiped out considerable numbers of slaves. Because the slaves were kept in such poor and inhuman conditions they were often unable to work on arrival in the Americas. Many died within the first three years of work in the sugar plantations. Some slaves resisted and jumped overboard. Others committed suicide by refusing to eat. Many of the slaves were crippled for life as a consequence of the way they were chained up on the ship.

An historian writing in 2001.

SOURCE B

An engraving from 1861 showing a slave being lowered into the hold of a slave ship.

SOURCE C

At last, when the ship, in which we were, had got in all her cargo, they made ready with many fearful noises, and we were all put under deck ... The stench of the hold, while we were on the coast, was so intolerably horrible, that it was dangerous to remain there for any time ... The closeness of the place, and the heat of the climate, added to the number in the ship, being so crowded that each had scarcely room to run himself, almost suffocated us ... the air soon became unfit for respiration [breathing], from a variety of loathsome smells and brought on a sickness among the slaves, of which many died ... This deplorable situation was aggravated by the galling [rubbing] of the chains ... and the filth of necessary tubs [toilets], into which the children often fell, and were almost suffocated. The shrieks of the women, and the groans of the dying, rendered it a scene of horror almost inconceivable.

Olaudah Equiano wrote this in 1789. At the age of eleven, he was captured by slave traders and was loaded onto a slave ship.

Question time

Look back at Sources A, B and C.

1   What do the sources tell us about the treatment of slaves in the 'Middle Passage'?

2   Discussion point. Slaves were regarded by slave traders as cargo. Why, then, did the traders not take better care of them?

British North America

From the beginning of the seventeenth century Europeans had settled on the eastern coast of North America (see the map below). In Virginia tobacco was grown and in New England settlers worked the land previously owned by Native Americans. In 1651, the British Parliament passed the Navigation Act which stated that all goods to and from the colonies must be carried on British ships. This was an important step in Britain's attempt to dominate trade. However, there was competition from the French and Dutch who were also trading in valuable goods such as spices and furs. This competition over trade spilled into war.

The British and French at war

In what is now Canada, French settlers threatened British control of North America. The French settled along the north banks of the St Lawrence River and controlled the valuable fur trade from their base in Arcadia. In 1713, the British gained control of Arcadia and Newfoundland by the Treaty of Utrecht. However, the British were still threatened by the French in North America. In 1745, the British and French fought over Nova Scotia and in 1753–4 they fought over the Ohio Valley.

In 1755, the Seven Years' War broke out between Britain and France (although it was not officially declared until 1756). Initially the French, under General Montcalm, defeated the British and took strategically important forts such as Fort William Henry in 1757. The crucial turning

British North America in the seventeenth century.

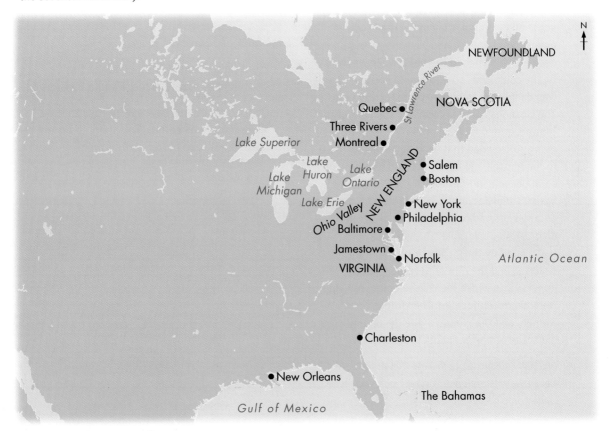

point of the war was the battle for Quebec, the heart of French Canada. The city of Quebec guards the mouth to the St Lawrence River, one of the most important trading routes into the centre of North America.

The task faced by the British Commander General Wolfe of capturing Quebec was a considerable one. Quebec could be reached only by climbing high cliffs or by a more roundabout route which was heavily guarded by the French. Wolfe and his army arrived by sea in June and set up camp at the Ile d'Orléans near Quebec. Wolfe was undecided about how to attack Quebec and his first attempt at capturing the city was defeated by the French.

The next plan adopted by Wolfe was far more daring. On the night of 12 September 1759, nearly 5000 soldiers were rowed up the river and they disembarked at the bottom of the steep cliffs at Anse de Foulon, only a couple of kilometres from the centre of Quebec. Without being detected, the British soldiers climbed the 60-metre high cliffs. The French were caught by surprise and lost the battle which followed on the Plains of Abraham outside Quebec, although Wolfe died in the assault. The French defeat at Quebec was followed by the surrender of Montreal in September 1760 and the passing of French Canada into British hands.

Digging deeper

The death of General Wolfe: myth or reality?

There is no doubt Wolfe's victory and death at Quebec made him a hero of the British Empire. However, to the French speakers of Quebec, Wolfe was a conqueror and an oppressor from a foreign land.

SOURCE A

Benjamin West's painting Death of Wolfe, *completed in 1770.*

SOURCE B

The order was given to charge. Then over the field rose the British cheer, mixed with the fierce yell of the Highland slogan. Some of the soldiers pushed forward with the bayonet; some advanced firing. The clansmen drew their broadswords and dashed on, keen and swift as bloodhounds. At the English right, though the attacking column [of French soldiers] was broken to pieces, a fire was still kept up, chiefly, it seems, by sharpshooters from the bushes and cornfields, where they had lain for an hour or more. Here Wolfe himself led the charge, at the head of the Louisbourg grenadiers. A shot shattered his wrist. He wrapped his handkerchief about it and kept on. Another shot struck him, and he still advanced, when a third lodged in his breast. He staggered, and sat on the ground. Lieutenant Brown, of the grenadiers, one Henderson, a volunteer in the same company, and a private soldier, aided by an officer of the artillery who ran to join them, carried him in their arms to the rear. He begged them to lay him down. They did so, and asked if he would have a surgeon. 'There's no need,' he answered, 'it's all over with me.' A moment after, one of them cried out, 'They run, see how they run!' 'Who run?' Wolfe demanded, like a man roused from sleep. 'The enemy, sir. Egad, they give way everywhere!' 'Go, one of you, to Colonel Burton,' returned the dying man, 'tell him to march Webb's regiment down to Charles river, to cut off their retreat from the bridge.' Then, turning on his side, he murmured, 'Now, God be praised, I will die in peace!' and in a few moments his gallant soul had fled.

Extract from a book by Francis Parkman in 1886. Parkman was a British writer in favour of the empire.

Question time

1 a Describe what you can see in the painting in Source A.

   b What do you think is the message of the painting?

2 Look back at Sources A and B.

   a What are the similarities and differences in these two accounts of General Wolfe's death?

   b How useful are the two sources as evidence for someone trying to find out about the death of General Wolfe?

The American War of Independence 1776–81

As well as being the most important issue in the British domination of North America, trade, and the taxation of trade, was to cause division between the British government and the British settlers in America. From 1776–81 Britain found itself at war with some of the colonists in what became a struggle for American independence from Britain.

The Seven Years' War with France, which ended in 1763, had been very expensive for the British government. Many politicians in Britain believed that the American colonists should help pay for the costs of the war, given the fact that it had been fought to protect them from the French settlers. In 1764 the British Parliament passed the Sugar Act which placed a tax on importing molasses (a dark juice processed during sugar refinement) into the colonies. In 1765 the Stamp Act placed a tax on the sale of newspapers, legal documents and even playing cards and dice.

These moves angered the American colonists. They did not have any representatives in the British Parliament to speak on their behalf. The cry of the colonists became 'No taxation without representation'. Although the Stamp Act was repealed (ended) in 1766, the opposition of the colonists provoked the British government into passing the Declaratory Act in March 1766. This act declared that the king and Parliament had the right to make laws in the colonies. The act provoked further tension, especially as the British government demanded the right to keep their troops in the colonists' houses.

The Boston Tea Party

In 1767 the Chancellor of the Exchequer in London, Charles Townsend, imposed duties (taxes) in the colonies on a number of goods. The money raised was used to pay royal officials in America. Tension and riots in Boston led to British troops being sent there in 1768 to control the violence. Their arrival was most unpopular and in March 1770 a riot led to five Bostonians being killed when British troops fired on the mob. Although the Townsend duties were relaxed, the tax on tea remained.

In December 1773 the East India Company attempted to land a consignment of tea in Boston. A group of Bostonians boarded the ship carrying the tea and threw it into the water. The government responded to this incident, known as the Boston Tea Party, by closing the port of Boston. The Prime Minister, Lord North, believed that the American colonists should accept the rule of Parliament, but by now many Americans would not accept the authority of the British government. In September 1774 representatives from the colonies met in Philadelphia to draw up a plan of action.

Events escalated. In April 1775 British troops marched to seize weapons reportedly hidden at the town of Concord. A Boston silversmith, Paul Revere, rode to Lexington to warn the locals of the advancing British troops. When the British arrived in Lexington, they were faced by an army of around 70 men, led by Captain John Parker. This was the trigger for the outbreak of the American War of Independence which lasted until 1781. Some important events in this war are:

- **June 1775**: The Battle of Bunker Hill. The first major battle between American and British forces. The British won but suffered heavy casualties.

- **July 1776**: The thirteen American colonies issued the Declaration of Independence (see page 14).

- **October 1777**: The Battle of Saratoga. The British were defeated and this encouraged France to join the war on the side of the American colonists.

- **October 1781**: The British General Cornwallis surrendered after the siege of Yorktown.

The Declaration of Independence

By the middle of 1776, many Americans had come to the conclusion that they should be fully independent from Britain. This idea was strengthened by the publication of the book *Common Sense* written by an English writer, Thomas Paine. On 7 June 1776 a member of Congress (the elected representatives of the people of America), Richard Henry, proposed that 'these United Colonies are and of right ought to be free and independent states'. Congress agreed and appointed a committee led by Thomas Jefferson to prepare a document entitled *The Unanimous Declaration of the Thirteen United States of America*.

SOURCE C

We hold these truths to be self-evident, that all men are created equal, that they are endowed by their creator with certain unalienable rights, that among these are life, liberty, and the pursuit of happiness. That, to secure these rights, governments are instituted among men, deriving their just powers from the consent of the governed. That, whenever any form of government becomes destructive of these ends, it is the right of the people to alter or to abolish it, and to institute new government ...

An extract from the Declaration of Independence.

The aftermath of war

The British lost the American War of Independence because:

- the quality of British military leadership in America was poor

- the intervention of France in October 1777 swung the balance in favour of the Americans.

However, for the British Empire the impact of the war did not last too long. The ideas known as mercantilism (see page 7) were falling out of favour and were being replaced by the ideas of Adam Smith. In his book *The Wealth of Nations*, Smith argued in favour of free trade. This means that countries could trade without restrictions, such as import and export taxes.

The loss of the American colonies meant that, from now on, the British would look to trade in the East. Other colonies were developed for different reasons. Convicts from Britain had been settled in Virginia in America, but now they would be settled in Australia.

Question time

What do you feel to be the most important cause and consequence of the American War of Independence? Explain your answer fully.

Digging deeper

The story of Deborah Samson

On both sides, women were fully involved in the American War of Independence. Their role, in the main, was as camp followers (people who followed the soldiers around the country) rather than as soldiers. However, there are examples of extraordinary women who masked their true identity in order to take part in the conflict. One of the best known of these women was Deborah Samson. Below are a selection of accounts about Deborah written by historians (note that they do not agree about the spelling of her name).

SOURCE D

In October of 1778 Deborah Samson of Plymouth, Massachusetts disguised herself as a young man and presented herself to the American army as a willing volunteer to oppose the common enemy [the British]. She enlisted for the whole term of the war as Robert Shirtliffe and served in the company of Captain Nathan Thayer of Medway, Massachusetts.

For three years she served in various duties and was wounded twice – the first time by a sword cut on the side of the head and four months later she was shot through the shoulder. Her sexual identity went undetected until she came down with a brain fever, then prevalent [widespread] among the soldiers. The attending physician, Dr Binney of Philadelphia, discovered her disguise, but said nothing. When her health was restored the doctor met with Robert's commanding officer and subsequently an order was issued for Robert Shirtliffe to carry a letter to General Washington.

When the order came for her to deliver the letter into the hands of the Commander-in-Chief, she knew that her deception was over. She presented herself at the headquarters of Washington,

trembling with dread and uncertainty. General Washington, to spare her embarrassment, said nothing. Instead he sent her with an aide to have some refreshments, then summoned her back. In silence Washington handed Deborah Samson a discharge from the service, a note with some words of advice, and a sum of money sufficient to cover her expenses home.

After the war Deborah Samson married Benjamin Gannett of Sharon and they had three children. During George Washington's presidency [George Washington became President of the United States of America after the war] she received a letter inviting Robert Shirtliffe, or rather Mrs Gannett, to visit Washington. During her stay at the capital she was granted a pension [regular sum of money], in addition to certain lands, which she was to receive as an acknowledgement for her services to the country in a military capacity as a revolutionary soldier.

From Daughters of America *(1982) by Phebe A. Hanaford.*

SOURCE E

It was Deborah's desire to avoid hard labour on the family farm that led her to impersonate a man and join the American army. Sampson first enlisted [joined the army] under the name Timothy Thayer early in 1782. When she failed to report for duty after a night spent drinking at a local tavern, her true identity was discovered. In May of 1782, she re-enlisted, this time in Captain George Webb's Co. 4th Massachusetts Regiment, under the name of Robert Shurtleff. She took part in several battles and in 1783 was named aide-de-camp to General John Paterson at West Point. Her identity was again discovered during the summer of 1783 by a physician who treated her when she became seriously ill. Shortly thereafter she was honourably discharged [let out] from the army. She subsequently returned to Massachusetts where she married.

From America's First Woman Warrior: The courage of Deborah Sampson *(1992) by Lucy Freeman and Alma Bond.*

SOURCE F

Deborah Sampson was the first known American woman to impersonate a man in order to join the army and take part in combat.

Deborah's youth was spent in poverty. For ten years as a servant she helped with the housework and worked in the field. Hard labour developed her physical strength. On 20 May, 1782, when she was 21, Sampson enlisted in the Fourth Massachusetts Regiment of the Continental Army at Bellingham as a man named Robert Shurtleff (also listed as Shirtliff or Shirtlieff). On 23 May, she joined the militia. Being 5 foot 7 inches tall, she looked tall for a woman and she had bound her breasts tightly to approximate a male physique. Other soldiers teased her about not having to shave, but they assumed that this 'boy' was just too young to grow facial hair. Sampson was sent with her regiment to West Point, New York, where she apparently was wounded in the leg in a battle near Tarrytown. She tended her own wounds so that her gender would not be discovered. As a result, her leg never healed properly. However, when she was later hospitalised for fever in Philadelphia, the physician attending her discovered that she was a woman and made discreet arrangements that ended her military career. Sampson was honourably discharged from the army at West Point on 25 October 1783 by General Henry Knox.

Deborah Sampson returned home, married a farmer named Benjamin Gannett, and had three children. After Paul Revere sent a letter to Congress on her behalf in 1804, she started receiving a US pension of the amount of four dollars per month.

An historian posting information on the Internet, 2001.

Question time

Look again at Sources D, E and F.

1   Distinguish between fact (something that can be checked) and opinion in each of the three sources. Place your findings in a chart like the one below:

Deborah Samson	
Facts	**Opinions**

2   Why do you think that there are conflicting stories about Deborah Samson?

3   Use the information given in the three sources to write a biography of Deborah Samson.

The Napoleonic Wars 1793–1815

Britain's success in war was the main reason for building a large empire. The last great colonial wars of the eighteenth century were the Napoleonic Wars which were fought against France on and off from 1793 until 1815.

There are a number of reasons why war broke out between Britain and France:

- In 1789 a revolution had taken place in France and a Republic (a country without a king or queen) was declared. The French King Louis XVI had attempted to escape from the revolutionaries but was captured, tried and executed in January 1793. This execution was condemned by politicians in countries such as Britain which were still monarchies. The British Prime Minister, William Pitt, called the execution of Louis XVI the 'foulest and most atrocious act the world has ever seen'.

- Pitt was also worried that the French had broken a treaty respecting the independence of the Netherlands.

Tension between the two countries reached such a peak that in February 1793 France declared war on Britain.

War on two fronts

The Napoleonic Wars were made up of two wars:

- War on land in Europe in which France fought against Britain's allies – Prussia, Austria and Russia. The British did not have a strong army and it was Pitt's policy to give loans and money to his allies to fight the French. This policy was not a great success.

- War in the colonies and at sea. In this war Britain was far more successful because its navy was superior to any other. Because of this success, Britain's empire was secure for most of the nineteenth century.

The French forces in Europe were ably led by a brilliant and ambitious young army officer, Napoleon Bonaparte. In 1796 and 1797 Napoleon conquered much of Italy and defeated Austria. In 1797 and 1798 it seemed as if the French might invade Britain. Morale was low as the mutiny in the British Royal Navy at Spithead in 1797 showed. A rebellion in Ireland in 1798 led by Wolfe Tone acted as a further threat to British security.

However, Napoleon did not feel that his army was capable of invading Britain successfully. Instead he planned to defeat Britain by destroying the British Empire. In 1798 he invaded Egypt and quickly defeated the army of the Egyptian rulers at the Battle of the Pyramids in July. Further progress was halted when the French navy was defeated at the Battle of the Nile by a fleet led by a young British Admiral, Horatio Nelson.

The Egyptian episode fits neatly into the pattern of the Napoleonic Wars. For most of the time, Napoleon's armies were victorious but the Royal Navy dominated the seas. Soon after the Battle of the Nile, Nelson won another famous victory at Copenhagen. In 1805 came his greatest triumph.

During this year Napoleon won a series of impressive victories against Britain's Austrian and Russian allies at Ulm and then at Austerlitz. However, at sea, again, it was a different story.

The threat of invasion and Trafalgar

Napoleon realised that the only way to defeat Britain was to gain control of the seas. By 1805 the danger of the invasion of Britain seemed even nearer. Along the British coast defensive towers known as Martello towers were built. Some of these towers can still be seen today. The fear that French spies had landed in England ahead of invasion led to suspicion of all newcomers. There is a story that in Hartlepool, a monkey that had come ashore after a shipwreck was seized by local fishermen. Not knowing what a French person looked like, they tried the monkey on a charge of spying for the French and executed it by hanging.

In March 1805 the French Admiral Villeneuve put together a French fleet in the West Indies and set sail for the English Channel in order to protect any invasion force. As his fleet sailed back to Europe, Villeneuve's ships were forced off course by the weather and took refuge in Cadiz harbour in Spain.

Napoleon had already formed an alliance with Spain in 1804 and on 21 October 1805, a joint French and Spanish fleet emerged from Cadiz harbour. They found a British Royal Navy fleet led by Admiral Nelson in *HMS Victory* waiting for them off the coast of Trafalgar in Spain. During the battle that followed, French naval power was destroyed – 18 out of the 33 French and Spanish warships were sunk. During the battle Nelson was mortally wounded but became a hero for many generations to come. The victory at Trafalgar marked the beginning of British naval supremacy throughout the nineteenth century.

Nelson's victories broke the power of the French navy which up until then had been the Royal Navy's most powerful rival. From 1806 Napoleon tried to starve Britain into defeat by preventing other countries from trading with it. This was known as the Continental Blockade. It did not work because after Trafalgar, the Royal Navy was powerful enough to protect British trading ships bringing goods to Britain from around the world.

Digging deeper

Did Nelson die a hero?

All societies have their heroes. The heroes of our generation include sportsmen and women, pop stars or television celebrities. War often creates heroes for people to idolise and look up to. The British hero of the Napoleonic Wars was undoubtedly Horatio Nelson.

During the Battle of Trafalgar, Nelson used the battleship *Victory* as his flagship. It was from this ship that his famous last order to his fleet was sent. Using semaphore flags he ordered, 'England expects that every man will do his duty'.

As the battle progressed, Nelson watched his plans unfold from the deck of the *Victory*. In the early nineteenth century, battleships would fire cannon at each other from close range. In the rigging that surrounded the masts of these ships, snipers would fire at those on enemy ships nearby. One such sniper managed to fatally wound Nelson.

Nelson's body was brought back to England, preserved in a cask of brandy. Although it was guarded night and day by a sentry, this did not prevent the sailors on the *Victory* draining the brandy from the cask through tubes of macaroni. As the level of brandy dropped, so the cask was filled with wine. Soon after his arrival back in England, Nelson was buried as a hero in St Paul's Cathedral in London.

Many stories were told of his death. Read the following accounts carefully.

SOURCE A

Horatio Nelson was a vain, arrogant man. It was arrogance that led him to leave his wife, Fanny Nisbett, and set up house with the glamorous Emma Hamilton. It was his vanity that led to his death. Wearing full dress uniform and all his medals, he was a sitting target for a French sniper as he strutted about on the deck of his flagship, *Victory*.

An historian writing in 2002.

SOURCE B

Such a battle could not be fought without sustaining a great loss of men. I have not only to lament, in common with the British Navy, and the British Nation, the Fall of the Commander in Chief, the loss of a Hero, whose name will be immortal, and his memory ever dear to his country: but my heart is rent with the most poignant grief for the death of a friend ... his Lordship received a musket ball in his left breast, about the middle of the action, and sent an officer to me immediately with his last farewell; and soon after expired.

From an account written by Vice Admiral Collingwood in his report on the Battle of Trafalgar to the Admiralty, 1805.

SOURCE C

If ever there was a man who deserved to be praised, wept and honoured it is Lord Nelson. His three great naval victories have eclipsed the brilliancy of the most dazzling victories in the annals of English daring.

The Times, 7 November 1805.

SOURCE D

The Death of Nelson *by Daniel Maclise, painted in 1859–64.*

What was the turning point for Napoleon?

In 1812, Napoleon's armies invaded Russia. However, defeat in Russia marked the turn in Napoleon's fortunes on the continent. As his enemies invaded France in 1814 Napoleon abdicated (stepped down) as French Emperor and was exiled to the island of Elba, off the west coast of Italy. The allies (Britain, Austria, Prussia and Russia) met in Vienna to arrange a peace treaty, thinking that the war was over. Napoleon, however, was determined to try one last time to defeat his enemies. He escaped from Elba, returned to Paris, raised an army and marched into Belgium. The allies raised an army to face Napoleon and they met on 18 June 1815 near the Belgian town of Waterloo.

At Waterloo the allied army was led by the Duke of Wellington and included soldiers from Britain, Holland and Prussia. The battle was a ferocious one. Throughout the day, the French threw wave after wave of soldiers against the allied lines; however the lines held. In the late afternoon the Prussians, led by General Blücher, arrived and the day was won. Napoleon surrendered a few days later, abdicated, and was exiled the second and final time to the remote island of St Helena in the Atlantic Ocean where he died in 1821.

The Napoleonic Wars.

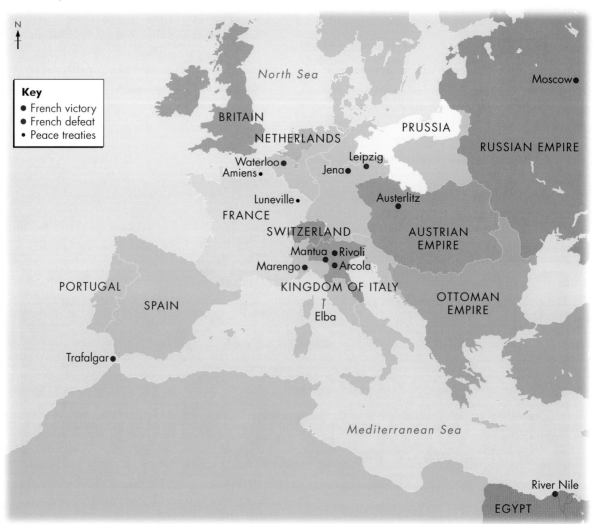

A timeline of the main events of the Napoleonic Wars

1793 France declares war on Britain and its ally, Spain.

1796–7 The French General Napoleon commands the French army in victories against the Austrians at Arcola, Rivoli, and Mantua.

1798 Napoleon conquers Egypt after the Battle of the Pyramids. The British admiral Lord Nelson defeats the French fleet at the Battle of the Nile.

1799 Napoleon becomes virtual ruler of France.

1800 Napoleon defeats the Austrians at Marengo.

1801 Peace with Austria at Luneville. Nelson defeats the Danish at the Battle of Copenhagen.

1802 Peace with Britain at Amiens. Napoleon breaks treaties and takes Piedmont and Switzerland.

1803 Britain declares war on France. Alliance between France and Spain.

1804 Napoleon crowns himself Emperor of France. Spain declares war on Britain.

1805 Napoleon is crowned King of Italy. Nelson defeats the combined French and Spanish fleets at Trafalgar but dies. Napoleon wins a major victory at Austerlitz.

1806 Napoleon's victory at Jena virtually destroys the Prussian army.

1807 Allied with Russia in the Treaty of Tilsit, France declares war on Portugal.

1808 The Peninsular War in Spain begins.

1809 The French defeat the Austrians at Wagram.

1810 France annexes Holland.

1812 Napoleon invades Russia. His Grande Armée retreats from Moscow and is destroyed.

1813 Napoleon is defeated at Leipzig in the Battle of Nations. France loses control of Germany.

1814 The British General the Duke of Wellington invades France from Spain. The allies enter France from Germany. Napoleon abdicates and is exiled to the island of Elba.

1815 The Congress of Vienna decides the terms of peace. Napoleon escapes back to France and raises an army. Napoleon is defeated at Waterloo and exiled to St Helena in the Atlantic Ocean where he dies in 1821.

Investigation

1 a Build up a fact file of the life story of Nelson. You should use the Internet and books in your library for your research.

   b Write an essay on why people at the time considered Nelson to be a hero. In your essay compare Nelson to anyone you look up to today.

2 An obituary is an account of someone's life, written after their death. Obituaries usually praise people but criticisms are often made, wrapped in praise. Research the life story of an individual from this period, such as Emma Hamilton, Napoleon or Wellington. Write an obituary for your person, taking note of the comment above. Remember obituaries usually praise but can subtly criticise.

India,1750–1948

The importance of India to the British Empire was in its wealth and trade. By 1900 India was so central a part of the empire that it became known as the 'Jewel in the Crown'. In 1948, India gained its independence from Britain.

The rise of the East India Company

In the sixteenth century, merchants from England began trading with India, buying cloth, spices and precious stones. Such was the importance of this trade that from the middle of the seventeenth century, the East India Company set up its own trading communities in a number of places on the Indian coast. Over time the East India Company became a powerful organisation. It controlled trade in many parts of India by making agreements with local princes (nawabs). By 1750 the company had built large bases at Madras, Calcutta and Bombay.

As in the Americas, the main rival for trade with the Indian sub-continent was France. During the Seven Years' War, while General Wolfe was capturing Quebec (see pages 10–12) an equally famous British general, Robert Clive, was defeating the French at the Battle of Plassey. The importance of this victory was that it destroyed French claims in India.

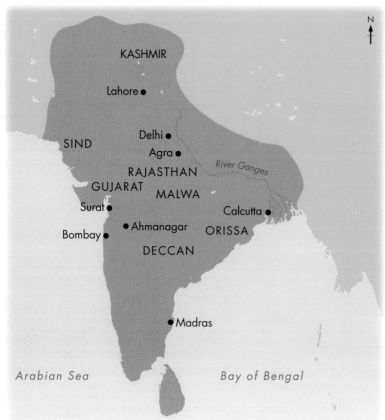

India in 1750.

SOURCE A

The barracks at Fort William, Calcutta. The Black Hole is behind the barred windows.

In 1756, the Nawab of Bengal, who was fighting on the side of the French, attacked the East India Company's Fort William at Calcutta and imprisoned the British men and women that he had captured. They were kept overnight in a cell and, because of overcrowding, a number of the prisoners died. The episode became known as the Black Hole of Calcutta.

Digging deeper

What really happened in the Black Hole of Calcutta?

The only written account of the imprisonment in Calcutta was by survivor John Holwell. He claimed 146 people were imprisoned in a small and airless dungeon at Fort William. The cell measured, according to Holwell, only 8 metres by 6 metres. As a result of conditions in the cell, by the next morning 123 of the prisoners had died. This story quickly spread to England where the Indians were portrayed as heartless and cruel.

SOURCE B

It is impossible that 146 people could have been accommodated in a room of this size. It is now agreed that Holwell greatly exaggerated his story. Indian historians have shown that the Nawab had no hand in this affair, and that the number of prisoners was no higher than 69. It may even be possible to argue that the episode of the Black Hole never happened.

An Indian historian writing in the 1990s.

SOURCE C

In Calcutta there was a small prison, six yards long by five yards broad. It was meant to contain only a few persons, and it was known as the Black Hole. The Nawab ordered all the prisoners to be locked up in this room. His soldiers forced them in at the point of the bayonet and shut the door. At six o'clock in the morning the door was opened. Twenty-three pale figures were all that came out. The rest were all dead. A pit was hastily dug, and the dead bodies, one hundred and twenty-three in number, were thrown into it.

From Stories from English History *(1891).*

SOURCE D

For over a century Holwell's story was used as an example of the uncivilised behaviour of native Indians and to justify the building of the British Empire. By the beginning of the twentieth century, Holwell's account was under serious attack. One scholar, J. H. Little, said the entire affair was a hoax designed by Holwell to make himself look like a hero. To call the affair a hoax is perhaps extreme. But looking at the evidence we can probably say the following about 20 June 1756 in the Black Hole of Calcutta.

Europeans were put in a cell during a long hot night in the aftermath of the capture of the city. The number varies but perhaps as many as 60 were placed in the Black Hole. Some Europeans died that night from suffocation, but many from the wounds received in the defence of the fort. Between 20 and 25 survived.

The local ruler, in the flush and confusion of victory, simply forgot they were there. British authorities let Holwell's exaggerations stand. The story was used to justify the enormous sacrifices needed to maintain the largest empire the world had ever seen. Thus, the Black Hole of Calcutta became one of the great imperial myths, designed to horrify later generations.

Adapted from A Moment In Time *(1993) by an American writer, Dan Roberts.*

SOURCE E

Then was committed that great crime, memorable for its singular atrocity [cruelty], memorable for the tremendous retribution [pay-back] by which it was followed. The English captives were left to the mercy of the guards, and the guards determined to secure them for the night in the prison of the garrison, a chamber known by the fearful name of the Black Hole. The space was only twenty feet square. The air holes were small and obstructed. The number of the prisoners was 146. When they were ordered to enter the cell, they imagined that the soldiers were joking; and, being in high spirits on account of the promise of the Nabob [Nawab] to spare their lives, they laughed and jested [joked] at the absurdity of the notion. They soon discovered their mistake. The captives were driven into the cell at the point of the sword, and the door was instantly shut and locked upon them.

Nothing in history or fiction approaches the horrors which were recounted by the few survivors of that night. They cried for mercy. They strove to burst the door. But the answer was that nothing could be done without the Nabob's orders, that the Nabob was asleep, and that he would be angry if anybody woke him. Then the prisoners went mad with despair. The day broke. The Nabob had slept off his debauch [excessive drinking], and permitted the door to be opened. But it was some time before the soldiers could make a lane for the survivors, by piling up on each side the heaps of corpses on which the burning climate had already begun to do its loathsome work. When at length a passage was made, twenty-three ghastly figures, such as their own mothers would not have known, staggered one by one out of the cell.

From Lord Clive, Critical and Historical Essays *(1843) by Thomas Babington Macaulay.*

Question time

Use Sources B to E in order to work out what really happened in the Black Hole of Calcutta.

1   In order to work out whether or not a source is giving us reliable evidence about something, we need to look at whether the author or artist was in a position to know what really happened, and what their motives were in recording the event. Which sources give us reliable evidence about what really happened in the Black Hole of Calcutta?

2   Historians should take account of all sources in some way, but are there any sources here you could ignore? Why?

3   Make a list of the words in all four sources that might make us think the authors are exaggerating. Why do you think they would have done this?

4   Do you think you have enough evidence here to write a reliable account of what really happened in the Black Hole of Calcutta? As an historian, is there anything more you would look for?

5   Now write your account, remembering to say how reliable the evidence on which you are basing your account is, and what weight you are giving to the available evidence.

British rule increases

The Battle of Plassey was a turning point for the East India Company. It changed from being a trading organisation to a company that had control of large areas of India. However, many East India Company employees were greedy and abused their power in order to increase their own wealth. This was done at the expense of Indians who suffered as a result.

At this time much of India was ruled by the Mughal emperors. In 1765 the company was given the right to collect tax in Bengal on behalf of the Mughal emperor. This decision was disastrous for the people of Bengal as the company officials taxed the people heavily. In 1769–70 a famine spread among the Indian population. The East India Company did nothing to help the starving and it is estimated that up to a third of the population of Bengal died in the famine. This was a dark episode in the history of India.

By the mid-1850s, the British (in the form of the East India Company) dominated all of India. Their control worried many Indians because the British saw themselves as superior. Heavy taxes and the replacement of Indian officials with European ones increased tension. In 1857, Indian soldiers in the British army staged a mutiny. The uprising lasted a year and thousands died. The British government decided that this could not be allowed to happen again and in 1858 the East India Company handed the running and control of India over to the British government.

Digging deeper

How did the British view Indian people?

The attitudes of the British towards the Indians were very important in the shaping the history of India in the eighteenth and nineteenth centuries.

These sources give us a comparison of British attitudes in India at the time.

SOURCE F

Many of those Britons who went to India quickly fell under the spell of Indian culture. Indeed, before the mutiny many Britons mixed socially with Indians and adopted many aspects of their day-to-day life, from language to dress. There are many examples to describe. In 1805, a young Scot called William Fraser arrived in Delhi. He quickly was attracted to Indian life. Within a few years he was the father of a number of children born to a number of Indian wives. Fraser's favourite activity was to go hunting lions barefooted, armed only with a spear. In the end he was shot dead by the Nawab of Loharu for having an affair with the Nawab's sister.

Fraser was by no means alone in his desire to seek better relations with the Indians. Sir William Jones was a judge in Calcutta who, in 1784, set up the Royal Asiatic Society to promote an understanding between the two cultures. Sir William learned the Indian language of Sanskrit and took to dressing in the loose white clothes worn by the Indians.

An historian writing in 2001 about relations between Indians and Britons before the Indian Mutiny in 1857.

SOURCE G

The racial arrogance of the British after the mutiny hurt the feelings of educated Indians and widened the gulf between ruler and ruled.

From The Break-up of British India (1969) by B. N. Pandey.

SOURCE H

Take up the White Man's burden –
Send forth the best ye breed –
Go, bind your sons to exile,
To serve your captive's need;
To wait in heavy harness,
On fluttered folk and wild
Your new-caught, sullen peoples,
Half-devil and half-child.

The White Man's Burden *(1898) by Rudyard Kipling.*

SOURCE I

The British in India were aloof [kept themselves to themselves], absorbed in their own concerns and tended to treat the Indian in a social or official capacity as a second class citizen. They avoided close contact with Indians of any description.

Written by J. Nehru, Prime Minister of India 1948–65.

Question time

Study Sources F to I.

What are the main differences between the attitudes described in Source F to those described in Sources G, H and I?

The Raj 1859–1948

The period of British rule in India after the mutiny, from 1859 until 1948, was known as the Raj. India was run by about 1000 British civil servants from the Indian Civil Service. The priority for the British government was to keep control of India, not to serve the interest of Indians. India had become a very important market for British goods, so in this period, transport was improved and railways were built across India.

On 1 January 1877 Queen Victoria was made Empress of India as a symbol – to both Britain and India – of British control. Queen Victoria never went to India, but sent a viceroy (the queen's governor) to rule in her name. Some Indians did not appreciate this idea. In 1885 a political party called the Indian National Congress Party was set up with the aim of persuading Britain to allow Indians to govern themselves. Their cause was helped by the decision of the British viceroy, Lord Curzon, to divide the state of Bengal in 1905. Violent protest broke out in Bengal against these reforms and the British government was forced to take note and listen to what the people were suggesting. A number of changes to how India was ruled were suggested, and in 1909 the Morley-Minto reforms were introduced. Lord Morley was the British politician in charge of Indian affairs in the British government and Lord Minto was Curzon's replacement as viceroy. Their reforms included Indians being on the viceroy's council, which meant that they would have a say in the running of the country. However, such initiatives did not go far enough to please Indian nationalists who kept up their campaign against British rule.

Question time

1   Draw up a timeline of events in India between 1750 and 1909.

2   How did British attitudes to India change in the period 1750–1900? Explain your answer using the information from the text and sources above. You could refer to issues like calls for change, social status and protest in your answer.

How did explorers and missionaries help create the empire?

Up until this point in the chapter we have seen how the British Empire grew as a result of the desire to trade and success in war. Before the 1860s, the empire was not very popular in Britain; many people felt that it was costing too much money for not enough gain. However, the lure of adventure and exploration meant that a number of people were determined to travel to areas of the world previously unexplored by Europeans. Many of these explorers were Christian missionaries who believed that it was their duty to take Christianity to the peoples of the non-Christian world. These missionaries ignored the value of the cultures of the non-Christian world, but in spreading Christianity they helped develop the idea that became popular at the time in Britain – that the empire was a force for civilisation.

Captain James Cook 1728–79

SOURCE A

Captain Cook taking possession of the Australian continent, on behalf of the British government, 1770.

One of the most famous explorers was Captain James Cook. A skilled seaman, Cook taught himself mathematics and astronomy, essential skills for a navigator. Cook was driven by the desire to explore and record his discoveries in the form of maps and charts, as much of the world was still uncharted. In 1768 Cook set sail in the ship *Endeavour* with the aim of exploring the Southern Seas in search of land which had not yet been explored by Europeans. In particular he was looking for the unknown continent which many thought stretched across the Southern Seas. On the voyage of the *Endeavour*, Cook had charts drawn of New Zealand and the eastern coast of Australia. These charts were vital for the British as they gave them superior information about the coasts and currents of the Pacific Ocean and this gave them an advantage over their colonial competitors.

Again in 1772 Cook led an expedition in search of the unknown continent as he still believed that there was a large land mass that covered the Southern Seas. Cook sailed as far south as the Antarctic. Then he turned north after having failed to find any such great continent.

In 1776 he set sail on his third and final voyage – an attempt to find a north-west passage to the Pacific by sailing around Canada and Alaska. It was during this expedition that Cook was killed in a skirmish with native Hawaiians while spending the winter on the island.

Digging deeper

The settlement colonies

The first European settlers in Australia, up to the 1840s, were mainly convicts – people who had been convicted of crimes in Britain and sent far away or deported. The last convicts were landed in West Australia in 1867. However, the promise of land and an escape from poverty meant that significant numbers chose to leave Britain and settle in new countries in the hope of making a better life for themselves. These countries became known to the British as 'settlement colonies'. From the 1850s the settlement colonies were given dominion status. This meant that they could rule themselves while staying part of the British Empire. Dominion status worked very well for those countries that were granted it. They could sell their goods anywhere in the British Empire but could also put taxes on goods coming into the country from abroad.

In the late-nineteenth and twentieth centuries large numbers of white European settlers emigrated to Australia, New Zealand, Canada and South Africa. In the early days, in order to settle on the land, they first had to take it. In some countries this was not done without a fight. In New Zealand, for example, from the 1840s to the 1870s a series of wars were fought with the native Maori people over land.

In the period between 1900 and 1914 the numbers of those emigrating peaked. In 1911, 455,000 people left Britain for foreign destinations. Not all were emigrating permanently but many were looking for a fresh start in a new country. Of this number, 41 per cent were bound for Canada, 18 per cent for Australia and 7 per cent for South Africa.

Mungo Park 1771–1806

Cook was one of many explorers who attempted to map areas previously unknown by Europeans. The reasons for this were clear – it gave your country an advantage in trade because raw materials and markets were more easy to find. Mungo Park explored the course of the Niger River in central Africa. When he returned to England he published *Travels in the Interior Districts of Africa* in 1799. This detailed many of the differences between African and European culture. In 1805 Park was sent by the British government to trace the Niger to its mouth. However, Park was attacked while on his journey and was drowned. His contribution was that he raised awareness in Britain of the existence of thriving cultures in central Africa.

David Livingstone 1813–73

David Livingstone was a missionary who, like many explorers in the nineteenth century, went to Africa with the aim of converting the native people to Christianity. He made a number of journeys to central and western Africa. His aims were many; among them were to introduce

Christianity there and to end the slave trade in Africa once and for all. Livingstone believed that he would be 'civilising' Africans by destroying their cultures and ways of life. This attitude is now considered racist but in Livingstone's time it was the view held by many. In 1858 he went to Africa 'to try and make an open path for commerce [trade] and Christianity'.

On his travels Livingstone explored the Zambezi River, coming across a magnificent waterfall which he named Victoria Falls in honour of Queen Victoria. In 1865 Livingstone set off on an expedition to find the source of the River Nile. After some time all news of him stopped. In 1871 the American newspaper *New York Herald* sent a correspondent, Henry Morton Stanley, to Africa to search for Livingstone. Eventually Stanley found Livingstone, greeting him with the famous words 'Dr Livingstone, I presume?'. Livingstone died in Africa in 1874. His legacy was that he made popular the idea of the missionary explorer.

Mary Henrietta Kingsley 1862–1900

Not all explorers shared Livingstone's views that Africa and the Africans should be converted to European ideas. By the end of the nineteenth century some Europeans were beginning to realise that African culture was not barbaric or uncivilised but the equal of European culture. This contradicted the views of the majority of Europeans in Africa who taught Africans to believe that all things European were superior. Mary Henrietta Kingsley was a European explorer who travelled extensively in West Africa between 1893 and 1895. Kingsley was fascinated with different African cultures. After her return to England in 1895 she wrote *Travels in West Africa*. In this book she argued that the Africans were 'a great world race … one that has an immense amount of history before it'. In 1899 Kingsley travelled to South Africa and took a job caring for Boer prisoners of war during the Boer War. She died of typhoid fever in 1900. Her contribution to the British Empire was that she helped to spread the idea that the cultural differences of the Africans were to be celebrated rather than crushed.

Cecil Rhodes 1853–1902

One of the most influential figures in the British Empire in the nineteenth century was Cecil Rhodes. He was not an explorer but a British immigrant to South Africa who had gone there to create his wealth in the diamond industry. By 1890 Rhodes was the owner of the leading diamond mining company in the world, Rhodes De Beers Consolidated Mines. He also owned companies which mined much of South Africa's gold and diamonds. His political power came from him being Prime Minister of the Cape Colony from 1890 to 1896.

Rhodes believed in the superiority of what was called the 'Anglo Saxon' race. His ambition was to spread the British Empire northwards and form a British block of land from the Cape to Cairo.

This was to be linked by a British-owned railway from the northern to the southern tips of the continent. Indeed, Rhodes had an ambition to spread the British Empire across the globe.

SOURCE C

I believe that we are the finest race in the world and that the more of the world we inhabit, the better it is for the human race ... The extension of the British Empire, for the bringing of the whole uncivilised world under British rule, for the recovery of the United States ... What a dream! But yet it is probable ...

Cecil Rhodes writing to a friend, W.T. Stead, in August 1891.

In the 1890s, Rhodes' company took the mining rights and land of Mashonaland, which was re-named Rhodesia. The only threat to British control of the region lay with the independent Transvaal Republic dominated by the people known as Boers, who were descended from Dutch settlers in the region. The Boers strongly disliked the British Empire.

The Boer War 1899–1902

In 1886 huge deposits of gold were discovered in the area known as the Rand in the Transvaal. Word spread and gold diggers flooded into the Transvaal, 30,000 of them being British. The Boers were now outnumbered by British settlers. The Boer leader, Paul Kruger, insisted that the settlers were not given full rights. In 1895, one of Rhodes' closest friends, Dr Leander Starr Jameson, launched a raid on the Transvaal, supported by Rhodes' money. The raid was launched with the aim of seizing the important city of Johannesburg for the British South Africa Company, but it was a failure and Rhodes had to resign as Prime Minister of Cape Colony. One result of the raid was that the Boers in the Transvaal were convinced that the British wanted to take over their country.

Tension between Boer and British increased to the point that in October 1899 the Boers invaded the Cape Colony. This was the start of the Boer War which was to last until British victory in 1902. It was to cost nearly 10,000 lives.

The impact of Rhodes on the growth of the British Empire was considerable. He was the driving force behind Britain's expansion of its empire in southern Africa and the exploitation of the wealth of these newly colonised lands.

Southern Africa at the time of Cecil Rhodes.

Digging deeper

Black people in South Africa

The Dutch settlers in South Africa, the Boers, had little sympathy for black Africans. The Boers did not believe that black people should own land or vote. When the Boer War broke out, most black people supported the British. They hoped that this would win them full rights across South Africa.

After the Boer War, the British government allowed elections to take place, but the number of black South Africans allowed to vote was restricted. The first election in 1910 was won by the South African Party, led by the Boer leader, General Botha. His aim was to gain independence for South Africa within the British Empire. He also wanted equality for Boer and English settlers. This new government cared little for black people.

In 1912 a group of black Africans formed the South African Native National Congress (SANNC). The leader of SANNC was J. I. Dube and its aim was to campaign for rights for black Africans.

Their concern about the racist nature of the Boer government was well founded. On 14 June 1913, Botha's government passed the Immigration Act that restricted the immigration of Indians into South Africa. Two days later it passed the Natives Land Act which attempted to further segregate black Africans from the European settlers by restricting the land they could own. The black people of South Africa had been betrayed by a British government that cared little for their plight.

What was the Scramble for Africa?

Until the late 1870s, most European governments showed little interest in ruling Africa. While some Europeans travelled there to convert the African peoples to Christianity, most governments saw little reason for controlling vast areas of a continent about which they knew very little. In the next 20 years all of that was to change. In the 1880s the British Empire in Africa grew slowly. In the 1890s there was a change of attitude and policy, with the British government taking a leading role in seizing new colonies in Africa. Most leading European powers also attempted to sieze parts of the African continent. Below are examples of Britain's role in what has become known as the Scramble for Africa.

Establishing control

West Africa. In the 1870s, Britain controlled a string of trading stations along the coast of West Africa in the Gambia, Gold Coast and Sierra Leone. These ports were important to Britain as they were useful in the campaign against the trade in slaves that still existed. British interest in areas of Africa was still dominated by private companies. In India, the East India Company had been the main reason for the growth of the British Empire there. The same was the case in the area around the River Niger in West Africa, where the most important British company was the United Africa Company.

By the mid-1880s France and Germany were expanding their interests in various parts of Africa. In 1885 the Berlin Conference on African affairs met and the leading powers decided which parts of the African continent would belong to which European country.

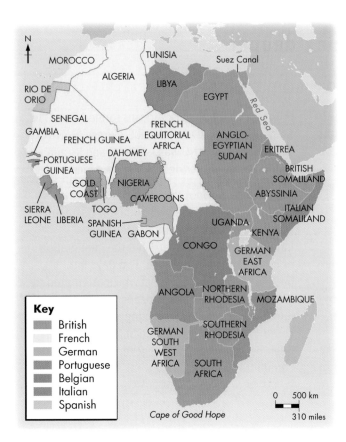

European possessions in Africa around 1900.

Key
- British
- French
- German
- Portuguese
- Belgian
- Italian
- Spanish

Egypt and The Sudan. In 1867, the British Prime Minister, Benjamin Disraeli, bought Britain a share in the Suez Canal. By the 1870s over 80 per cent of the shipping using the canal was British. Very quickly the canal became a crucial link in communications between Britain and India because it enabled ships to make a short cut via the Red Sea, instead of the much longer journey around the Cape of Good Hope, the southern tip of Africa. In 1875 the Egyptian ruler, Ismail, fell deeply into debt and announced that he wanted to sell his shares in the Suez Canal. Disraeli bought Ismail's shares for £4 million. Britain now owned a majority share in the canal.

Some Egyptians resented this strong British involvement. In 1882 an Egyptian army officer, Colonel Arabi, led a nationalist uprising under the slogan 'Egypt for the Egyptians'. An economic crisis in the country increased the resentment and made Arabi's cause even more popular amongst Egyptians. The view of the British was different. They feared that Arabi's uprising would threaten British interests.

In 1882 the British Prime Minister, William Gladstone, sent a military force to the country to restore order and to protect British business interests. Egypt's neighbour, Sudan, was also in a state of unrest. In 1881 a *jihad* (holy war) had been declared by the Muslim leader, the Mahdi, against the British. A force under General Gordon was sent to the Sudanese capital, Khartoum, but Gordon was killed in February 1885. It was not until the Battle of Omdurman in 1898 that the British managed to gain control of Khartoum and the Sudan. Britain had gained control of Egypt and Sudan.

Question time

Work in small groups. Look again at the information on pages 27–30. In your groups discuss the following:

1   What were the different motives of these people?

2   What was their impact on the British Empire in Africa?

3   Which of them do you think was the most significant to the development of the empire? Explain how you have come to this conclusion.

Assessment section

Study the sources below and then answer the questions that follow.

SOURCE A

A British poster from 1900, showing a Boer from the Transvaal kneeling before Britannia.

SOURCE B

What is the meaning of keeping safe the road to India? It seems to mean this; that a little island at the end of the world [Britain], having possessed enormous territory at the other end of the world [India] thinks that it can possess or control all the territory in between. That is a monstrous claim.

Adapted from a speech by William Gladstone in 1874.

SOURCE C

When he [the manufacturer] wants a new market for his adulterated [bad quality] Manchester goods, he sends a missionary to teach the Gospel of Peace. The natives kill the missionary; he flies to arms in the defence of Christianity; conquers for it and takes the market as a reward from heaven.

George Bernard Shaw, a playwright and political thinker of the late-nineteenth and early-twentieth centuries.

SOURCE D

Think it over yourself, Percy. Can you thrash most fellows your own age? Can you run as far and as fast as most of them? Can you take a caning without whimpering over it? Do you feel, in fact, that you are able to go through fully as much as any of your companions?... It is pluck and endurance, and the downright love of adventure and danger, that have made us masters of the great part of India, and up until now makes us the ruler of most of it.

From Through the Sikh War *(1893) by G.A. Henty. His books were written for schoolchildren and glorified the empire.*

SOURCE E

The aim of every schoolboy is to love his country more and more, to praise its control over many parts of the globe, to support Britain's brave soldiers in battle and to thank God England made him such a happy child.

Adapted from The School History of England *(1911) by Rudyard Kipling.*

1   Using all the sources, what impression do you get about the attitudes of the British towards the empire in the nineteenth century?

2   Compare Source A with Sources B and C. What are the similarities and differences between them?

3   Study Sources A and C. Why do these interpretations differ?

4   Study all the sources. Which of the sources do you consider *most* useful and which do you consider *least* useful to an historian studying British attitudes to the empire? Explain why you have come to your conclusion.

5   In your view, which two individuals contributed most to the growth of the British Empire? For each individual explain what their role was and why he or she was so important.

6   'Trade built the British Empire.' To what extent do you agree with this statement? Explain your answer fully using examples to back up your ideas.

Further reading

Dale Anderson *The American Revolution* (Evans Brothers, 2002)

Leon Ashworth *British History Makers: Horatio Nelson* (Cherrytree Books, 1997)

Tom Monaghan *The Slave Trade* (Evans Brothers, 2002)

Social and economic change 1750–1900

Between 1750 and 1900 Britain's economy and society was to change out of all recognition. As the population boomed towns and cities grew at an incredible rate. This is called urbanisation. In these towns and cities the Industrial Revolution took hold and new industries grew, blackening the air with the soot from thousands of steam-driven machines. The countryside also changed as the demand for food grew. The pace of life changed as the new steam trains roared through countryside and cities alike.

Population growth and its impact

The increase in the population in the period 1751–1901 was remarkable. Nowadays the size of the population stays roughly the same, but in those 150 years the number of people living in England and Wales doubled, doubled and nearly doubled again! As historians we have to ask the question, why?

Year	Population of England and Wales (millions)	Year	Population of England and Wales (millions)
1751	6.5	1831	13.9
1761	6.7	1841	15.9
1771	7.2	1851	17.9
1781	7.5	1861	20.0
1791	8.3	1871	22.7
1801	8.9	1881	26.0
1811	10.2	1891	29.0
1821	12.0	1901	40.8

The population of England and Wales, 1751–1901.

Counting the population

Every ten years in Britain there is a census – a count of the population. The first census took place in 1801. Any figures for the population before 1801 are estimates. The most useful source of information for estimating the size of the population before 1801 is parish registers. Every parish kept records of those people who were baptised, married or buried in the parish. However, there are problems with using parish registers to estimate the size of the population:

● not everybody was a member of the Church of England

● the Church of England was slow to set up new parishes in the industrialising cities

● in some areas the registers were kept more accurately than in others.

From 1801 the census provides historians with a more accurate series of statistics. However the censuses of 1801, 1811, 1821 and 1831 were undertaken by local officials, without central direction, and it is possible that these figures are incomplete. The Civil Registration Act made the registration of births, deaths and marriages compulsory from 1 July 1837. Therefore the 1841 census was the first which could be checked against other evidence.

Between 1750 and 1850 the population of Britain rose dramatically. There are a number of possible contributing factors for this.

A fall in the death rate

The death rate is the number of people who die per thousand of the population in each year. Some historians have argued that the death rate fell at this time because of better agriculture (which meant more food), more work, better pay and better medicines. However, this was not really the case until late in the nineteenth century. It is true that medical advances such as vaccination were beginning to halt the spread of diseases like smallpox, but these advances were slow. The new cities of the nineteenth century were dirty, polluted and full of terrible housing. It is clear that any fall in the death rate is not enough on its own to explain the population increase.

Immigration

There was a lot of immigration into Britain, in particular from Ireland in the 1840s after the Irish famine. However, there was also a lot of emigration to America and the countries of the empire known as the settlement colonies (see page 28). Significant numbers of Scots left their home country for places like Canada and New Zealand as the land there was cleared of people and was available for the profitable enterprise of sheep farming. Between 1851 and 1901 over 4.5 million people emigrated from England and Wales.

Birth rate and early marriage

Probably the most important reason for the increase in the population was the fact that people got married younger. The growing economy meant that young people did not have to wait so long before they could afford to get married. In the nineteenth century most people waited until they were married before they had children. The younger they got married, the more children they had. In 1750 the average age of marriage was around 26 years old. By 1850 that figure had fallen to around 23 years old. In areas where the economy was dominated by the textile or mining industries, the average age of marriage was 20 years old. The reason for this is clear – these industries offered workers higher wages and a stable job.

Activity time

1   Draw a bar chart showing the population figures for England and Wales in the period 1751–1901.

2   How quickly did the population grow in each decade? You might need a calculator to work this out.

    Here is an example of how to work out the rate of growth between decades, using the figures for 1861 and 1871:

    22.7 m (the 1871 figure) – 20.2 m (the 1861 figure) = 2.5 m

    $$\frac{2.5\,m}{20.2m} \times 100 = 12.38 \text{ per cent increase}$$

3   Use the figures you have calculated about the rates of population growth to pick out the decade in the nineteenth century with:

    a   the largest growth in population

    b   the smallest growth in population.

    In your own words identify why this might be the case.

4   Try to find out what your local village, town or city was like in the nineteenth century. There are a number of questions you could ask about it:

    ●   Did the population rise and if so by how much?

    ●   What was the main source of employment?

    ●   Are there any nineteenth-century (or even earlier) buildings that survive?

    To do this research you might use your school or local library or the Internet.

Digging deeper

What was life like in London in the 1850s?

The information so far in this section has been mainly in the form of facts and figures. However it is important for historians not to lose sight of the fact that these figures represent real people. In 1851–2 *London Labour and the London Poor* was published in instalments by a writer called Henry Mayhew. This book contained his observations about life in London in the middle of the nineteenth century. It shows that Londoners in the 1850s lived their lives on the streets; buying, selling, stealing and begging. In 1862 Mayhew's work was finally completed and stretched to four volumes. Mayhew was a journalist by training so he managed to describe people on the London streets in vivid detail. These are just a few of the characters he encountered. When you have read the descriptions, discuss why Mayhew's observations are so important to historians.

SOURCE A

I then talked to her about the parks, and whether she ever went to them. 'The parks!' she replied in wonder, 'where are they?' I explained to her, telling her that they were large open spaces with green grass and tall trees. Her eyes brightened up a little as I spoke; and she asked 'Would they let such as me go there – just to look?'

Although the weather was severe she was dressed in a thin cotton gown, with a thin shawl wrapped around her shoulders. She wore no covering to her head, and her long rusty hair stood out in all directions. When she walked she shuffled along, for fear that the large carpet slippers that served her for shoes would slip off her feet.

Mayhew's description of a watercress girl.

In the 1850s, the River Thames was the main sewer for the city. Despite this, a large number of Londoners earned their living wading in the mud of the river banks, looking for small pieces of coal, chips of wood, or any sort of refuse washed up by the tide. The mud-larks were of all ages, from young children to the very old. To Mayhew these people were the worst in appearance of all the Londoners he saw.

SOURCE B

It cannot be said that they are clad in rags, for they are scarcely half covered by the tattered, indescribable things that serve them for clothing; their bodies are grimed with the foul soil of the river, and their town garments stiffened up like boards with dirt of every possible description.

Mayhew's description of a mud-lark.

SOURCE C

An engraving of a mud-lark.

He was a short stout fellow with a face like an old man's ... I have seldom seen so dirty a face, for the boy had been sweating and then had wiped his cheeks with his muddy hands. Mike wore no shoes, his coat had been a man's and its tails reached to his ankles, one of the sleeves was missing and a dirty rag was wrapped around the arm instead. The boy's parents had died before he was ten and his brother had introduced him to crossing sweeping. Mike explained how he made his money. 'On a good day when it's poured o'rain and then leave off sudden, and made it [the road] nice and muddy, I've took as much as ninepence. There's about ten of us in our gang. If we sees one of our pals being pitched into by other boys we goes up and helps him. At twelve at night we goes up to the Regent's Circus and we tumbles there [do gymnastics] to the gentlemen and the ladies. The most I ever got was sixpence at a time.'

Mayhew's description of crossing sweepers. One way in which adults and children could make money was to sweep clean a number of road crossings. On a rainy day the crossing sweepers would clear away the mud in order for people to cross the road without getting too dirty. Mayhew interviewed many crossing sweepers including this boy, called Mike.

Town /city	1801	1841	1901
Glasgow	77	287	904
Liverpool	82	299	685
Manchester	75	252	645
Norwich	36	62	112
York	17	29	78

The population of towns and cities, 1810, 1841 and 1901 (figures in thousands).

The impact of the population rise

The most obvious impact of the growth of industry and the increase in population was the growth in the size of towns and cities like London, which were full of the types of people described by Henry Mayhew. However the growth in the population in those towns and cities depended on the jobs available for people there. The chart on the left shows that some towns and cities boomed while others grew more slowly.

Living conditions

Conditions in the new towns and cities were terrible for many people. The demand for housing meant that old houses were divided up into rooms which were then divided up again. Builders constructed new houses out of poor materials. In many cities, houses were built back-to-back, with two rows of houses sharing one roof. Families were crowded into rooms and cellars. Such poor housing was a matter of concern to a number of people at the time.

A whole family is often accommodated in a single bed, and sometimes a heap of filthy straw and a covering of old sacking hide them in one undistinguished heap. Frequently we found two or more families crowded into one small house, containing only two apartments [rooms], one in which they slept, and another in which they ate. Often more than one family lived in a damp cellar, containing only one room, in which twelve to sixteen people were crowded. Often they also kept pigs and other animals in these rooms.

Observations of Dr J. P. Kay, published in 1832. He is describing housing in Manchester.

Overcrowding and poor sanitation (drinking water and sewage disposal) meant living conditions were worse than we could imagine. In many cities there was almost no sanitation. Privies (lavatories) were shared by a large number of families. Most often the privies would empty into a local stream or river which would also serve as the water supply.

In 1844 the German philosopher, Friedrich Engels, described conditions in courts. These were buildings crammed together with a small court in the middle.

SOURCE F

The worst courts were those reached by going through Long Millgate. On reaching them one is confronted by a degree of dirt and revolting filth, the like of which is not to be found elsewhere. In one of these courts, just at the entrance, there is a privy without a door. The privy is so dirty that the inhabitants of the court can only enter or leave the court after wading through puddles of stale urine and excrement.

Friedrich Engels' description of a court in Manchester, 1844.

The water supply in most cities was terrible and often contaminated by human waste. Most people got their water from wells, streams or pumps in which the water was dirty. It was not until the 1890s that piped water into houses was the normal arrangement in all towns and cities. In the 1840s, water was supplied by private companies who cared little for the quality of the water. In 1894, it was calculated that only 5 per cent of homes in industrial towns had a bath.

SOURCE G

A slum in Victorian London.

Leeds is very badly supplied by its public water works which was built forty years ago when the town was much smaller. Therefore around 12,000 people receive water from the waterworks. Another 60,000 have no water supply except from wells and rainwater. The water is taken from the river near Leeds Bridge and forced up by its waterwheel to reservoirs. Its quality is very bad.

From a report about the quality of water in Leeds in the 1830s.

Disease in the cities

Because of poor sanitation and overcrowding, disease swept through the new cities. Smallpox killed large numbers each year. The faces of those who survived were marked for the rest of their lives by deep scars. Tuberculosis was another killer which affected the lungs and caused around 50,000 deaths a year. Another common killer was typhus which was spread by lice and attacked the intestines.

One of the worst diseases was cholera. Originally from Asia and caused by infected water, cholera spread rapidly in the filthy cities of Britain. In 1831 the disease made its first appearance in Sunderland. The epidemic that followed across England killed 32,000 people. At the time, the cause of the disease was not known. The symptoms of cholera were sickness and diarrhoea. The disease was deadly within a very short period of time.

In 1848–9 the cholera epidemic struck London with an even greater ferocity, with over 53,000 people dying in a few months. The last great outbreak of cholera was in 1866 in London when 15,000 died. Although little was known about what caused cholera, guesses were made early on that it was linked to bad conditions.

On 26 May the first case of cholera occurred in Blue Bell Fold, a dirty cul-de-sac containing about twenty houses inhabited by poor families. Blue Bell Fold lies on the north side of the river between it and a polluted stream that carries the waste from mills and dyehouses [where clothes were dyed]. The first case occurred in a child two years of age who was in perfect health the day before. He suddenly became ill on the morning of 26 May and died at 5pm the same day. If the board would refer to the map with this report they will see that the disease is worst in the parts of the town where there is often no sewage system, drainage or paving.

From a report by a Dr Bacon to the Leeds Board of Health in 1833.

Despite the terrible conditions, very little was done to improve the situation in the cities. There were a number of reasons for this lack of action:

- **Ignorance** Little could be done to prevent diseases like cholera as long as there was ignorance of their causes. Until the 1860s most people believed that cholera was caused by 'bad air'.

- **Laissez-faire** Many politicians believed in *laissez-faire*, that it was best to leave things alone to sort themselves out and that it was not the role of government to interfere.

- **Taxation** Most local authorities and central governments did not want to raise taxes to pay for improvements.

The responsibility of society

Slowly many Victorians recognised that it was the responsibility of society to provide decent housing and good public health for the working people.

By the 1860s, medical research began to make the link between disease and water. In 1854 Dr John Snow showed that cholera was carried by water, however he could not explain how. In 1864, the French scientist, Louis Pasteur, proved that bacteria caused disease. He also demonstrated that the way to kill bacteria was to expose it to heat, using a process that is now called pasteurisation. In the 1880s and 1890s, the German scientist, Robert Koch, identified the microbes which caused cholera, typhoid and other diseases.

Although the government did little to improve housing, there were attempts to build housing of quality by some employers and philanthropists. (A philanthropist is someone who uses his or her money to help improve the lives of others.) One such example was George Peabody who set up the Peabody Trust in 1860 to provide cheap and affordable housing. By 1900 around 150,000 people were housed in Peabody accommodation. Some employers thought that it was their responsibility to build good quality housing for their workers. For example, at the end of the nineteenth century, George Cadbury built the village of Bournville near Birmingham for his chocolate factory workers.

Edwin Chadwick

Some important individuals believed that it was the role of government to improve conditions in the cities. One of these was Edwin Chadwick. He was a Commissioner of the Poor Law (see pages 44–5). One of Chadwick's priorities was to ensure that the tax people had to pay to look after the poor – the poor rates – was kept low. He was worried that too many of the poor were dying which led to poor rates having to support orphaned children and pay funeral expenses. His conclusion was that poor living conditions led to high poor rates. In 1842 in a report called *Sanitary Condition of the Labouring Population* he suggested that the government should intervene and create local authorities with the power to improve sanitation. He also supported the idea of clean water being crucial to good health.

Chadwick's ideas upset many people who did not like the idea of central government telling local government what to do. *The Times* newspaper launched a bitter campaign against Chadwick and his ideas with the result that they were ignored. In 1848 another outbreak of cholera changed people's minds and a Public Health Act was passed by Parliament. This allowed people in a local area to set up Local Boards of Health. However their powers were still limited.

Digging deeper

Dr John Snow and the spread of cholera

Dr John Snow worked in Soho in central London. As a junior doctor he had seen the effect of the cholera outbreak in the north-east of England in 1831 and was determined to find the source of this disease. Snow did not believe those who said that cholera was in the air. In 1849 he wrote a book suggesting that the disease was spread by water. However he had no proof.

In 1854 Snow's chance came to test his idea, as cholera broke out in Soho. The disease rampaged through the alleyways and courts at the heart of London. Within nine days seven hundred people had died in an area around one particular street. In the next street, however, virtually nobody died. To Snow this was proof of the fact that the disease could not have been spread by the air.

SOURCE J

Snow's map of deaths from cholera around Broad Street in London. The dark areas show where the dead people had lived.

Snow's research narrowed the deaths down to one common factor. All those who died had drunk the water from a pump in Broad Street. Men who drank beer at work in a local brewery survived as did those in the area who travelled to a different pump to get their water supply.

The final piece of evidence was the story of a woman who lived near the Broad Street pump but then moved away to Hampstead. Although she liked the area she had moved to, she preferred the taste of the water from the Broad Street pump. Therefore she bottled water from the pump and had it delivered to her new home. The day after she drank the bottled water she died. Her niece, who came to visit, also tasted the water and died. Snow was convinced his ideas were right and he persuaded the authorities to take the handle off the pump, which they did. The cholera in that part of London stopped.

Despite such clear evidence most people did not believe Snow. Snow's problem was that he could show that cholera was linked to water but could not explain why this was so. Slowly local authorities and doctors began to believe him.

Snow died in 1858 but his ideas were more widely accepted after the 1866 cholera outbreak. This was linked to the actions of a waterman who allowed unfiltered water containing sewerage from a cholera-infected household to pass into the drinking supply. The 1875 Public Health Act marked a turning point – local government was given responsibility to build sewers, reservoirs, public lavatories and ensure fresh clean water supplies.

Poverty and the Poor Laws

From Elizabethan times a series of laws organised help for the poor. This poor relief was organised at a local level by 15,000 parishes. In each parish a poor rate came from householders to pay for poor relief. At the end of the eighteenth century, the poor were divided into three groups:

- the 'able-bodied' poor who could not find work and needed it to be provided for them

- beggars who did not wish to work

- the 'impotent poor', such as the old or the sick who needed to be looked after.

In the 1780s and 1790s the poor were greatly affected by bad harvests, lack of regular work, low wages and rising food prices. A particular problem in the 1790s was the rise in the price of bread as a result of the Napoleonic Wars. So in some areas the amount paid to the poor was set according to the price of bread and the size of their families. One of the most famous of these sytems was set up by the magistrates of Speenhamland in Berkshire in 1795. This system was copied by other parishes.

The end of the Napoleonic Wars in 1815 saw agricultural depression which was to have a serious effect on the numbers of poor (see page 50). After 1815, around 400,000 servicemen returned to Britain looking for work but many of them remained unemployed.

Falling wheat prices and high poor relief spending in the 1820s and 1830s led to many ratepayers arguing that there should be a change in how the poor were managed. The works of a number of writers backed up this view.

- Reverend Thomas Malthus claimed that a growing population would increase more quickly than food supply and so would result in famine.

- Adam Smith in *Wealth of Nations* (1776) suggested that the Poor Laws stopped the economy working properly by preventing people moving around the country looking for work.

- Jeremy Bentham argued that the old Poor Law was inefficient and actually encouraged poverty. His ideas were influential and convinced many, including Nassau Senior and Edwin Chadwick (see page 42), who were to work on changing the system.

How did people react to unemployment?

In 1830-1 a wave of violence swept the rural south and east of England. Farm buildings were burned, farmers were attacked and machines were damaged in rioting which came about because of low wages and unemployment. The unrest was known as the Swing Riots. Many politicians felt that it proved that the system of looking after the poor didn't work. In 1832 the government set up the Royal Commission on Poor Laws, headed by the Bishop of London. Its task was to investigate the administration of the Poor Law and suggest alterations to it. The commission set about its task by collecting information on how the Poor Law worked. Twenty-six assistants travelled around the country collecting data. Edwin Chadwick and Nassau Senior were the main authors of the commission's report which criticised the existing system of poor relief. Its priority was to improve the administration of the Poor Law, not to deal with the issue of poverty. As a result, the following reforms were put in place.

- The 15,000 parishes were combined to form 640 Poor Law Unions. Each union had to build a workhouse.

- Workhouses gave relief to the poor, but conditions there were made deliberately harsh so few people would want to go there.

- A Poor Law Commission based in London was set up to ensure that the Poor Law was administered in the same way across the country.

The new Poor Law, especially the workhouses, was very unpopular with the working classes. The regime in the workhouses was very strict. Married couples were separated, children were housed apart from their parents and discipline was harsh. In some workhouses conditions were appalling. In the Andover workhouse in 1845, paupers were keeping animal bones to suck because they were so hungry. Although workhouses were set up in most towns, throughout the nineteenth century most people were given help outside the workhouse. This was called outdoor relief.

1 Most people in the mid-nineteenth century, including Edwin Chadwick, believed that diseases like cholera were carried through the air in droplets. This was known as the Miasma Theory. How might a supporter of John Snow have tried to convince people like Chadwick that cholera was spread through water?

2 What did the government do to tackle the problems of poor sanitation?

3 Produce a piece of descriptive writing with the title 'The conditions of towns and cities in 1850'. You should try to include the following aspects:

- the growth of towns and cities
- sanitation
- housing and overcrowding
- disease.

The important point to remember when writing descriptively is that you must explain yourself clearly. Remember to support what you say with evidence.

Agricultural change 1750–1900

The open field system

In the sixteenth century, most arable land (land used for crops) in England, especially in the Midlands and East Anglia, was organised in what was known as the open field system:

- large fields were divided into strips

- farmers would farm strips in each of the fields

- fields would be sown every year with wheat, barley and oats

- each field would have a different crop each year and one year in three it would be left fallow (with nothing growing in it)

- crops would be rotated (changed) every year to allow the soil to recover some of its goodness

- common land on which all the villagers could graze their animals would be available near the village

- meadows and woodlands were also common land; from the meadows, villagers could take hay; from the woodlands, they could collect wood for fires and building and keep their pigs there.

The open field system worked well as the means of feeding a stable population, but there were disadvantages. Farmers' strips were often scattered far and wide so time was wasted travelling between them. The arrangement of the strips meant that there was little possibility for innovation (new ideas) or the use of new machines. This meant that land was often badly drained and less productive than it could have been. Seed was sown by hand, most often by the broadcasting method, where seed was simply thrown onto the ground.

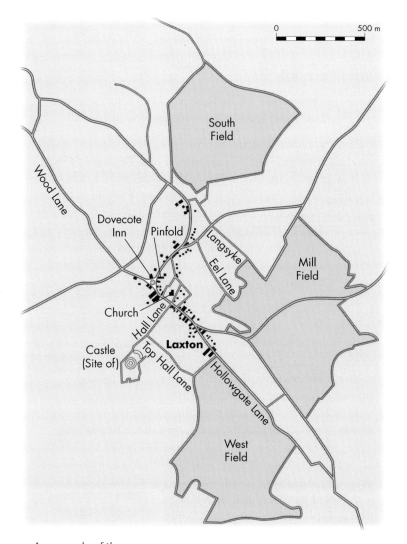

An example of the open field system of farming. Each of the three large fields would be divided into many strips of land.

Another problem was that disease could spread fast amongst the animals on the common land. Also, a lack of winter fodder meant that animals had to be slaughtered, and only the very fit animals that could breed well were kept.

By the eighteenth century, changes were taking place that were to lead to a revolution in agriculture.

- The population began to rise steadily.

- Urbanisation resulted in a larger number of people who did not grow their own food. Therefore demand for food increased.

- Throughout the eighteenth century, the price of food remained stable, so farmers needed to look for new ways to make more money.

- There had been a scientific revolution in the seventeenth century. Many farmers now wished to apply the lessons of science to agriculture.

- Between 1765 and 1792 there were a number of bad harvests. This encouraged farmers to look for ways to improve production of food.

- From 1793–1815 Britain was at war with France. During this war the French ruler Napoleon attempted to blockade Britain, to prevent food coming into the country. The demand for food from British farms rose considerably.

Enclosure

From the turn of the eighteenth century the number of villages that saw their fields enclosed began to increase rapidly. Enclosure was when a field, made up of a number of strips, was surrounded by a fence or a hedge. The move from the open field system to enclosed fields was a very important change to how the land was farmed. Until 1801, when the general Enclosure Act was passed by Parliment, it was quite a slow process.

- Before 1750 most fields were enclosed after agreement of the villagers.

- After 1750 enclosure of a village's fields was often hotly contested. It could only take place if 80 per cent of the landowners in a parish agreed.

- The next step was for landowners to petition Parliament for permission to enclose their land. At that time Parliament was dominated by landowners who were usually very keen to pass Enclosure Acts so that they could make more money.

- After passing an Enclosure Act, Parliament would appoint commissioners to examine all the claims and then decide who got which land.

Enclosure meant that more land, including common land, was put under cultivation (planted with crops). The owners of the new fields could experiment with new farming methods. However, enclosure was expensive – hedges, ditches, drains and roads cost a considerable amount to maintain. Many farmers lost their strips and could not afford to enclose the land given to them. Many were forced to sell their land, often to wealthy landowners, and work as labourers. As a result many more large farms were created. While the enclosures meant that new farming methods could be tested, other people sought to improve agriculture in other ways.

The improvers

There were some farmers who worked to improve the land. Most of them had farms in the east of England where soils are lighter and therefore easier to farm. Their ideas helped different and better methods of agriculture to develop. However the spread of ideas was slow and many farmers could not afford to make changes until well into the nineteenth century. Some of the more important improvers are described below.

Jethro Tull (1674–1741)

Tull believed that the broadcasting method of sowing seed was wasteful. His answer was to invent the seed drill in 1701. This new machine would sow seeds by drilling into the earth and then cover the holes. Tull was also concerned about the problem of weeds killing crops. In 1714 he invented the horse hoe which pulled up weeds as it was dragged through the earth by horses.

Digging deeper

How important was Jethro Tull?

Many of those who lived at the same time as Jethro Tull dismissed his ideas as those of a crank. This view has been accepted by many historians. However there are others who judge Tull in a far more positive light.

SOURCE A

Tull taught the need of keeping the earth between the row of plants well raked so that air and moisture could penetrate the roots. He experimented with manures. He improved draining methods. Though Tull's methods were criticised at the time, his principles were responsible for a widespread improvement in agriculture.

The historian, Pauline Gregg, writing in 1949.

In the progress of scientific farming Tull is one of the most remarkable of pioneers. His method of drilling wheat and roots in rows was not generally adopted till many years after his death. But the main principles which he laid down in his *Horse-Hoeing Husbandry* (1733) proved to be the principles on which was based an agricultural revolution in tillage [cultivation of land]. The 'greatest individual improver' that British agriculture had ever known, he sought to discover scientific reasons for observed results of particular practices.

Extract from The Pioneers and Progress of English Farming *(1888) by Lord Ernle.*

Tull was against the practice of putting manure [as fertiliser] on the land because he thought that manure contained the seed of weeds. He believed that hoeing was enough to keep the soil fertile and that it was not necessary to feed the land with nutrients as well. At the time of Tull's death in 1741, his ideas had had little effect on farming.

The historian, Simon Mason, writing in 1984.

Tull was a strange person. Some of his activities would not meet with the approval of modern farmers; he claimed, for example, that he had grown thirteen successive crops on the same ground without manure. Tull's reputation has been exaggerated.

An historian writing in 2001.

Charles 'Turnip' Townshend (1725–67)

Townshend was a Secretary of State (like today's Foreign Secretary) who retired to his Norfolk estate in 1730 and set about making changes to how his farm was worked. He encouraged the farmers who rented land on his estate to improve their soil by mixing it with a clay called marl. Townshend's most famous innovation was the four-crop rotation. Instead of a fallow field, Townshend copied the Dutch by encouraging a rotation of turnips, barley, wheat and clover. The turnips and clover put goodness back into the soil and provided animal feed for the winter. Unlike the crop rotation of the open field system, there was not the waste of a fallow year.

Thomas Coke (1754–1842)

From 1776 Coke owned a farm at Holkham in Norfolk. He was not an innovator but he encouraged new developments. He held festivals at which people could come and see new techniques of farming.

Robert Bakewell (1725–95)

The quality of farm animals by the mid-eighteenth century was still poor, as they were often too thin to provide much meat. Bakewell experimented by cross-breeding animals. He cross-bred the Lincoln and Longhorn sheep to produce the New Leicester variety. This provided better and more meat. He did the same with cattle and horses. However, as with Tull, his ideas spread very slowly.

Arthur Young (1741–1820)

The reason why Bakewell's ideas spread slowly was that communication was still poor. The significance of Arthur Young was his tireless work in campaigning to spread information about farming innovation. In 1784, he set up his magazine, *Annals of Agriculture*, which was full of ideas about new farming techniques. Such was Young's reputation that in 1793 he became secretary of the newly-created Board of Agriculture.

The aftermath of the Napoleonic Wars

The Napoleonic Wars (1793–1815) had a great impact on the development of agriculture:

- food prices rose and farmers rushed to enclose the land – during the war around 3 million acres were enclosed

- as prices rose, so did farmers' incomes and they were able to spend money on new machinery and develop new techniques of farming.

The Corn Laws 1815

Many farmers borrowed heavily to improve their farms and had not paid back their debts by the time the war was over in 1815. These farmers were worried that the end of the war would see a rush of foreign wheat or corn come into the country. Therefore they demanded that Parliament protect them with taxes on foreign wheat. At that time Parliament was dominated by landowners who were happy to agree to this. In 1815 the Corn Laws were passed. These stated that no foreign wheat was allowed to enter the country until the price of British wheat had reached 80s (shillings) a quarter.

Despite the protection given to agriculture by the Corn Laws, the price of wheat fell after 1815. This fall in price was the result of a surplus of wheat. In many areas of the countryside violence was increasing because of growing unemployment, low wages and hunger. In 1816 there were riots in East Anglia. In 1830–1 even more serious disturbances, the Swing Riots (see page 45), took place across the wheat-growing areas of the south and south-east of England in protest at the introduction of farm machines which the rioters felt might take their jobs. The rioters wrecked machines and burned farms to the ground.

Not all agriculture suffered from the depression after 1815. There was a growing demand for food, as the population was rising (from 11 million in 1815 to 15 million in 1836). Many farmers introduced mixed farming – a mixture of arable (crops) and pasture (animals). Also new ideas continued to emerge about how to improve farming. Collectively these became known as High Farming, and included the use of the fertiliser guano (bird droppings) from islands in the South Atlantic and the cultivation of a variety of crops. In some areas farming was improved with better drainage which meant that land would be more productive. In 1846 Prime Minister Robert Peel introduced the Agricultural Drainage Act which provided government loans for landlords to pay for the drainage of their land.

A meeting of the Royal Agricultural Society at Bristol in 1842, where farmers are inspecting new agricultural machinery.

The Golden Age of farming, 1850–73

In 1846 the abolition of the Corn Laws removed the protection for farmers from foreign competition. However, farmers were able to deal with a reduction in prices because of improvements in the following areas:

- **Machinery** One of the most important changes in agriculture was the introduction and wider use of steam-powered machines. Steam threshers had been introduced in the 1820s and 1830s and by 1880 two-thirds of the corn harvest was threshed by machine.

- **Fertilisers** Also important in improving productivity was the increasingly widespread use of fertilisers. In 1843, J. B. Lawes showed that treated crushed animal bones could make excellent fertiliser. Farmers began to keep larger herds which therefore produced more natural dung. The result of the growth in fertilisers is clear – from the late 1830s to the late 1850s, wheat yields increased by 50 per cent.

- **Demand** A growing population provided the demand for agricultural goods. Imports of foreign wheat in this period continued to rise, from an average 484,000 tonnes a year from 1846–8 to 2 million tonnes a year from 1869–75. However, demand was greater in Britain than foreign imports could satisfy. Most important to the growth in agriculture were the developments in transport. The new railways linked food-producing areas with expanding and prosperous towns.

The Great Depression and its effects on agriculture c. 1871–1914

In this period, wheat prices fell and those who relied on wheat suffered. The summer weather from 1875–8 was very wet, resulting in bad harvests which in turn damaged the profits of arable farmers. As a result, wheat declined in relative importance to other crops. By 1904, the price of wheat had fallen.

This can partly be explained by the fact that the cost of importing wheat fell dramatically with the improvement in transport, especially shipping. As the prairies of the USA were opened up for wheat production from the late 1860s, so the cost of bringing this produce to Europe fell.

Other aspects of farming also experienced competition. The introduction of refrigerated ships meant that meat from around the empire could be frozen and delivered cheaply to meat markets in London. By 1895 around a third of all meat sold in Britain came from abroad.

Those farmers who could change their business to meet demand stayed prosperous and successful. In some areas such as Cheshire, farmers turned to dairy production. In 1870–6, the output of milk in Britain was worth £27 million or 13.8 per cent of agricultural output. By 1904–10 this had risen to £36.5 million or 23.5 per cent of total output. The demand for milk was high and it was not suitable for importation. Home-produced milk could be rapidly transported to market by the railways and would arrive fresh at market.

Question time

1 Sources A to D on pages 48–9 give different impressions of the impact of Jethro Tull on farming.

- In your book put the heading 'How important was Jethro Tull?'.

- Underneath it draw a table with two columns, labelled *Similarities* and *Differences*.

- In each column give examples of how the sources agree and differ.

Here is an example of a similarity:

Sources A and B agree that Tull was an important improver. Source B states that he was the 'greatest individual improver' while Source A claims that the result of his work was a 'widespread improvement in agriculture'.

2 Use your table from question 1 to answer the question: Should Jethro Tull be considered a great improver? Use the evidence from Sources A to D to back up your argument.

3 Which was the most important eighteenth-century agricultural change outlined in this section? Give a reason for your choice and say why you think that it is more important than the others.

4 A turning point is a point after which things are clearly different. Choose what you think are the two main turning points in nineteenth-century agriculture. Explain why you have chosen each turning point.

Industrial change

By 1900 most goods in Britain were made in factories. By goods we can mean anything from linen tea towels to cotton clothes or fine pottery. This was not the case in 1750. Industry took place on a much smaller scale, mainly in very small workshops or even at home. It needed changes and developments in a number of areas to make the switch from workshop to factory possible.

- **Demand** The growth in population meant a greater demand for goods.

- **Power** The workshops and early factories used water power. By 1900 the most important source of power was steam.

- **Fuel** The development of steam power meant an increase in demand for coal. Improvements were needed to overcome the problems that restricted the amount of coal obtained.

- **Transport** In 1750 most goods were carried by road or by river. By 1900 canals and then railways had become the most important means of transport.

- **Entrepreneurs and innovation** For change to take place it was necessary for individuals to take risks, build factories, invent new technology and make new machines.

- **Natural resources** None of the developments could have taken place without improvements in the production of iron. This was a very important natural resource of the Industrial Revolution because machines, engines and bridges were made out of iron.

- **Colonial expansion** The expansion of overseas colonies increased the supply of cheap raw materials and gave access to a ready market for manufactured goods.

- **Engineering** None of the changes could have taken place without the work of engineers such as George Stephenson or Isambard Kingdom Brunel.

Steam power

The early factories were powered by waterwheels and were located next to rivers. Gradually steam replaced water as the foremost source of power in the Industrial Revolution Age. The process of developing a steam engine capable of meeting the needs of industry took decades.

The first steam engine was developed to pump water out of the bottom of coal mines. Designed by Captain Thomas Savery in 1698, it could pump water up about 10 metres. In 1712 Thomas Newcomen improved upon Savery's machine. He built a steam engine that could pump water up 100 metres.

In the 1760s a Scot called James Watt was mending a Newcomen engine when he realised a way in which it could be improved.

The Sun and Planet gear steam engine.

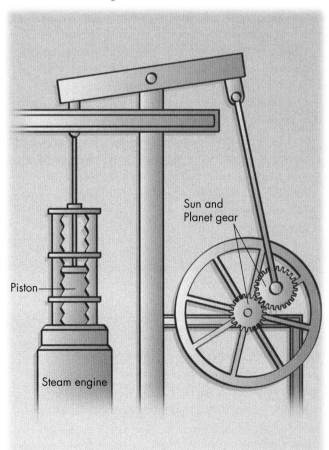

Sun and Planet gear

Piston

Steam engine

By 1781 Watt had managed to design a steam engine that could turn a wheel, the so-called Sun and Planet gear.

The importance of Watt's engine was that he had linked steam power to motion. However, his invention did not mean that every factory quickly changed to steam power – far from it. In 1800 there were only around 500 of Watt's machines in use. However, by 1850 steam power was far more widespread, especially in the cotton industry. It also had a crucial role in the development of the railways because steam was the power used to drive the engines.

Iron and steel

Iron and then steel were the materials of the Industrial Revolution. Their production on a large scale made engineering, transport and industrial change possible. The main changes in the iron and steel industries between 1750 and 1900 were in the scale of production. Developments came about because of:

- an increase in demand from growing industry and transport
- the work of entrepreneurs to improve technology.

Both the iron and steel industries faced a number of problems but hard-working inventors came up with solutions.

Problem	Solution
Before the eighteenth century, the main fuel used for smelting iron (turning iron ore into molten–liquid–iron) was charcoal. As wood became scarcer so charcoal was in short supply.	In 1709 Abraham Darby introduced coke smelting which meant that the iron industry no longer depended on charcoal. Coke is a fuel made from coal. It was used to heat the iron ore (which is a rock) to a temperature at which the metal turns to a liquid and is extracted from the rock.
By the mid-eighteenth century, the demand for iron was greater than the supply. This was because impurities in pig iron (iron just out of the mould) had to be beaten out in a workshop. This took a long time, and often dented the iron.	In 1783 Henry Cort's puddling and rolling process melted down the pig iron by burning coal. It then allowed the flames to burn out the impurities without spoiling the iron. The iron was then stirred (puddled) and a spongy iron was created which could be used to make large sheets of iron.
Much of the iron industry had been traditionally located near streams and rivers which provided water power but only in a limited amount. The work in these small workshops was done by hand.	The iron industry used other inventions to improve the industry and increase the scale of production. In 1775 ironmaster John Wilkinson used Watt's steam engine to work the bellows of his furnace. Equally important was John Naysmyth's invention of the steam hammer in 1839. This could bash out huge sheets of iron to be used in making bridges and ships.
Steel was slow to produce as it took up to three hours to convert iron into steel by burning off impurities. It could only be made in small quantities in crucibles (pots) without becoming uneven and blistered.	In 1856, Henry Bessemer first introduced his convertor which reduced the cost of making steel. Bessemer's convertor could produce steel in larger quantities. The molten (liquid) iron was oured into the convertor and the pimpurities were burned away. The waste material (slag) was then poured off and the steel was poured out.

Problem	Solution
Bessemer's convertor was not covered and, therefore, lost heat.	The open-hearth furnace was devised by William Siemens and refined by French ironmaster, Pierre Martin. It was more efficient method of making steel and could make steel on a smaller scale than Bessemer's convertor. Cold air was passed through heated chambers and the hot air then removed the impurities in the iron. Other materials such as carbon were added to produce steel.

Henry Cort's puddling and rolling process.

Year	Coal output
1750	5.0
1800	11.0
1850	49.4

Total UK coal output, in millions of tonnes, 1750–1850.

The coal industry

The increasing demand for coal was due to a number of reasons:

- a growing population which used coal for heating
- the building of the railways and the running of steam trains
- the growth of the iron industry
- the development of coal gas lighting which used coal to produce the gas.

As a result of this increase in demand, it was necessary to dig deeper mines so more coal could be extracted. The growth in the output of coal between 1750 and 1850 can be seen in the table on the left.

For mines to be dug deeper, certain problems had to be overcome.

Problem	Solution
As the pits were dug deeper so miners came across pockets of methane gas. This could cause terrible explosions underground. In 1708 a disaster at Wear Colliery resulted in 69 miners being killed. In the mines the air was often stale and difficult to breathe. It was clear that for miners to be able to go deeper they needed better ventilation and safe lighting.	The problem of explosions underground was tackled by John Buddle who, in 1810, attempted to use trap doors to introduce fresh air to various parts of the mine. Buddle also introduced a mechanical ventilator to pump stale and potentially explosive air out of the pit. To improve the safety of lights in the mines, the scientist, Sir Humphrey Davy introduced the Davy Lamp in 1815. This worked on a simple principle of using a gauze to surround the light, preventing heat from escaping and causing an explosion. Despite these solutions, mining was still a dangerous occupation.

Women and children in the mines

In the early-nineteenth century, thousands of women and children worked underground in mines. A number of politicians were very concerned about this. The most influential of these was Lord Shaftesbury, a great social reformer of this era. In 1840 he led an investigation into the working conditions of women and children in the mines. As a result of his report, the 1842 Mines Act banned women and children under ten from working underground. In 1850, inspectors were appointed to make sure that the laws were kept. This was followed by a law in 1860 which prevented boys under twelve working down the mines unless they had been educated and could read and write.

Digging deeper

Working in the mines

Lord Shaftesbury's report in 1840 into the conditions of work for women and children in the mines shocked polite Victorian society. As the following extracts show, it was full of details about the exploitation of women and children, and it was accompanied by a book containing pictures.

SOURCE B

I have been working below [the ground] three years on my father's account. He takes me down at two in the morning, and I come up at one or two the next afternoon. I go to bed at six at night to be ready for work the next morning. I have to bear my burden up four traps or ladders, before I get to the main road that leads to the pit bottom. My task is four or five tubs. Each tub holds 4.25 hundredweight. I fill five tubs in twenty journeys. I have had the strap [been beaten] when I did not do my bidding [as he was told].

Ellison Jack, aged eleven, Loanhead Colliery, Scotland.

SOURCE C

A woman hauling coal, from the book that accompanied Lord Shaftesbury's report.

SOURCE D

She has first to descend a nine ladder pit to the first rest ... to draw up the tubs of coal filler by the bearers. She then takes her creel [basket] and carries it on her journey to the wall face. She then lays down her basket, into which the coal is rolled. Often it is more than one man can do to lift the burden to the pit bottom ... This one journey exceeds the height of St Paul's Cathedral. It not unfrequently happens that the tug [strap] breaks and the load falls on the females who are following.

Extract from the report by the sub-commissioner R. H. Franks, 1842. He is describing the work of a woman underground.

SOURCE E

I'm a trapper in the Gawper pit. It does not tire me, but I have to trap without a light, and I am scared. Sometimes I sing when I have a light, but not in the dark. I dare not sing then. I don't like being in the pit.

Sarah Gooder, aged eight.

SOURCE F

Lord Shaftesbury visiting a mine in 1842.

SOURCE G

I have a belt around my waist, and a chain passing between my legs, and I go on my hands and feet. The road is very steep, and we have to hold a rope, and when there is no rope, anything we can catch hold of. There are six women and girls in the pit I work in. It is very hard for a woman. The pit is very wet where I work, and the water comes over our clog tops always, and I have seen it up to my thighs. It rains in at the roof terribly. My clothes are wet through almost all day long.

Betty Harris, aged 37. She had worked drawing [pulling carts of] coal for fourteen years.

SOURCE H

The bald place upon my head is made by thrusting [pushing] the corves [carts]. I hurry the corves a mile and more underground and back; they weigh 5 hundredweight. I hurry 11 a day. The getters that I work for are naked except for their caps. They beat me with their hands if I am not quick enough. The boys take liberties with me sometimes. I am the only girl in the pit. There are about 20 boys and 15 men. All the men are naked [because of the heat underground]. I would rather work in a mill than in a coal pit.

Patience Kershaw who was seventeen years old. She was a hurrier, someone who pushed tubs of coal.

As a result of the report, the Mines Act of 1842 was passed. Introduced by Lord Shaftesbury, the act ran into strong opposition in Parliament from mine-owners. However, as a result of the Mines Act, no women were allowed to work in the mines and no child under the age of ten was to be employed at all. Women could only work above ground. Not all women welcomed these changes – some would have preferred to work underground where wages were better.

Question Time

Study Sources B to H.

1 What picture of the mines did Lord Shaftesbury want to portray in his report?

2 What would shock the readers of the report?

3 What might the following people have thought about the Mines Act:

● mine owners

● parents

● working children

● woman miners?

Textiles

It was not just in the mines that women and children worked. They also worked in the textiles industry. There were several stages in the textile process.

● **Cleaning** – first the wool or raw cotton had to be cleaned before use.

● **Carding** – the raw material had to be brushed with boards so the fibres were untangled.

● **Spinning** – the fibres then had to be pulled and twisted. This was done by using a spinning wheel. The result was thread.

● **Weaving** – the thread was then used to make cloth. This is called weaving and was done on a loom. Two kinds of thread were needed, the warp thread that went across and the weft thread which was tied vertically on the loom.

In 1750 most of the textile process took place in the home. The workers would spin thread or weave cloth and then sell their produce to merchants. The benefit of this system was that the workers could work from home. The disadvantage was that cloth was expensive because the manufacturing process used a lot of labour.

Change to the factory system

The change from the domestic system (where people worked at home) to the factory system was the result of the work of a number of inventors. These men came up with solutions to practical problems.

Problem	Solution
The weaver working at home could only pass the shuttle (which held the thread) by hand. This meant that cloth could only be woven as wide as the weaver's reach.	In 1733, John Kay invented the flying shuttle. Kay put wheels on the shuttle and a spring to propel it across the loom so that wider cloth could be made and at a faster rate.
Kay's flying shuttle meant that it took six spinners to supply one weaver.	In 1767 inventor James Hargreaves came up with the idea of a spinning machine – the spinning jenny – that could spin eight or sixteen times the amount of a normal spinning wheel. At first Hargreaves was unpopular with spinners who feared that his machine might put them out of work.

SOURCE I

The flying shuttle, invented by John Kay.

SOURCE J

The spinning jenny, invented by James Hargreaves.

Problem	Solution
Despite Hargreaves' invention there was still a shortage of good quality thread.	In 1769 Richard Arkwright started using his new invention, the water frame. This machine worked by rollers drawing out the thread. The thread produced by the water frame was strong. However the machine was too large to be placed in spinners' homes. In 1771 Arkwright and his business partner, Jedediah Strutt, built their first factory at Cromford in Derbyshire. They soon found a way of powering their frame with water power. The factory system had begun.
The thread spun by the jenny and water frame was too rough and was not suitable for high quality cotton products.	In 1779 Samuel Crompton invented the mule. This machine could spin much more finely than any other machine. It also had to be located in factories, as it needed to be driven by stream or water. As a result bigger factories were built, and Crompton's mule was improved by Richard Roberts who made the machine fully automatic.
Spinning was now linked to the factory system, but weavers still worked at home.	In 1785 Edmund Cartwright invented the power loom that could weave automatically.

The result of these inventions was to make cotton easier to produce and with less labour, so the price of cotton goods fell. This in turn meant that demand went up, so more cotton was produced. The table below shows how much the cotton industry grew between 1750 and 1850.

	1750	1850
Imports of raw cotton	1.5 million kg	300 million kg
Value of cotton exports	£45 000	£30 million

Digging deeper

Richard Arkwright: Inventor or businessman?

In 1769 Arkwright patented his water frame. When something is patented it means that an idea is registered with the government. This means that nobody else can use that idea without paying money to the inventor. Arkwright claimed that the idea for the water frame was his and that he was a master innovator. However, in 1785 he lost the patent to his machine. A clockmaker he had been working with in the 1760s, John Kay, said that the water frame was his idea.

SOURCE L

Arkwright is a tyrant [someone who frightens and attempts to dominate others]. Surely you should agree that such a tyrant should not be able to rule over such a large factory as the one he has built in Manchester.

The comments of a fellow cotton manufacturer, Matthew Boulton, in 1782.

SOURCE M

He married your mother and began business for himself. He was always thought to be very clever in the wig-making business. All of those who knew him thought him to be an ingenious man [someone with plenty of new and exciting ideas].

From a letter by Thomas Ridgeway in 1799. Ridgeway was writing to Arkwright's son.

SOURCE N

Arkwright appears to be a man of great understanding and he knows the way to make people do their best. He puts on dances and parties for his workers. This means that they work hard and are sober throughout the rest of the year.

The comments of a visitor to Cromford Mill in 1781.

Question Time

Study sources K to N.

1   What do you think were the characteristics of Arkwright that made him such a good businessman?

2   Which sources do you think are exaggerating about Arkwright? Explain your answer.

Before improvements in steam engine technology, most of the new textiles factories such as Richard Arkwright's mill at Cromford in Derbyshire (built in 1771) relied on water power. The move towards larger cotton factories was partly the result of a shift from water to steam power. As a result of this change factories were moved from near sources of water power into towns and cities.

Of 1600 cotton mills in England in 1838, 1200 were based in Lancashire. This part of the country was perfect for cotton manufacture for the following reasons:

- the climate is damp which meant that the threads were less likely to snap

- there are plenty of rivers in Lancashire that could be used for the washing and dyeing of cotton

- raw cotton could easily be imported into Lancashire via the port of Liverpool.

The innovations in machinery were more suitable for use in the cotton industry than in any other. By 1850 it was cotton that had become the first industry to move to a factory system on a wide scale. Between 1851 and 1870, the cotton industry enjoyed extremely rapid growth. By the 1870s Britain was exporting cotton goods worth, on average, £71·5 million per year. Britain did not produce raw cotton and had to rely on imports from places like America. During the American Civil War (1861–5) the supply of raw cotton dried up which caused a temporary cotton famine. From the 1870s, the British cotton industry was in danger from competition from cotton industries in Europe and in America.

Digging deeper

How harsh was the factory system?

One of the results of setting up factories was a strict regime of discipline. Children were employed at a very young age to work the machines. They were especially prized because they could get under the machines and their small hands could tie broken threads. Hours were long – often the working day would start before six in the morning and not finish until nearly eight in the evening. Children were beaten if they dozed off to sleep or made mistakes.

An historian writing in 2001.

12 June 1844: A boy died in Manchester after his hand had been crushed in the wheels of a machine.

15 June 1844: A youth from Saddleworth died of dreadful injuries after being caught in a machine.

24 July 1844: An Oldham girl died after being swung round fifty times in machinery belting, every bone in her body being broken.

Extract from Manchester Guardian *between 12 June and 3 August 1844.*

A nineteenth-century engraving of the workers inside a cotton mill.

SOURCE R

Q What age are you?
A Twenty-three.

Q Where do you live?
A In Leeds.

Q When did you begin work at the factory?
A When I was six years old.

Q What were your hours of work in the mill?
A From five in the morning till nine at night.

Q For how long a time in one go have you worked that length of time?
A For about half a year.

Q Are you deformed as a result of this work?
A Yes, I am. Since the age of thirteen.

From the report of the Select Committee on Factory Children's Labour, 1832. The evidence of Elizabeth Bentley, a doffer. Her job was to replace the full bobbins on the spinning-machine and replace them with empty ones.

At this time, there were a number of Factory Acts which attempted to lay down rules about the following:

- the age of children working in the factories
- the education of children working in the factories
- fencing of machinery
- the hours people worked

Inspectors were sent to check that the acts were being introduced.

 Activity time

Read the sources through with a work partner. Try to draw up your own Factory Act. Introduce at least one point for each of the bullet points above. Then check it against the chart below.

Legislation	Main points
1802 Health and Morals of Apprentices Act	Children were limited to 12 hours of factory work a day. Children were to be given religious instruction.
1819 Factory Act	No child under 9 could be employed in a cotton factory. Children between the ages of 9 and 16 were not allowed to work more than a 12-hour day.
1833 Factory Act	Children between 9 and 14 were restricted to 8 hours work a day with 2 hours of compulsory education. Those under 18 could work only 12 hours a day. Four inspectors were appointed.
1844 Factory Act	Dangerous machinery was to be fenced. Children under the age of 13 could not work more than $6\frac{1}{2}$ hours a day.
1853 Factory Act	The working day for adults was limited to 6am–6pm or 7am–7pm with a $1\frac{1}{2}$ hour break. This made a working day of $10\frac{1}{2}$ hours.
1874 Factory Act	The working day for adults was limited to 10 hours and a half day on Saturday.
1878 Factory and Workshops Act	Factories and workshops were placed under general government inspection.

Transport

Neither agricultural nor industrial developments could take place without a reliable transport system. The eighteenth century saw a number of changes which meant that goods could be carried in bulk and faster.

The roads

A Royal Mail coach on the approach to Kew Bridge in London. There is a toll gate on the bridge.

Roads in the seventeenth century were in a very bad condition. They were poorly drained and full of holes. Improvements in road transport sprung from the creation of turnpike trusts in the eighteenth century. These were new or improved roads built by private companies who then charged a fee or a toll for people to use them. The trusts spent money on the improved road-building techniques of those engineers as John McAdam and Thomas Telford. By 1823 McAdam had repaired up to 2000 miles of road. The improvement of road foundations and better drainage meant that roads could carry heavier traffic loads. In 1750 there were 3400 miles of turnpike

trust roads built by 143 different trusts. By 1836 this figure had risen to 22,000 miles of roads built by 942 trusts.

Journey time by coach from London to ...	Mid-1750s	Mid-1830s
Oxford	2 days	6 hours
Manchester	4–5 days	19 hours
Edinburgh	10–12 days	45 hours

The improvement in road transport led to improvements in communication such as a better postal system and personal travel. The reduction in journey times by the mid-1830s led to a boom in the coaching industry, as shown in the table on the left.

In 1740 there had been one coach a week from London to Birmingham, by 1829 there were 34 a day. Coaching was controlled by large firms which became very big and successful. The largest companies in London were owned by W. J. Chaplin, E. Sherman and B. W. Horne, who together provided around four-fifths of the main coach services. By 1838, Chaplin's coach services employed 2000 people and used 1800 horses. The growth of personal travel was not matched by an increase in goods carriage. There were large companies such as Pickfords but they were the exception rather than the rule.

The building of canals and railways affected road travel. Long distance passenger travel was hit by the growth of the railways. However, many road companies worked with the railway companies, for example in 1840 coaching companies such as Chaplin and Horne became agents for the Grand Junction railway. Similarly, Pickfords managed to adapt by working in conjunction with the London and Western Railway from 1847. Some road companies were ruined by the competition. In 1841, the Bath mail coaches were withdrawn with the opening of the Great Western Railway.

In the period 1837–50, the revenues of the turnpike trusts fell by a third. In local areas some turnpike trusts tried to cover increasing debts by raising their charges. Sometimes this sparked off violence (see below).

Digging deeper

The Rebecca Riots 1843–4

In the countryside of west Wales, tenant farmers lived in very poor conditions. Distress was made worse by the introduction of the 1834 Poor Law which increased the poor rates paid by householders and set up workhouses (see page 45). Another source of discontent was the fact that even though 80 per cent of the population did not belong to the Anglican Church they still had to pay a tithe (a tax) to it.

When the turnpikes were first built in west Wales, the trusts helped the farmers by not charging them for using the roads to transport their goods. However, in the 1840s the trusts began to fear a decline in profits because of the rise of the railway and they started to charge farmers tolls.

The winter of 1838–9 was particularly severe and this was followed by a poor harvest in 1839. In Pembrokeshire in 1838 more toll gates were erected on the roads and higher tolls were charged. Of the new gates erected, four were near the village of Efailwen.

This move sparked off the so-called 'Rebecca Riots'. On the night of 13 May 1839, the toll gate keeper was confronted by a group of men dressed as women who attacked the gates and the new toll house. Their strange dress was partly disguise but partly religious. Most people went to chapel and had a good understanding of the Bible which explains why they were acting the part of Rebecca in attacking the toll gates (see Source B).

> **SOURCE B**
>
> And they blessed Rebekah and said unto her, thou art our sister; be though the mother of thousands of millions, and let thy seed possess the gates of those which hate them.
>
> *From The Bible, Genesis 24, verse 60.*

Attacks on turnpikes continued from 1842–4. By May 1843 the attackers had got so confident that gates inside one town, Carmarthen, were destroyed. In June, 'Rebecca' and 'her daughters' attacked the Carmathen workhouse. The authorities acted against what were becoming ever more violent attacks. On 6 September 1843 at Pontarddulais a crowd of over 100 Rebeccaites was ambushed by police and soldiers. Seven people were arrested and tried. One of the leaders of the attack, John Hughes, was sentenced to 20 years' transportation to Australia. After an attack on Hendy Toll House, information was given to the police that led to the arrest of John Jones and David Davies. In December 1843, they and 39 others were tried. John Jones was sentenced to transportation for life, David Davies to 20 years' transportation.

These arrests marked the end of the Rebecca Riots. However, the government did not ignore the demands of the protesters. A committee was set up to improve the quality of the roads and reduce tolls in west and south Wales.

Question time

What do the Rebecca Riots tell us about west and south Wales in the late 1830s and early 1840s? Discuss this with a partner, then write your ideas down.

The canals

In the eighteenth century, it was difficult to move bulky goods by road. If possible, heavy goods such as coal would be transported by boat along the coast or on rivers. However, many coal mines were not close to the sea or a river. The answer to this problem was canals. The first canal of the industrial age was finished in 1761 and ran from the mouth of the Duke of Bridgewater's coal mine at Worsley into Manchester. This sparked the building of a number of other canals. Each canal was built in response to local business demands, for example, the Trent and Mersey canal, built by James Brindley and completed in 1777, had been partly financed by the maker of pottery, Josiah Wedgwood.

Between 1791 and 1794, 42 canals were built, costing £6 million. By 1840 there were 4000 miles of navigable waterways in Britain. Although transport on the canals was slow, they carried a large amount of Britain's industrial goods. The importance of the canals was that they helped in the development of coal, iron, pottery and other industries which needed raw materials to be carried long distances.

However, canals were not an ideal means of transport. They had been built to different designs which meant that it was sometimes difficult to adapt from one canal to another, because canals came in different widths and sizes. The most important cargo carried on the canals was coal, and those canals which did not link to a mine ran the danger of not making enough money.

In the 1840s, canals were used to transport goods needed for the building of the railways. However, it was the building of the railways that posed the greatest threat to the canals. Most damaging was the slow pace of travel on the canals – it could take 36 hours to send cotton the 20 miles from Liverpool to Manchester. The railways could do this journey in a couple of hours. The result was that, after the 1850s, the canals fell into a long decline. They still carried goods short distances but the golden age of the canals had now gone.

The railways

The railways were the result of improvement in the production of iron (for the track) and in steam and engineering (for the engines). The Stockton to Darlington railway opened in 1825 and broke new ground in that it used a steam engine, *Locomotion*, built by the engineer, George Stephenson. The potential for successful investment and the slowness of the canals led to the planning of new lines, including one between Liverpool and Manchester. The line's engineers, George and Robert Stephenson, managed to tackle the problems of how to cross a twelve-mile bog by laying heather and timber foundations, and how to get through solid rock by blasting their way through.

In 1829 a competition was held to decide on the engine for the new line and this was won by George Stephenson's engine *Rocket*. The Liverpool to Manchester line was opened in 1830 although not without a disaster on its opening day. The president of the Board of Trade, William Huskisson, was hit by *Rocket* and killed. Despite this, the line was a success, carrying 400,000 passengers in its first year, as well as freight and goods.

Year	Miles of railways
1833	208
1840	1,497
1850	6,559
1870	15,537
1900	21,855

Miles of railway in the UK in selected years, 1833–1900.

In the 1830s and 1840s the main lines of the English railway system were built. Important routes were completed, linking London to the rest of the country. The most important were:

- the London–Birmingham line built by Robert Stephenson and opened in 1838

- the London–Bristol line built by Isambard Kingdom Brunel and opened in 1841.

Between 1844 and 1847, there was a rush of railway building. Large armies of construction workers known as navvies (see pages 70–1), undertook huge engineering feats. The government was aware of the importance of the railways. In 1840, under the Railway Regulation Act, companies intending to build a new line had to inform the Board of Trade which would then inspect the line. Companies also had to report their toll rates and accidents.

In 1844 the Railway Act meant that railway companies had to provide at least one train a day with cheap third class travel which stopped at every station and charged one penny per mile. The government also intervened in the debate over the size of the track gauge (width), the so-called 'Battle of the Gauges'. The standard size used by the Stephensons was 4 feet 8.5 inches but the Great Western railway completed by Brunel had a broader gauge of 7 feet. In 1846 the Gauge Act stated that the standard width for all railway lines was to be the narrower gauge.

After 1850 the railways continued to expand with new lines being opened. In 1863 the first London Underground line was opened from Paddington to the City. More underground lines were opened, including the Circle line in 1884.

A scene depicting the opening of the Stockton to Darlington railway line, 1825.

The railways had an important impact on the development of the British economy.

- They stimulated demand in iron, coal and the brick industry.

- Railway construction in the 1840s was a major industry in itself. From 1845–9, average annual employment on the railways was 172,000. In May 1847 this stood at a peak of 256,509.

- The more efficient transportation of fresh produce had an impact on diet and the availability of food in cities.

- The growth in railways led to changes in the financial markets. The London Stock Market expanded and new stock exchanges opened, for example, in Liverpool and Manchester in 1836, in Glasgow in 1844, and in Leeds and Birmingham in 1845.

- The coming of the railways changed towns and cities. The building of railway stations in the centre of towns and the miles of track required large areas of land.

- The railways opened up the possibility for people to travel. In 1851 the Great Exhibition at Crystal Palace in Hyde Park in London attracted crowds from around the country, many of the visitors travelling to London by train. Excursions offered by railway companies created opportunities for cheap holidays. Blackpool and Southport on the west coast grew rapidly because the inhabitants of the towns and cities of the industrialised North were able to travel there for their holidays. By 1871, Blackpool received 500,000 visitors a year. Other holiday towns such as Eastbourne on the south coast and Windermere in the Lake District did not exist before the railway had made their construction economically viable.

SOURCE D

One of the displays in the Great Exhibition at Crystal Palace in 1851.

Digging deeper

What were navvies really like?

Machines did not build the railways – they were built by hand. Men known as navigators or 'navvies' did the work. The tunnels, cuttings and laying of lines was done by hand with the help of gunpowder. Many navvies who worked on the railways had worked building the canals. In the peak of railway building in 1845, there were 200,000 navvies working on building railway lines. They gained a reputation of being hard drinkers, fighters and gamblers.

SOURCE E

We are sorry to announce that a labourer who was working on the building of the railroad at Edgehill, where the tunnel is to come out and join the surface of the ground, was killed on Monday last. The poor fellow was in the act of undermining a heavy head of clay, 14 or 15 feet high, when the mass fell on him, and literally crushed the bowels out of his body.

From Liverpool Mercury, *10 August 1827.*

SOURCE G

I have not seen anything uglier on my travels than the mass of labourers [navvies]. They are three times more brutal because of the three times the normal wages they are paid. The Yorkshire and Lancashire men are believed to be the worst and the Irish the best behaved. The postman tells me that the Irish send some of their earnings home. The English, who eat twice as much beef, drink the rest of their wages in whisky and send nothing home.

From the observations of Thomas Carlyle in 1846.

SOURCE H

There are many navvies who, after twenty years of digging and hard work have, by the sweat of their own brow, been able to buy valuable estates.

Adapted from History of the English Railway *(1851) by John Francis.*

SOURCE F

A railway cutting and navvies at work, building the London–Birmingham railway in the 1830s.

SOURCE I

The audience of the court contained a number of navvies. They were surprised at the severity of the sentence against Hobday, fifteen years in Australia. Hobday simply turned round and laughed at his sentence. He is a remarkable man and typical of the navvies. He is of normal height but his broad shoulders give evidence of immense strength. His look is frightening. Every feature indicates a life of crime. His rough hair is matted. We understand that he has not slept in a bed or worn a hat for nine years. His custom is to put on new boots and never remove them until they have fallen to pieces. His clothes are treated the same way except that he changes his shirt once a week.

Adapted from Carlyle Patriot, *February 1846. The newspaper is commenting on a court case involving a navvy called Hobday.*

SOURCE J

Some navvies slept in huts made out of damp turf. Others formed a room of stones without cement, placed thatch or reeds across the roof and took possession of it with their families. In such places from 9 to 1500 were crowded for periods of up to six years, living like brutes.

Adapted from History of the English Railway *(1851) by John Francis.*

Activity time

1 a Using Sources E to J write down seven statements to describe the navvies. Back each statement up with a quote from a source. Here is an example:

Some navvies were careful with their pay and saved it over years. Source H states that they had 'been able to buy valuable estates'.

   b Imagine the year is 1851. You are a newspaper journalist writing a report about the navvies. Your readers are fascinated with the navvies and your report is to give them as much information as possible. Quote from the sources in the report.

Question time

1 Draw a table with two columns headed *Social* and *Economic*. Having read the information in this section put the different impacts of the railways in the correct columns.

2 What was the most important impact of the railways? To answer this you need to argue which of the two was more important, the economic impact or the social impact.

Progress in Victorian England

The reactions of Victorian England to such rapid social and economic change were mixed. To some the country was entering an age of progress. To others the changes in society posed many questions.

1837–50: Conflict

This period is summed up by uncertainty and conflict. Although this was the period in which the railways and factories were built, it was also a period of depression. In the late 1830s harvests were bad and hunger was widespread. In 1834 a new system for giving assistance to the poor was introduced (see pages 44–5). This meant that the able-bodied poor had to go into a workhouse if they were to receive financial aid. Families were split apart and the poor were put to work.

In *Oliver Twist* (1837) by Charles Dickens, the writer showed the horror of conditions in the workhouse for orphaned children like his main character, Oliver.

Charles Dickens was not the only one to speak out. The Chartist petitions (pages 88–9) frightened many people who feared that the country was falling apart. That was not the case but many writers wrote about a divided society. They came from many walks of life, from the future Conservative Prime Minister, Benjamin Disraeli, to the popular novelists, Charles Dickens and Elizabeth Gaskell.

SOURCE A

'Say what you like, our Queen reigns over the greatest nation that ever existed.'

'Which nation?' asked the young stranger, 'for she reigns over two.'

The stranger paused; Egremont was silent, but looking inquiringly.

'Yes,' resumed the stranger after a moment's interval, 'Two nations … who are ignorant of each other's habits, thoughts and feelings, as if they were dwellers in different zones, or inhabitants of other planets; who are formed by different breeding, are fed by different food … are not governed by the same laws.'

'You speak of …' said Egremont, hesitatingly.

'The Rich and the Poor.'

From Sybil *(1845) by Benjamin Disraeli. In this extract Morley is arguing with Lord Egremont.*

The work of Elizabeth Gaskell is hard-hitting. In the novel *Mary Barton* (1848) she described the despair of the 1840s. In the extract in Source B, Gaskell's character, Mary, is looking after her father who is unemployed.

SOURCE B

And by and by Mary began to part with things at the pawn-shop [a place where goods could be exchanged for cash]. The smart tea tray, and tea-caddy, long and carefully kept, went for bread for her father. He did not ask for it or complain but she saw hunger in his shrunk, fierce, animal look … She often wished that he would apply for relief from the Guardian's relieving office … Once when she asked him as he sat grimed, unshaven and gaunt after a day's fasting over the fire, why he did not get relief from the town, he turned round, with grim wrath, and said, 'I don't want money, child! Damn their charity and their money! I want work and it's my right, I want work'.

From Mary Barton *(1848) by Elizabeth Gaskell.*

It was not just in novels that division and bad feeling was shown. A number of writers visited large cities such as Manchester and reported on the conditions there. Doctors such as Dr James Shuttleworth-Kay described the impact of cholera, typhoid and other diseases. Some of these writers attempted to use their information for political reasons. Their observations added to the debate about the condition of England.

However, there was no revolution in England against poor conditions. The Chartists' petition of 1848 did not lead to the government being overturned.

Digging deeper

Reactions to the railway: Charles Dickens

In 1847 Charles Dickens published his work *Dombey and Son*. The extract below is one of the most famous reactions to the railway from the time.

Question time

1 Describe the image Charles Dickens is giving of the railways.

2 Why do you think that he gave this impression?

SOURCE C

Away with a shriek, and a roar, and a rattle, from the town, burrowing among the dwellings of men, and making the streets hum, flashing out into the meadow, mining in through the damp earth, booming on in darkness and heavy air, bursting out again into the sunny day so bright and wide; away, with a shriek and a roar, and a rattle, through the fields, through the woods, through the corn, through the hay, through the chalk, through the mould, through the clay, through the rock ... like as in the track of the remorseless monster, Death!

Through the hollow, on the height, by the heath, by the orchard, by the park, by the garden, over the canal, across the river, where the sheep are feeding, where the mill is going, where the barges are floating, where the dead are lying, where the factory is smoking, where the stream is running, where the village clusters, where the great Cathedral rises, where the bleak moor lies ... away with a shriek, and a roar, and a rattle, and no trace to leave behind but dust and vapour, like as in the track of the remorseless monster, Death.

Adapted from Dombey and Son *(1847) by Charles Dickens.*

1850–75: Mid-Victorian stability

The mid-Victorian years were far more stable. This period began with the Great Exhibition held in London in 1851. Opened in May of that year by a proud Queen Victoria, the exhibition was a celebration of Britain's industrial and technological supremacy. The patron of the exhibition was the Queen's husband, Prince Albert. He encouraged the greenhouse maker and gardener, Joseph Paxton, to build a huge glass house in Hyde Park for the exhibition. This became known as Crystal Palace (see Source D on page 69). In total, about six million people visited the site.

In this period, many workers were unhappy with the conditions in which they worked and the pay they received. Occasionally violence broke out as in the 1866 Sheffield Outrages when workers who made cutlery went on strike. Some workers formed trades unions to represent them in discussions with employers. In 1868 all the unions sent representatives to the first meeting of all the trades unions, the Trades Union Congress.

Peaceful trades unions were seen by Parliament as a force for good and in 1871 the Trades Union Act recognised the right to set up a union. There was also important political change in this period. In 1867 the Second Reform Act had given the vote to the urban working class. This gave the push for the government of William Gladstone to introduce the 1870 Education Act. This encouraged the creation of School Boards to set up elementary (primary) schools where there were none.

There were many great writers of this period. One of the widest read and most important was Mary Ann Evans, although to most people that name would mean nothing. Mary Ann Evans understood her society very well and felt that she would have a better chance of being published if she wrote under the name of a man. She chose the name George Eliot. Her books such as *Adam Bede* (1859), *Mill on the Floss* (1860), *Silas Marner* (1881) and *Middlemarch* (1872) are set in the English Midlands. Eliot does not only reveal a deep understanding of how life in the provinces worked, her books also contain characters who ask questions about the meaning of life itself.

1875–1901: The late-Victorian age

This period was one of greater worry and anxiety than that of the mid-Victorian period. It was the age of empire (Chapter 1) but also a period of increasing foreign competition, especially with the booming economies of Germany and the United States of America growing so quickly.

Charles Booth and Seebohm Rowntree wrote about the poverty in London and York in the 1890s. They showed that, at some time in a year, around a third of the population lived below what was called the poverty line, the basic minimum required to live.

The late-Victorian period saw more unrest among workers. In the late 1880s, trades unions for unskilled workers like dockers were formed. These unions posed a new threat and increased tension in society. This period saw the increase in the popularity of socialism, the belief that the wealth of the country was unfairly distributed and this had to be changed.

Not all was uncertain. This period saw the emergence of a number of composers and performers whose influence lasted well into the next century. Much of their music has come to represent Victorian life.

- **W. S. Gilbert (1836–1911) and A. Sullivan (1842–1900)** The combined talents of writer, Gilbert, and composer, Sullivan, resulted in some of the most popular music of the late-nineteenth century. They produced a series of light operatic works which included *The Pirates of Penzance* (1879) and *The Mikado* (1885). Very quickly Gilbert and Sullivan's works became popular and they are still performed today.

- **Henry Wood (1869–1944)** The importance of Henry Wood was as the conductor of a series of classical music concerts held every year in London that became known as The Proms. Many young musicians were given the chance by Wood to play in a major orchestra for the first time. The Proms are still held today.

- **Edward Elgar (1857–1934)** It took Elgar, a composer, some time to become established internationally. However, a breakthrough in his career came when he wrote the *Imperial March* for Queen Victoria's Diamond Jubilee in 1897. The following year he wrote a series of musical portraits of people he knew, known as the *Enigma Variations*.

Football

One of the most important cultural developments in the Victorian period was the emergence of the modern game of football. Before the 1850s, football was a violent and rough game with few rules. A version of the game was played at public schools and in 1823 William Webb Ellis, a boy at Rugby School, picked up the ball and ran with it. So was born the game of rugby.

In the 1850s, attempts to draw up rules for football were made in Cambridge and Sheffield. In 1862 the Cambridge rules set out that each team should have eleven players. These rules were adopted by the Football Association, set up in 1863. They still allowed the ball to be handled although by 1870 most of the rugby-style rules had been dropped.

New clubs

In the Midlands a number of clubs were formed in the 1860s – Nottingham in 1862 (later Notts County), Nottingham Forest in 1865 and Chesterfield in 1867. In 1871, the secretary of the Football Association came up with a novel idea, to hold a cup competition. In 1872 the first FA Cup was held with fifteen teams entering, including one from Scotland.

Soon the game took hold in the industrial North. One of the reasons for this was the 1874 Factory Act that allowed workers to be given a half day on Saturday. This left Saturday afternoon free for leisure. In 1874 Aston Villa, Blackburn Rovers and Bolton Wanderers were formed. Four years later, workers at the Lancashire and Yorkshire Railway Company's engine depot at Newton Heath set up a club of that name. Later Newton Heath was to change its name to become one of the most famous clubs in the world, Manchester United.

The Football League

In 1884 the Football Association accepted that players could be paid for playing. The pressure was now for clubs to arrange fixtures on a regular basis. In 1888 the Football League was set up with twelve founder members. Six of these were from Lancashire, five were from the Midlands and one was from Stoke. There were no clubs from the South. In the 1890s the new league was to be dominated by Preston North End (known as the Invincibles), Aston Villa and Sunderland.

THE HON: A: F: KINNAIRD:
CAPTAIN OF THE "OLD ETONIANS"
THE ENCLOSURE
S: A: WARBURTON.
CAPTAIN OF THE BLACKBURN OLYMPIC
CROSSLEY KICKING THE DECISIVE GOAL
THE PRESIDENT PRESENTING THE CUP

SOURCE D

The 1883 FA Cup Final.

The FA Cup

The game of football was fast becoming popular and was attracting bigger crowds. One of the most popular competitions was the FA Cup. At first it was dominated by amateur teams such as the Old Etonians and Old Carthusians. In 1883 the Cup was won by Blackburn Olympic (soon to become Rovers) and from then to the end of the century it was contested by professional clubs from the North. From 1872–92 the Cup final was held at the Kennington Oval (where test match cricket still takes place). However, the attendance at the Oval for the 1892 final was 25,000 and the authorities felt that the numbers were too large.

The following year the final was held at Fallowfield in Manchester in front of a crowd that was officially 45,000 spectators. It is likely that at least double that number attended, many children creeping under the turnstiles or climbing over the fences. Little interest was shown in football in the south of England until a non-league side, Tottenham Hotspur, managed to reach the FA Cup Final in 1901.

Digging deeper

The FA Cup final of 1901

The Cup Final of 1901 marked a turning point in the history of football. Clubs from the North and South had met in the final of the FA Cup before but the southern teams had been amateurs. Since the creation of the League in 1888 no southern team had been in the First Division. Tottenham Hotspur were from the southern league. In 1901 they had won through to the final to meet one of the giants of the Football League – Sheffield United.

The final was to take place at Crystal Palace on 20 April 1901. The country had only just emerged from the long period of mourning after the death of Queen Victoria in January 1901. It was a bright sunny day and a huge crowd of 114,815 paid to see the game. The fans from Yorkshire had chartered 75 trains to take them to London to support their team. Children and adults climbed trees in order to get a better view. Despite the huge numbers of people the atmosphere was friendly. The only sour note pointed out by a local reporter was that some of the crowd un-sportingly made 'hooting' noises at the referee.

The game got off to a quick start and United scored first, Priest netting after fifteen minutes. Spurs equalised with a headed goal from Brown and the score was even at half time. Five minutes after the interval Brown scored with a shot that was greeted with 'thunderous applause'. However, two minutes later, a strange decision by the referee cast a shadow over the game.

Sheffield United attacked the Spurs goal almost straight away. Their left wing, Lipsham, crossed the ball and the Spurs' goalkeeper, Clawley, fumbled the ball behind him and then knocked it out for a corner. The referee's assistant, who was in a good position, signalled a corner. The referee, who was nowhere near the ball, signalled a goal. Both teams played out the rest of the game that finished an anti-climax. The replay at Burden Park Bolton the following Saturday saw a 3–1 victory for Spurs.

The first of the great FA Cup finals of the twentieth century had taken place. The number of people watching signalled the arrival of a national sport, the passion for which has lasted until this day.

Question time

What are the similarities and differences between Cup Final day in 1901 and today?

Assessment section

SOURCE A

A COURT FOR KING CHOLERA.

An illustration from Punch *showing the conditions in London in the 1850s.*

SOURCE B

In one cul-de-sac in Leeds there are 34 houses, and in ordinary times, there dwell in these houses 340 persons, or ten to every house. The name of this place is Boot and Shoe Yard, from whence the commissioners removed in the days of cholera, 75 cartloads of manure, which had been untouched for days.

From an inquiry entitled The State and Conditions of the Town of Leeds, *1842.*

SOURCE C

Suitable housing did not exist and additional numbers of people were crammed into every nook and cranny, from attic to cellar, of old properties or cottages quickly built with little or no access to light and air. Water and sanitation were not provided at all and, where they were, the water supply was often mixed up with sewerage.

Adapted from The Making of Victorian England *(1965) by G. Kitson Clark.*

1 Look at Source A. What image of conditions in the cities does the artist present?

2 Look at Source B. What were the particular public health hazards described in Source B?

3 Look at Source C. How does this source support the picture painted of cities given in Sources A and B?

4 Describe the impact of the building of the railways.

5 Choose from agricultural revolution, industrial revolution or transport revolution.

   a Describe the actions of one important individual who had a part in one of these revolutions.

   b What was the effect of that individual's work?

Research

Your favourite or a local football club might be one which was founded before 1914. If so, try to find out as much as you can about the history of the club. Ask the following questions and present your findings in a project or as part of a wall display.

- Who set the club up?
- Which league did they play in?
- Where did they play?
- Did they win any trophies?

Further reading

Geraldine Symons *The Workhouse Child* (Puffin, 1976)

Jeffrey Trease *No Horn at Midnight* (Macmillan, 1995)

Barabara Willard *Priscilla Pentacost* (Hamilton, 1970)

Political change 1750–1900

Throughout the period 1750–1900 the British political system was challenged by those who wanted change. Some wanted change because they believed that a certain situation was morally wrong, for example, slavery. Others demanded change for economic reasons, such as the work of the Anti-Corn Law League in the 1830s and 1840s to have the Corn Laws abolished.

The most important demand of many groups throughout the period was that the voting system should be changed. The middle class, working class and women, at one time or another in the nineteenth and early-twentieth century, all claimed the right to vote in elections. These demands were made for many reasons, often because people felt that having the vote would improve their economic position.

The abolition of slavery

You have read in Chapter 1 about the economic importance and inhumanity of slavery. Those in Britain who opposed slavery demanded the following:

- the abolition of the British slave trade – the capture, sale and transportation of slaves in British boats from Africa to colonies in the Americas

- the end to slavery in British colonies – the practice of human beings owning other human beings.

The abolition of the slave trade in Britain and the British Empire provides a good example of how and why the political system accepted demands for change. Many of those who opposed slavery did so for religious reasons. Two groups in particular were to play an important part in the campaign against slavery and the slave trade.

- **The Quakers** These were members of a religious group that was formed in the seventeenth century. Central to their faith was a belief in peaceful action. In 1783 a committee of Quakers was set up which included Thomas Clarkson, who was to become a leading member of the campaign to abolish slavery. The role of this committee was to uncover and publicise the horrors of the slave trade.

- **The Evangelicals** Members of the Church of England and other Protestant Churches, the Evangelicals believed that it was the responsibility of the individual to live a Christian life. In the 1780s, a group of influential Evangelicals met at the house of MP (Member of Parliament) and banker, Henry Thornton. Known as the Clapham Sect, they campaigned over issues like public manners and the abolition of the slave trade. One of the leading members of the Clapham Sect was a Yorkshire MP called William Wilberforce. In 1787 Wilberforce helped set up the Society for Effecting the Abolition of the Slave Trade (otherwise known as the Anti-Slavery Society).

Wilberforce and the abolitionists

William Wilberforce became the leading voice in Parliament for the abolition of slavery. As a member of the Church of England, he was allowed to sit in Parliament, unlike the Quakers who were barred until 1828. The abolitionists had support from a wide cross-section of the country including a number of MPs such as the influential statesman Charles James Fox. However, there were many in Parliament whose interests were bound up with the slave trade and they argued that abolition would harm their business and damage the empire. Their main argument was that freed slaves would be more expensive to employ than slave labour. Abolition would thereby drive up the price of sugar from the plantations.

In 1791, Wilberforce introduced his first parliamentary bill proposing the abolition of the slave trade. It met with fierce opposition and was defeated. In 1793 the Napoleonic Wars against France began (see pages 17–21). Those who supported the slave trade argued that the ships carrying slaves around the British Empire served as training vessels for the top quality seamen who were vital for victory against France.

Wilberforce was not to be intimidated and in 1807 his campaign was partially successful. Parliament agreed to abolish the slave trade in the West Indies. MPs voted for abolition for a number of reasons. Many believed that the slave trade was no longer necessary because there were now enough slaves in the British West Indies to maintain the production of sugar.

SOURCE A

An engraving from a series published by Leeds Anti-Slavery Society in 1853, showing two slaves being branded by a slave-owner.

By 1820, most European countries and the USA had abolished the slave trade. However, this did not prevent the slave trade continuing. After the end of the Napoleonic Wars in 1815, Royal Navy ships were used to stop illegal slave-trading. Any slave boats intercepted were returned to Sierra Leone (in Africa) and the slaves were freed. The fact that slavery still existed offended many in Britain. In 1823, the Anti-Slavery Society embarked on a high profile campaign to have slavery abolished altogether. Their cause was helped by uprisings amongst slaves in the West Indies.

The most important sugar-producing island in the West Indies was Jamaica. In 1831 a slave uprising broke out across the island. The main reason for this was a rumour that had spread among the slaves that they had been given their freedom by King William IV but were still being held in slavery by the plantation owners. The rebellion was led by the Baptist minister, Samuel 'Daddy' Sharpe. After four months the rebels were overpowered and their leaders were executed. The events in Jamaica

Leeds Anti-slavery Series No. 23.

SLAVE-BRANDING.

worried the new government in Britain led by Earl Grey, and in May 1833 Lord Stanley (the Colonial Secretary) introduced the Abolition Bill that was passed on 28 August. These were the main terms of the Act:

- for a six-year period from 1834 to 1840 slaves should serve an apprenticeship after which they would be given full freedom

- commissioners would distribute up to £20 million in compensation to slave owners

- all children under six years of age should be set free immediately.

Digging deeper

Mary Prince

The campaign against slavery included the use of propaganda – information in support of a cause – on both sides. Those who opposed slavery circulated the accounts of ex-slaves. It was hoped that by doing this they would stir up the conscience of MPs and influential people to move against slavery. One such account published in London in 1831 was that of Mary Prince.

Mary was born into slavery in Bermuda in around 1788. In her early years she was owned by a kind-hearted, good woman who treated all her slaves well. However, at the age of twelve, Mary and her family were taken to be sold at a slave auction. Her new master and mistress whipped and beat their slaves regularly. Mary was beaten with ropes and cow skin whips. In her story she told of how she was brutally treated. 'He [the master] tied me upon a ladder, and gave me a hundred lashes with his own hand.' Her next master was equally brutal. '[He] has often stripped me naked, hung me up by the wrists, and beat me with the cow skin.'

Mary's evidence shocked many in England, especially the fact that the slave owners behaved in such a violent manner.

Mary's next owner (in Antigua) was kinder to her. There she managed to put aside $100 made from selling goods such as coffee to ship captains. She also joined the Moravian Church and married a free man (an ex-slave who has been granted his freedom), Daniel James. Mary travelled to England with her owners when they took their son to school, and in England she found she was a free woman. She eventually left her master and mistress, but could not return to the West Indies for there she would still be a slave. Her husband remained in Antigua.

Some people in England argued that the slaves were happy with their position as slaves. Mary fiercely argued against this. Mary's evidence became a part of the campaign to end slavery in the empire.

SOURCE B

An illustration from Mary Prince's book The History of Mary Prince: A West Indian Slave *(1831).*

SOURCE C

... there is no modesty or decency shown by the owner to his slaves; men, women, and children are exposed alike. Since I have been here I have often wondered how English people can go into the West Indies and act in such a beastly manner ... All slaves want to be free ... to be free is very sweet ... They can't do without slaves they say. What's the reason why they can't do without slaves? They don't have them in England.

From The History of Mary Prince: A West Indian Slave *(1831)*.

Question time

1 Put the title in your book 'The abolition of slavery'. After reading through the section list the arguments for and against abolition. Then you should list the reasons why slavery was abolished.

2 Why do you think the evidence of Mary Prince had such an impact on those interested in the abolition of slavery?

Reform of the vote

The political structure in 1815

At the top of the political structure was the monarch. The king from 1820–30 was George IV and from 1830–7 William IV. The king had the power to appoint prime ministers. However the king had to take notice of the wishes of Parliament and would often appoint as prime minister the politician with most support in Parliament. From 1815–28 the prime minister was Lord Liverpool.

Parliament was divided into two Houses, the House of Lords and the House of Commons. Both were dominated in 1815 by the families who owned most of the land in the country.

The House of Lords

This House was filled with peers – those who inherited a title from an ancestor – for example Duke or Earl. The House of Lords was dominated by the landowners.

The House of Commons

The House of Commons had 658 Members of Parliament (MPs). Most MPs represented an area of the country known as a constituency. MPs were elected by voters. However the number of voters in constituencies varied. In some areas those who had the suffrage (those who could vote) were those who paid certain taxes. In other areas those who had the vote were those who owned certain pieces of land.

As Britain increasingly dominated large parts of the world, so the British system of rule by Parliament was widely admired and adopted. However there were many in Britain who pressed for change in the system. This change did not come about rapidly.

In the eighteenth century, elections to the House of Commons were controlled by a small group of landowners. The system of electing MPs was

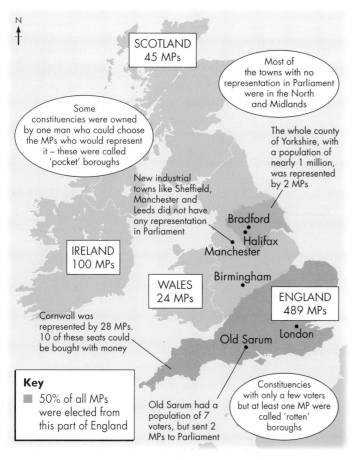

The following labels appear on the map:

SCOTLAND 45 MPs

Most of the towns with no representation in Parliament were in the North and Midlands

Some constituencies were owned by one man who could choose the MPs who would represent it – these were called 'pocket' boroughs

The whole county of Yorkshire, with a population of nearly 1 million, was represented by 2 MPs

New industrial towns like Sheffield, Manchester and Leeds did not have any representation in Parliament

Bradford
Halifax
Manchester
Birmingham

IRELAND 100 MPs

WALES 24 MPs

ENGLAND 489 MPs

London

Old Sarum

Cornwall was represented by 28 MPs. 10 of these seats could be bought with money

Constituencies with only a few voters but at least one MP were called 'rotten' boroughs

Old Sarum had a population of 7 voters, but sent 2 MPs to Parliament

Key
■ 50% of all MPs were elected from this part of England

The Electoral System in 1815.

not the same everywhere in the country and often corrupt. These were some of the weaknesses of the system:

- Many constituencies (an area that MPs are elected to represent) were controlled by wealthy landlords. These landlords, such as the Duke of Newcastle, chose who was going to be the MP. These constituencies were called 'pocket boroughs'.

- In some constituencies such as Old Sarum in Wiltshire or Dunwich in Suffolk there were hardly any voters. It was very difficult to justify why these areas had an MP. These constituencies were called 'rotten boroughs'.

- In some constituencies, such as Preston in Lancashire, the electorate (the number of people able to vote) was large but in others, including East and West Looe in Cornwall, the number of voters was very small. This made the system unfair and unrepresentative, as it did not take into account the number of people voting in each constituency. The new industrial cities such as Manchester and Leeds had no MPs to represent them.

- In many constituencies votes were bought. As a result elections were often rowdy affairs.

Digging deeper

Election day

Before reform, in many constituencies there was no contested vote on election day. This meant that people could not choose who they wanted to vote for. This was because the MP for the constituency had already been chosen. This was common because contested elections were expensive for the candidates (as there were often a few hundred voters to bribe). On election day the supporters of each side would descend on the market square and hustings (where candidates make speeches in the hope of persuading people to vote for them) would be held at which the candidates would make speeches to a large and often drunken crowd. Fights were common. Charles Dickens includes a description of election day in his book *Pickwick Papers*, written in 1836–7.

SOURCE A

'The night before the last day of the last election here, the opposite party bribed the barman at the Town Arms, to hocus the brandy and water of fourteen electors who had not yet voted but had stopped for a drink.'

'What do you mean by "hocusing" brandy and water?' inquired Mr Pickwick.

'Putting laudanum [an alcoholic substance containing the drug opium] in it,' replied Sam.

'Blessed if she didn't send them all to sleep till twelve hours after the election was over. They took one man up to the booth, in a truck, fast asleep, by way of an experiment, but it was no go – they wouldn't poll him; so they brought him back and put him to bed again.'

Sam is explaining to Mr Pickwick the kind of mischief that happens at election time.

SOURCE B

'It's a very bad road between here and London,' says the gentleman – 'Here and there it is a heavy road,' says my father. 'Especially near the canal, I think,' said the gentleman – 'Nasty bit that here,' says my father – 'Well Mr Weller,' says the gentleman, 'you are a very good driver of your horses. We are all very fond of you, Mr Weller, so in case you should have an accident when you're bringing these voters down here, and should tip them over into the canal without hurting them this is for yourself.' My father thanked them, had another glass of wine and took the money offered.

'You wouldn't believe it,' said Sam, 'that on the very next day when he came down with the voters his coach was upset on that very spot and they were all turned into the canal.'

'And got out again?' asked Mr Pickwick.

'Why,' replied Sam very slowly, 'I rather think one old gentleman was missing; I know his hat was found, but I am not certain whether his head was in it or not.'

Sam is telling Mr Pickwick a story about his father who was hired to drive a coach full of electors down from London to vote in an election.

SOURCE C

'You have come down here to see an election – eh? Spirited contest, my dear sir, very much so indeed. We have opened all the public houses in the place. It has left our opponent nothing but the beer-shops – masterly policy, my dear sir, eh?' The little man smiled complacently [in a self-satisfied way], and took a large pinch of snuff.

'And what is the likely result of the contest?' inquired Mr Pickwick.

'Why, doubtful, my dear sir, rather doubtful as yet,' replied the little man. 'Fizkin's people have got three-and-thirty voters in the lock-up coach-house at the White Hart.'

'In the coach-house!' said Mr Pickwick, much astonished.

'They keep 'em locked up there till they want 'em,' resumed the little man. 'The effect, you see, is to prevent our getting at them. Even if we could, it would be of no use, for they keep them very drunk on purpose. Smart fellow, Fizkin's agent – very smart fellow indeed.'

'We are pretty confident, though,' said Mr Perker, his voice sinking almost to a whisper. 'We had a little tea-party here, last night – five-and-forty women, my dear sir – and gave every one 'em a green parasol when she went away. Five and forty green parasols, at 3s7½d each. Got the votes of all their husbands, and half their brothers. You can't walk half a dozen yards up the street, without encountering half a dozen green parasols.'

Mr Pickwick is talking to Mr Perker, one of the candidate's agents.

Question time

Pickwick Papers was Charles Dickens' first book. It was published in weekly instalments and became very popular.

1 What are Dickens' criticisms of the electoral system?

2 Obviously Dickens has exaggerated some of the stories to make people laugh. Is the evidence provided here about the electoral system still to be trusted?

The debate about political reform

Those in favour of political reform:

SOURCE D

An engraving by William Hogarth called An Election Entertainment, *Febuary 1755. Hogarth wanted to portray the drunkenness, violence, bribery and deception that often accompanied elections in Britain.*

- The group known as the Whigs, who favoured changing Parliament by redistributing seats to areas without MPs. The Whigs were supported by large landowners who wanted to protect the power of Parliament from the monarchy. Eventually the Whigs became the Liberals as they turned into a more disciplined political party.

- Radicals who wanted to go further and give larger numbers of the population the vote.

Those against political reform:

- The Tories, who were supported mainly by country gentlemen. They thought that reform would lead to demands for further change. Most Tories pointed to the chaos of the French Revolution of 1789 as an example of what might happen if the political system were changed. A few 'liberal' Tories accepted the need for some reform.

The issue of parliamentary reform dominated politics from the end of the Napoleonic Wars to 1832. In 1815, the French Emperor, Napoleon, was defeated by the British and Prussians at the Battle of Waterloo (see page 20) and the Napoleonic Wars that had begun in 1793 were finally at an end. However, instead of bringing years of peace and stability at home, the period following 1815 was one of unrest and violence.

- The end of war against France meant unemployment for many of the 400,000 soldiers who returned to Britain looking for work.

- In East Anglia in 1816 riots broke out, property was destroyed and those desperate for food brought terror to the region. The banners they carried demanded 'bread or blood'.

- Industrial areas were hard hit by unemployment. In the West Midlands around 20 per cent of the working population were receiving poor relief (money handed out to the poor by parishes).

The message in radical newspapers and journals was that the hardship of the people was due to an unfair political system. Only when the political system had been changed would the condition of the working people improve.

One of the most famous incidents – known as the Peterloo Massacre – occurred at St Peter's Field, Manchester, on 16 August 1819. A large and peaceful crowd of 100,000 people had gathered with banners displaying slogans such as 'Love', and 'Cleanliness, Sobriety, Order and Peace'. They hoped that their demonstration would encourage Parliament to consider political reform. The size of the crowd and the growing feeling amongst the magistrates that they might face a rebellion led to the local yeomanry (armed soldiers) attacking the crowd with their sabres (swords). Eleven people were killed and a further 421 were injured. Of the injured, around 100 were women or girls.

Question time

1 What is a rotten borough?

2 From what you have read, do you think the electoral system in 1815 was fair?

3 a Which groups wanted reform?
   b Why was this?

4 a Which groups were against reform?
   b Why was this?

Digging deeper

The reaction to Peterloo

The Massacre of Peterloo *by the eighteenth-century artist, George Cruickshank, published in 1819.*

SOURCE F

I believe that you are a downright reformer. Some of you reformers ought to be hanged, and some of you are sure to be hanged – the rope is already around your necks.

A magistrate's address to the accused after the disturbance at Peterloo, printed in The Times, *27 September 1819.*

SOURCE G

These are the people all tatter'd and torn,
Who cursed the day wherein they were born,
On account of taxation too great to be bourne,
And pray for relief, from night to morn,
Who, in vain, petition in every form,
Who, peaceably meeting to ask for reform,
Were sabred by Yeomanry Cavalry, who
We thanked by THE MAN, all shaven and shorn,
All cover'd with orders-and all folorn.

The Political House that Jack Built. *This popular rhyme of late 1819 was based on the old nursery rhyme* The House that Jack Built.

SOURCE H

... prompt, decisive and efficient measures for the preservation of the public peace.

The government's description of the magistrate's action, 1819

SOURCE I

Over the field were strewn caps, bonnets, hats, shawls, and shoes and other parts of male and female dress, trampled, torn and bloody. The yeomanry had dismounted – some were easing their horses's girths ... others were wiping their sabres [swords].

A description of St Peter's Field by the radical, Samuel Bamford.

Question time

Study Sources E to I.

1   What were the contrasting reactions to Peterloo as shown in the sources?

2   Why were there these contrasting reactions?

Time for change

In 1830 the Whigs, led by Earl Grey, took power. They were committed to parliamentary reform. Other factors made the case for reform more urgent:

- from 1829–32 there was an economic recession

- harvests were poor and there was widespread unrest such as the Swing Riots that swept the southern and eastern counties in 1830–1 (see page 45)

- in the industrial centres that were not represented in Parliament, such as Leeds and Manchester, demands grew for political reform.

The First Reform Bill was introduced in March 1831. In it Lord Grey proposed increasing representation of the people in the new industrial cities by giving the vote to about 300,000 new voters and redistributing seats from many boroughs to the growing towns and cities. The bill was passed in the House of Commons by one vote but was defeated in the House of Lords. In April 1831 the General Election resulted in victory for the pro-reformers.

In September 1831, the Second Reform Bill was introduced into the House of Commons. Again it was passed by the House of Commons, but was rejected by the House of Lords. The reaction in the country was widespread violence.

In March 1832, the House of Commons passed the Third Reform Bill. With the country in a state of unrest, Earl Grey advised the king to appoint enough new peers to the House of Lords to see that the bill was passed. However, eventually William IV persuaded those peers in the House of Lords who objected to reform to allow the bill to pass. The bill became the Great Reform Act in June 1832. Its main points were:

- in the counties (countryside) the vote was given to adult males owning freehold property worth at least 40s (£2) per year or land worth at least £10 per year

- in the towns the vote was given to adult males owning or occupying property worth at least £10 per year.

In the end the changes made to the electoral system were not that great. A new political system had not been created. The working class were not given the vote and the old political groups kept their power and influence.

Chartism

From 1832 the new Parliament introduced many reforms. However, many people still felt excluded from the political system, in particular the working class who were not given the vote in 1832. Some of the reforms passed by the new Parliament were seen as threatening to the working class. The most obvious example of this was the New Poor Law of 1834 that set up workhouses for the poor in which conditions were often extremely harsh (see pages 44–5).

The Six Points
OF THE
PEOPLE'S
CHARTER.

1. A VOTE for every man twenty-one years of age, of sound mind, and not undergoing punishment for crime.
2. THE BALLOT. – To protect the elector in the exercise of his vote.
3. NO PROPERTY QUALIFICATIONS for Members of Parliament – thus enabling the constituencies to return the man of their choice, be he rich or poor.
4. PAYMENT OF MEMBERS, thus enabling an honest tradesperson, working man, or other person, to serve a constituency, when taken from his business to attend to the interests of his country.
5. EQUAL CONSTITUENCIES, securing the same amount of representation for the same number of electors, instead of allowing small constituencies to swamp the votes of larger ones.
6. ANNUAL PARLIAMENTS, thus presenting the most effectual check to bribery and intimidation, since though a constituency might be bought once in seven years (even with the ballot), no purse could buy a constituency (under a system of universal suffrage) in each resulting twelvemonth; and since members, when elected for a year only, would not be able to defy and betray their constituents as now.

The Six Points of the People's Charter.

In 1837 the London Working Men's Association led by Francis Place and William Lovett drew up a charter of demands that was published in May 1838. This group became known as Chartists. They demanded:

- universal suffrage (vote)
- secret ballots
- no property qualifications for MPs
- payment of MPs
- constituencies of equal size
- annual Parliaments.

As economic conditions worsened, so the campaign for these demands gathered strength. From 1837–42 there was an economic recession. Unemployment increased, and wages for those who were in employment were cut. An example of a group who suffered were the cotton spinners in Glasgow. In April 1837 the spinners went on strike. During the strike a strike-breaking spinner was shot dead. Five Glasgow spinners were accused of his murder and were transported to Australia. Support for the spinners was at the heart of the Chartist campaign in Glasgow in 1838.

In May 1838 the National Petition that became the People's Charter was launched in Glasgow. There were huge demonstrations in favour of the Charter held in Birmingham, Manchester and London. A National Convention met in London in February 1839. The Chartists now considered various points including using strikes and violent means to get their way. Tensions rose throughout the country. Mass meetings were held at Hartshead Moor (21 May) and Kersall Moor (25 May) amongst others.

Tensions between the Chartists and authorities were high. On 4 July 1839 a riot broke out in the Bull Ring, Birmingham, after police were called in to break up a Chartist meeting. Many Chartist leaders including William Lovett were arrested.

On 12 July the Charter was presented to Parliament. Containing over 1,280,000 signatures it was rejected by 235 votes to 46. This rejection angered many Chartists who were now determined to use other means to get the vote. In early November 1839, a crowd of around 7000 colliers and ironworkers led by John Frost descended on the Welsh town of Newport. This led to the Newport Rising.

Digging deeper

The Newport Rising, 1839

The rejection of the Charter was a bitter blow to its supporters. Across Britain, Chartists met to discuss their next move. In some areas feelings ran high, especially in South Wales. There, support for the Charter had been strong. Many workers in the iron and coal mines of the area saw it as a way of reducing the considerable power of the mine owners. In 1838 a local draper [cloth-seller] and Justice of the Peace, John Frost, was chosen to be a delegate to the Chartist Convention. When the Charter was rejected, Frost returned to South Wales and began to make plans with others for an armed uprising in Newport. The aim behind the rising was to release imprisoned Chartists and to win the political rights so recently denied.

During the night of 3 November 1839 over 7000 Chartists marched through the night armed with weapons from muskets to clubs, determined to see the Charter accepted by whatever means. However, the authorities had been tipped off and a force of heavily armed police, special constables and 32 soldiers from the 45th regiment awaited them in the Westgate Hotel. Amongst the ranks of the Chartists were many with high hopes for the coming struggle.

The Chartists arrived in Newport at about 9am and made their way through the town until they reached the Westgate Hotel. The fighting that followed lasted around 20 minutes with 14 Chartists losing their lives and 50 being wounded. Among the dead was George Shell (see Source A). In February 1840, Frost and the other five leaders of the rebellion were imprisoned and then transported into exile.

SOURCE A

Dear Parents, I hope this will find you well, as I am myself at this present. I shall this night be engaged in a glorious struggle for freedom, and should it please God to spare my life I shall see you soon; but if not, grieve not for me, I shall have fallen in a noble cause. Farewell!

George Shell, an eighteen-year-old from Pontypool writing to his parents on the night of 3 November 1839.

SOURCE B

Chartist rioters, led by Frost, fire on magistrates at the Westgate Hotel in Newport.

1842 Charter

Despite the fact that most of the Chartist leaders were in prison, support for the movement continued. A second Charter was presented to Parliament in May 1842 and contained over three million signatures. Again, Parliament rejected the petition by a large majority. In the summer of 1842, there was a wave of industrial unrest in the North that became known as the Plug Riots. Many of the strike leaders had been Chartists and the authorities responded to the violence with another round-up of known members of the movement. By the end of 1842 around 1500 Chartists had been charged with various offences. Although some Chartists were violent, it should not be seen as a violent movement. Fergus O'Connor is often described as a 'physical force' Chartist, as he was willing to use violence as the means of achieving the points on the Charter. However, O'Connor's main weapon against Parliament was the newspaper that he edited, *The Northern Star*.

1848 Charter

In 1848 the new Whig government led by Lord John Russell was immediately faced with the prospect of economic distress as the result of a poor harvest. In 1848 a revolution in France gave encouragement to those who hoped for some kind of uprising in Britain. Support for Chartism again grew. Fergus O'Connor addressed meetings across the country, including one at Kennington Common in south London in front of a crowd of 20,000 people. A Chartist Convention was called in April 1848 and the following strategy was agreed:

- a petition was to be presented to Parliament after a mass public meeting

- if the petition was rejected a National Assembly would be summoned which would sit until the main points of the Charter were accepted by Parliament.

The authorities reacted with alarm at the proposed events. The Chartist march to Parliament was banned by the police in April. The Duke of Wellington was put in charge of the defence of the capital and 85,000 special constables were enrolled. The queen left London for the Isle of Wight. The meeting duly went ahead on 10 April at Kennington Common. O'Connor spoke to the 20,000-strong crowd advising them that the procession had been forbidden. The Charter containing 2 million names was presented to Parliament and was promptly rejected. Chartism had failed and after this the movement died out. However, in the coming sixty years, five out of the six points of the Chartist petition were to be adopted.

Digging deeper

Was Chartism an economic or a political movement?

Historians differ very much in their opinions about the true nature of the Chartist movement. Here is a selection of arguments from people writing at the time and the view of historians.

SOURCE C

It was a purely political movement – Chartism – which was mainly responsible for uniting the workers against their oppressors. The whole working class is behind the great Chartist assault on the middle class.

Extract from The Condition of the Working Class in England *(1844) by Friedrich Engels. The German philosopher was a communist who believed in and hoped for a working-class revolution.*

SOURCE D

Chartism was a political movement based largely on economic grievances. The strength of the Chartist movement fluctuated with the movements of trade, and was apparent in the peak months of unemployment.

From A Social and Economic History of Britain, 1760–1980 *(1949) by Pauline Gregg.*

SOURCE E

Impatience engendered [caused] by fireless grates and breakfastless tables, was the driving force of much of Northern Chartism.

From The Chartist Movement *(1917) by Mark Hovell.*

SOURCE F

Chartism was a political movement ... A political movement doesn't simply reflect distress and pain. It is distinguished by the shared belief of its members that the only solution to the problem of distress is a political one.

Adapted from Language of Class *(1982) by Ralph Stedman Jones.*

SOURCE G

Knaves will tell you that it is because you have no property, you are unrepresented [do not have the vote]. I tell you that on the contrary, it is because you are unrepresented that you have no property ... your poverty is the result not the cause of you being unrepresented.

Bronterre O'Brien, a Chartist, writing at the time of the petitions.

SOURCE H

This question of universal suffrage was a knife and fork question after all; this question was a bread and cheese question; ... and if any man asked him what he meant by universal suffrage, he would answer, that every working man in the land had a right to have a good coat to his back, a comfortable abode [home] in which to shelter himself and his family, a good dinner upon his table, ... and as much wages for that work as would keep him in plenty.

From a speech made in September 1838 at Kersall Moor by Joseph Rayner Stephens, a Chartist leader in the north of England.

Question time

Some of the sources on the previous page suggest that the main cause of Chartism was the economic conditions suffered by the working class. Other sources argue that Chartism was a struggle for political rights.

1 Find evidence from the sources to back each of these opinions.

2 What is *your* opinion? Choose from the three options below and justify your choice using evidence from the sources.

a Chartism was the result of economic distress.

b Chartism was a struggle for political rights.

c Chartism was a struggle for political rights but had economic causes.

Political leaders and political parties

Robert Peel (1788–1850)

Robert Peel was one of the most significant prime ministers of the nineteenth century. He is famous for using his place in the political system to introduce change. The reasons for change, however, were to protect the system rather than to challenge it.

The son of a factory owner, Peel entered the House of Commons in 1809 as a Tory. He was an impressive politician and in 1812 was made Irish Secretary. This was an important job for someone who was only 24 years of age. In 1801, the Irish Parliament had been abolished and Ireland was ruled from Westminster with the Irish Secretary having considerable power. Most Irish people were Catholics although there was an important Protestant minority. However, Catholics could not vote in elections and, while he was Irish Secretary, Peel supported this idea.

SOURCE A

From 1822–7 Peel served as Home Secretary under the Prime Minister, Lord Liverpool. He introduced many new measures to improve the legal system including the abolition of capital punishment (the death penalty) for many offences. Peel was then appointed Home Secretary in the government led by the Duke of Wellington between 1828 and 1830. In 1829 Peel set up the Metropolitan Police Force in London. The nicknames of the new policemen were 'peelers' or 'bobbies' after their founder. Also in 1829 Peel backed an even more controversial measure, that of Catholic Emancipation, something he had been against when he was Irish Secretary. Many Tories opposed this move of granting Catholics the vote and giving them full civil rights (equality with Protestants). Peel, however, believed that if Catholics were not given full rights there would be serious unrest in Ireland.

Robert Peel.

In 1834 Peel published the Tamworth Manifesto which laid out the principles for his brand of Conservatism. In November 1834, Peel was asked to be prime minister by the king. Peel then called an election at which he issued the Tamworth Manifesto. He resigned in April 1835. However, in this time he managed to propose the reform of the Church of England. In 1841, Peel and the Conservative Party won a victory in the General Election. At this time the country was in crisis. Economic hardship had created the conditions in which Chartism flourished (see page 89). The Corn Laws were in place to protect wheat farmers by taxing foreign wheat coming into the country. Many thought they were unfair as they kept the price of bread high. Many also believed that protectionism damaged the economy, arguing that Britain would only truly prosper with free trade. In 1838 the Anti-Corn Law League was set up to campaign against the Corn Laws.

Peel believed that the way to improve the economic and social crisis in the country was through financial reform. In 1842 he re-introduced income tax, which had been abolished in 1816, as a way of making richer people pay more tax. Limited social reform took place with the Mines Act of 1842 (which restricted the work of women and children in mines) and the Factory Act of 1844 (which introduced inspectors into factories and brought in new safety measures).

In October 1845 it was clear that the potato crop in Ireland had been damaged by fungus and the prospect of famine loomed (see page 95). Peel had already become convinced that the Corn Laws were no longer necessary for the protection of farmers and that they were an unnecessary cause of social division.

In May 1846 the Corn Laws were repealed but at a huge political cost to Peel. Two-thirds of the Conservative Party opposed him. Repeal of the Corn Laws marked the end of Peel's political career – the Conservative Party was bitterly divided and his government collapsed in June 1846.

Four years later Peel died after being thrown from his horse. The extent of public distress at the news of his death was a reflection of how highly he was thought of by people of all classes.

Question time

1   Describe Peel's achievements while he was prime minister.

2   Explain the meaning of the term 'protectionism'.

Digging deeper

The Irish famine

By the mid-1840s the population of Ireland was over eight million. Some people lived in the major towns and cities of Dublin, Belfast or Cork but most lived in the countryside. Large numbers lived in the far west of Ireland on landholdings. These were small farms rented by peasant farmers. The main crop grown was the potato, and around a third of the population relied on this as their sole source of food.

The summer of 1845 was warm and the hopes for a good potato harvest were high. However, in October, when the potatoes were dug from the ground, they quickly disintegrated into a pulp. Across Ireland the potato crop was devastated by potato blight. The next year the crop failed again. The result was disastrous for the peasant population. As reserves of potatoes were used up, hunger set in. Those who visited the scenes of distress were appalled (see Source B).

In Britain there was widespread sympathy for the victims of the famine. Robert Peel, the prime minister until June 1846, set up a Relief Commission and imported £100,000 of American corn to help relieve the famine. Because many peasants could not afford to buy the corn he ordered work schemes on roads that would employ people for cash. By August 1846, around 650 voluntary committees had been set up to help the needy. However, Peel was followed as prime minister by Lord John Russell. Russell did not share Peel's belief that the government should hand out food. Many in Ireland tried to help but by early 1847 thousands were dying. Eventually the government set up soup kitchens in March 1847, but still the famine continued.

In 1847, the potato crop was healthy but small. In 1848, famine ravaged the country once more. Many tenants were evicted from their homes by heartless landlords. Those who could attempted to emigrate to England or the USA. Conditions on board what were known as the 'coffin' ships

were dreadful. In all around 1.5 million Irish people emigrated while around 1.4 million died of starvation or disease. The famine left a legacy of bitterness against the British that remains to this day.

SOURCE B

I ventured through that parish this day, to ascertain [check] the condition of the inhabitants, and although a man not easily moved, I confess myself unmanned [disturbed] by the extent and intensity of suffering I witnessed, more especially among the women and little children, crowds of whom were to be seen scattered over the turnip fields, like a flock of famished crows, devouring the raw turnips, and mostly half naked, shivering in the snow and sleet, uttering exclamations of despair, whilst their children were screaming with hunger. I am a match for anything else I may meet with here, but this I cannot stand.

An account from 1846 by Captain Wynne, an official in West Clare, Ireland.

Investigation

Historians disagree about the reasons for the Irish potato famine and the British reaction to it. Your task is to explore the Internet for different interpretations.

To begin with, try looking at the websites for this investigation at

www.heinemann.co.uk/hotlinks.

Find accounts of the famine from the time and accounts written later by historians. How do they compare in their interpretations?

Benjamin Disraeli (1804–81)

Benjamin Disraeli.

In 1867 leading Conservative politicians such as the Chancellor of the Exchequer, Benjamin Disraeli, believed that reform was inevitable. His aim was to introduce a reform that would suit the Conservative Party by trying to change constituency boundaries so that they would win more seats. He also wanted to boost Conservative morale; they had not been in power for around twenty years. Disraeli believed that by introducing limited reform he would prevent more radical reform by the Liberals.

The result was the Second Reform Act of 1867, another step on the road to full democracy. These were the main features:

- nearly one million extra electors, mainly town-based householders, could vote
- all householders in towns were given the vote
- in towns of less than 10,000, voters lost one of their two MPs.

Disraeli became leader of the Conservative Party in 1868. He was an impressive speaker and a widely read author. His background was Jewish although he was a member of the Church of England. He believed in change as a means of defending tradition. Disraeli was prime minister twice, briefly in 1868 and then 1874–80. During his second period in office his government introduced a number of important reforms.

- The 1874 Factory Act reduced the number of hours employees worked in a day and introduced the half-day on Saturday.
- The 1874 Public Worship Regulation Act halted the use of Catholic practices in Church of England services.
- The 1875 Artisans' Dwelling Act allowed local authorities to knock down slum housing.
- The 1875 Public Health Act brought together all previous laws on issues such as sewerage systems and drains.
- The 1875 Sale of Food and Drugs Act set out rules against bad food being sold.
- The 1875 Conspiracy and Protection of Property Act allowed unions to demonstrate peacefully.
- The 1875 Employers and Workmen Act put employers and employees on the same legal footing.
- The 1876 Education Act set up committees to encourage children to attend school. This was partly due to pressure from the Church of England which wanted to fill its schools.

In foreign policy Disraeli encouraged the growth of the British Empire. In 1875 he bought a large share in the Suez Canal. This was important as it provided a short cut to India (see page 32).

However, Disraeli did not intervene in Irish affairs. From 1879 a severe agricultural depression hit Britain and Ireland. Disraeli's government did little to help those suffering the effects of this.

William Gladstone (1809–98)

At first Gladstone was a Conservative, but eventually became a Liberal. He was Chancellor of the Exchequer 1852–5 and 1859–66. In that time he introduced a series of budgets that firmly established the principle of free trade. He cut duties on imports and also cut income tax. In his time as chancellor he established the principle that public money should be spent wisely and without waste.

In 1868 Gladstone became prime minister, a post he was to hold four times. His first ministry lasted to 1874 and saw some important changes based on ideas of social justice and administrative efficiency.

- In 1869 Gladstone ended the privileges of the Protestant Church of Ireland. This was called disestablishment.

- Gladstone laid the foundations of a national education system with the 1870 Elementary Education Act.

- Army reforms of 1871 led to an increase in the size of the army and made it more efficient. Gladstone insisted that promotions in the army should be based on merit.

- The 1872 Licensing Act introduced licences for inns and public houses.

- Trade unions were given legal rights with the 1871 Trade Union Act although violence in strikes was made illegal.

William Gladstone.

- The legal system was improved with the 1873 Judicature Act.

- Public health improved with the 1872 Public Health Act.

Gladstone's Liberal Party lost the 1874 General Election but he became prime minister again 1880–5. His second period as prime minister was not as successful as the first, but he did manage to extend the vote further with the 1884 Representation of the People Act. This Act extended the vote in the countryside and added another 2.6 million male voters to the electorate. Gladstone also passed an important act for Ireland, the 1881 Land Act. This gave tenant farmers important rights including the right to a fair rent.

Gladstone was again prime minister in 1886 and 1892–4. In these years he concentrated on the issue of Ireland. Many Irish politicians campaigned for Home Rule, in other words an Irish Parliament in Dublin to run Irish affairs rather than being run from the Houses of Parliament in London. Ireland was still suffering social problems, especially over the issue of land.

By 1886 Gladstone was convinced that Home Rule for Ireland would help to solve Ireland's problems. However, this idea was unpopular with many in his party who believed that Home Rule would undermine the empire and give power to the Irish Catholics. The Conservative Party also opposed Home Rule. In 1886 and 1893 Gladstone tried to introduce Home Rule but both times he failed.

Digging deeper

Gladstone, Disraeli and Queen Victoria

For nearly half a century, Gladstone and Disraeli were personal and political rivals. They had very different personalities and did not like each other. This dislike was made greater by the very different relationship they each had with Queen Victoria.

In this period, the queen was an important political figure. Disraeli's natural charm and flattery of the queen was well received. In April 1876 he made her Empress of India – she approved of this with great enthusiasm. Her response was to write that Disraeli was 'full of poetry, romance and chivalry' [politeness].

Victoria's view of Gladstone was entirely different. In a letter to one of her daughters, in 1876, she wrote that he was 'so very arrogant, tyrannical and obstinate with no knowledge of the world or human nature'. She also accused him of being 'that half madman' and 'not quite sane'. Her dislike of him came partly from a suspicion of his policies – she preferred Conservative politicians. More importantly she

disliked Gladstone because he was a serious man who did not flatter her and was quite blunt. Queen Victoria once said, 'He addresses me like a public meeting'. He wrote her long memos that she did not understand and had to get her secretary to summarise. Disraeli's correspondence was full of flattery with terms like 'our beloved sovereign'.

The relationship between the three was further complicated by the hatred Disraeli had for Gladstone. He detested his political rival and in letters to his friends, Disraeli accused Gladstone of being mad. Gladstone protested that he did not hate Disraeli, but there is evidence to show that he had little liking for his rival. He accused him of lacking principles and called him 'the worst and most immoral minister since the early part of the century'.

When Disraeli died in 1881 the queen sent two wreaths of primroses (her dead husband's favourite flowers) for his coffin. She ignored Gladstone's funeral in 1898.

Activity time

Choose one from Peel, Disraeli or Gladstone. Investigate in detail his life and political career.

1   Write an obituary for your chosen politician.

2   Write a speech to be read in the House of Commons upon the retirement of your chosen politician.

Women in the nineteenth and early-twentieth centuries

The introduction of factories changed the way in which some women worked in the nineteenth and early-twentieth centuries. Upper-class women continued not to work, but the job opportunities for working-class and, eventually, middle-class women broadened.

- Women continued to work in the home as they had always done, and in industries traditionally associated with women, such as hat- or dressmaking.

- New industries led to the appearance of wage-earning women in the factories of the new industrial areas. Many of the new industries relied on women. In 1911, for example, there were around 600,000 women working in the textile industries.

- Towards the end of the nineteenth century, the opportunity for quite well-paid work in the service sector became available to women, for example, as telephonists or shop assistants.

Patterns of employment

In the nineteenth century, large numbers of women worked as domestic servants. In 1891 around 1.8 million women worked for other people in jobs ranging from cook to washerwoman. Many more women worked in their own homes, bringing up a family and running their own household. However, millions of women worked outside the home, either because they were unmarried or the money brought in by their husbands was not enough to support the household.

In many industries women were excluded from skilled work. In the view of most in society the woman's place was in the home, and the emergence of wage-earning women in male-dominated industries caused concern to many men. Many working men also feared women taking their jobs, particularly as women were cheaper to employ.

The widely-held view was that women and men dominated different spheres of life. The woman's sphere was the home; the man's sphere was considered to be that of politics, intellectual life and full-time employment. This view of women helps to explain why women were not given the vote in national elections although they did have the vote in some very limited areas of public life.

- In 1834 the Poor Law Amendment Act gave women the right to vote for Poor Law Guardians (those who dealt with the poor in a local area).

- Women also had the right to vote in local elections. By 1900 there were about one million women eligible to vote at council and parish elections.

- In 1907 women were given the right to stand as candidates at county council elections.

As early as 1792, Mary Wollstonecraft had argued for the right of women to vote in her publication *A Vindication of the Rights of Women*. As a greater number of men were given the vote by the Reform Acts of 1867 and 1884, so the argument that women should be given the vote was strengthened. In 1867 the National Society for Women's Suffrage was set up to campaign for the vote at national elections to be given to women.

The suffragists

The cause of women and the vote is often associated with violent protest. However not all the protest was violent. There were many peaceful suffragists, so-called because they believed that women had a right to the suffrage, that is, the vote. Perhaps the most effective campaigner on the issue of women and the vote was Millicent Fawcett. She believed that women could be given the vote through the power of logical argument. If, argued Fawcett, Parliament made laws that women had to obey, then women should take a part in making those laws. Similarly, if women employed men as, for instance, their gardener, then surely they should have the same voting rights as the gardener. Many women joined organisations committed to peaceful means, such as the National Union of Women's Suffrage Societies (NUWSS). By 1914, the NUWSS had a membership of 50,000 and was active in campaigning against anti-suffrage candidates at by-elections.

The suffragettes

In 1903 a leading campaigner for the vote for women, Emmeline Pankhurst and her daughters, Christabel and Sylvia, set up the Women's Social and Political Union (WSPU). Their members were called 'suffragettes' and their aim was to persuade the government to allow women to vote. The WSPU adopted the usual tactics of political campaigning such as marches, rallies and meetings. They gained a distinct identity, with their purple, white and green campaigning colours being highly visible on posters, banners and leaflets. However, the WSPU also decided to use more direct and militant tactics to try to get more publicity for votes for women. From 1909, suffragettes attacked the property of those they felt were their opponents. Windows were smashed and some buildings deliberately destroyed by fire.

Between 1911 and 1912 there was a lull in the violence while the WSPU waited to see if Parliament would respond to their pressure. When it failed to do so the violence resumed, with some protestors being arrested and put in prison. Imprisoned suffragettes who went on hunger strike were force-fed. When this was shown not to work the government changed its tactics. In 1913 the Prisoner Temporary Discharge (popularly knows as the 'Cat and Mouse') Act was introduced. It allowed those on hunger strike to be temporarily released. When their health had improved they could be re-arrested. The WSPU was important but there were many divisions in the group and a public backlash against its violent tactics caused it to become weakened by 1914.

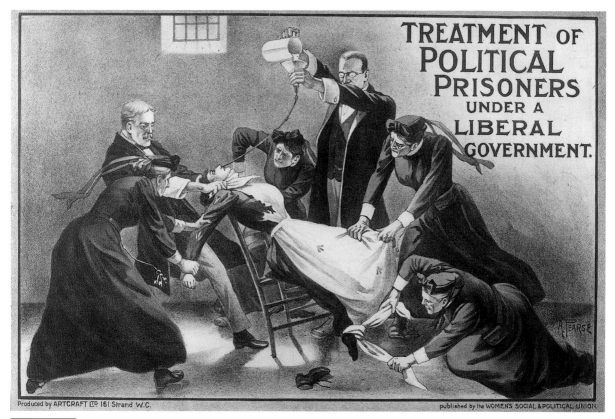

TREATMENT OF POLITICAL PRISONERS UNDER A LIBERAL GOVERNMENT.

Produced by ARTCRAFT LTD 161 Strand W.C.

published by the WOMEN'S SOCIAL & POLITICAL UNION

A poster published by the WSPU, campaigning against the force-feeding of suffragettes.

Women working in a munitions factory during the First World War.

Women get the vote

Before 1914 there were some attempts by MPs to change the law to give some women the vote, but these bills were defeated. By the end of the First World War, in 1918, some women had been given the vote. This was for the following reasons.

- During the First World War the suffrage movements threw all their energy into the war effort. Not only that, women made a vital contribution to the war effort. This was recognised by the newspapers and other media which portrayed them in a positive light. It is likely that this had an effect on attitudes towards women and the vote.

- Most politicians realised that women's suffrage was inevitable. The suspension of the suffragist and suffragette campaigns made it easier for those politicians like Herbert Asquith, who had been against women's right to vote, to change their minds and to give women the vote.

- The appointment in 1916, of the pro-suffrage Prime Minister David Lloyd George, meant that women were more likely to get the vote.

- By 1916 all political parties believed that they could benefit from women being given the vote.

The 1918 Representation of the People Act gave the vote to all women over the age of 30 who were either married, local government voters or householders. Many were still excluded from voting, including those who had worked as part of the war effort during 1914–18. The act resulted in a female electorate of around 8.5 million and was another important change in politics. In November 1918 the Eligibility of Women Act was passed, allowing women to stand as candidates in the General Election of December 1918. The first women elected was Countess Markiewicz, who was elected to stand for Sinn Fein. However, she refused to accept the legitimacy of the Westminster Parliament and did not sit as an MP. The first woman to sit as an MP, Nancy Astor, was elected in 1919. In 1928 women were finally given equal voting rights with men.

Digging deeper

Emily Wilding Davison – suicide or accident?

In 1913 Emily Wilding Davison, a suffragette, threw herself under the king's horse at the annual horse-race called the Derby. Did she know that she was going to die? Or was she carrying out a protest that went horribly wrong?

SOURCE C

With a fellow suffragette, Emily had planned a Derby protest without tragedy – a mere waving of the purple, white and green flag at Tattenham Corner, which, by its suddenness, it was hoped would stop the race. Whether from the first her purpose was more serious, or whether a final impulse altered her resolve, I know not. Her friend declares that she would not thus have died without writing a farewell message to her mother. Yet she sewed the WSPU colours inside her coat as though to ensure that no mistake could be made as to her motive when her dead body should be examined.

Adapted from evidence given by the suffragette Sylvia Pankhurst, daughter of Emmeline Pankhurst, after Emily's death.

SOURCE D

She stood alone there, close to the white-painted rails where the course bends round at Tattenham Corner; she looked absorbed and yet far away from everybody else and seemed to have no interest in what was going on around her. A minute before the race started she raised a paper of her own or some kind of card before her eyes. I was watching her hand. It did not seem to shake. Even when I heard the pounding of the horses' hoofs moving closer I saw she was still smiling. And suddenly she slipped under the rail and ran out into the middle of the racecourse. It was all over so quickly. Emily was under the hoofs of one of the horses and seemed to be hurled for some distance across the grass. The horse stumbled sideways and its jockey was thrown from its back. She lay very still.

An account by a suffragette eyewitness, Mary Richardson, in 1913.

SOURCE E

Emily Davison clung to her conviction [belief] that one great tragedy, the deliberate throwing into the breach of a human life, would put an end to the intolerable torture of women. And so she threw herself at the king's horse, in full view of the king and queen and a great multitude of their Majesties' subjects.

Emmeline Pankhurst describing Emily Davison's death in her autobiography My Own Story, *(1914).*

SOURCE F

Anmer [the horse] struck the woman with his chest, and she was knocked over screaming. Blood rushed from her nose and mouth. The king's horse turned a complete somersault, and the jockey, Herbert Jones, was knocked off and seriously injured. An immense crowd at once invaded the course. The woman was picked up and placed in a motor car and taken in an ambulance to Epsom Cottage Hospital.

From The Daily Mirror, *5 June 1913*

SOURCE G

Waiting there in the sun, in that happy scene, among the heedless crowd, she had in her soul the thought, the vision of wronged women. That thought she held to her; that vision she kept before her. Thus inspired, she threw herself into the fierce current of the race. So greatly did she care for freedom that she died for it.

Adapted from Votes for Women, *12 June 1913*.

SOURCE H

Mother was ill from her second hunger-strike when there came the news of Emily Davison's historic act. She had stopped the king's horse at the Derby and was lying mortally injured. We were startled as everyone else. Not a word had she said of her purpose. Taking counsel with no one, she had gone to the racecourse, waited her moment, and rushed forward. Horse and jockey were unhurt, but Emily Davison paid with her life for making the whole world understand that women were in earnest for the vote. Probably in no other way and at no other time and place could she so effectively have brought the concentrated attention of millions to bear upon the cause.

Adapted from Unshackled *(1959) by the suffragette, Christabel Pankhurst.*

Question time

Did Emily Davison commit suicide or was her death a tragic accident? Explain your answer to this question, backing your ideas up by either quoting from or referring to the sources.

3 Assessment section

The repeal of the Corn Laws was a controversial event. Peel's reasons for repealing the Corn Laws have been the subject of much debate.

PUNCH'S MONUMENT TO PEEL.

From Punch, *published after Peel's death in 1850.* Punch *was a popular and widely read magazine. The original caption reads 'Cheap Bread'.*

[For Peel] it was the achievement [of repealing the Corn Laws] that mattered, not the price that had to be paid for it. Over almost a decade he had seen the Corn Laws grow into a bitter social issue. He had made his mind up that the problem had to be solved.

Adapted from the work of a twentieth century historian, Norman Gash.

[Peel] is so vain that he wants to figure in history as the settler of all great questions [in this case the Corn Laws].

Adapted from a letter by Benjamin Disraeli, written in December 1845. Disraeli was a member of Peel's Conservative Party and was the leading critic of the policy of repeal of the Corn Laws.

1   Look at Source B. Why, according to this source, did Peel repeal the Corn Laws?

2   Look at Source C. How and why does Source C differ from Source B in explaining why the Corn Laws were repealed?

3   Look at who produced Sources B and C. How might this explain why their versions of events are different?

4   'The Corn Laws were repealed as a result of famine in Ireland.' Comment on this statement, using all the sources and your own knowledge.

Who was the greatest?

This activity should be done in pairs or in larger groups. Here is a list of political figures mentioned in this chapter:

William Wilberforce, Robert Peel, Benjamin Disraeli, William Gladstone, Emmeline Pankhurst, Millicent Fawcett, Mary Wollstonecraft.

There are many arguments about which of these people was the greatest political figure of the nineteenth and early-twentieth centuries. The choice is yours. For each political figure you must identify and write down the following:

● what were his/her achievements

● why should he/she be admired

● how did his/her actions change the country

● what were his/her less attractive features?

You may need to use your school library or the Internet to do some research. When you have done this you should be able to present an argument explaining who you think was the greatest and why. Write this argument in your book and then present it to the rest of your class.

Chose a turning point

During the nineteenth century there were a number of highly significant turning points including the Great Reform Act of 1832, the abolition of slavery in 1834 or the repeal of the Corn Laws in 1846.

Your task is to chose what you think is the most important political turning point of the period covered by this chapter. When you have made your choice you should do the following:

● describe the turning point

● explain why its impact is so significant.

Further reading

Malcolm Chandler *Votes for Women, c.1900–28* (Heinemann, 2001)

R.G. Grant *Lives in Crisis: the African–American Slave Trade* (Hodder Wayland, 2002)

4 The First World War 1914–18

The impact of the First World War on European culture and civilisation was enormous. It shaped the development of the twentieth century and involved destruction and slaughter on a previously unimaginable scale. It scarred and traumatised a whole generation. In its wake came revolution and upheaval.

Why did the First World War break out?

The Austro-Hungarian Empire and the Balkans at the outbreak of war in 1914.

The First World War broke out in the Balkans region in south-east Europe. Very quickly it turned into a European, and then a world war.

A Balkans war

The spark for war came in the Balkans – Romania, Bulgaria, Serbia, Montenegro, Albania and Greece. This corner of Europe had been part of the Ottoman (Turkish) Empire for many centuries. However, the power of the Ottoman Empire had begun to decline in the nineteenth century. This gave hope to those nationalities in the region that wanted greater independence.

- The Austro-Hungarian Empire was very keen to establish its influence over the Balkans region. Within its empire there were many different nationalities, including Serbs. The last thing it wanted was for Serbia to grow in influence because that might unsettle the Serbs in its empire.

- The Russians also had an interest in the area as they saw themselves as protectors of Serbia and the Serbs. This was because the Russians and Serbs were Slavs, sharing similar languages and customs. The Russians also felt it their duty to protect the many Orthodox Christians of the

Balkans region. This Pan-Slavism (a belief in the unity of the Slav peoples) was seen as a threat by the Austrians. The Russians also wanted to extend their interest in the area because they hoped to have some kind of control over the Dardanelles Straits, which would give them guaranteed access to the Mediterranean.

Since 1878 Austria had been running the provinces of Bosnia-Herzogovina (just north of Montenegro) although they technically belonged to the Ottoman Empire. The population of these provinces was racially mixed but it contained many Serbs. In 1908 the Austrians formally annexed (took over) Bosnia-Herzogovina. The Serbs and Russians were furious at this action. However, neither was strong enough to act and in 1909 Russia and Serbia had no choice but to formally recognise the annexation.

In 1912 and 1913 the Balkans Wars (a series of wars between Balkan states) saw Serbia emerge as the stronger state. This worried many Austrians who felt that Serbia would need to be restrained. Eventually tension between the Austro-Hungarian Empire and Serbia spilled into war. The murder of Archduke Franz Ferdinand in June 1914 was the excuse for war that the Austrians were looking for.

A European war

To understand how the countries of Europe became involved we must look back to 1870 when the Prussian army invaded France and won a series of crushing victories. On 18 January 1871, the new German Empire was proclaimed at Versailles near Paris. The Franco-Prussian War of 1870–1 had seen the humiliation of the French army, most spectacularly at Sedan in north-east France. As part of the peace treaty signed at Frankfurt, the French were forced to pay Germany reparations (compensation). They were also forced to hand over the wealthy regions of Alsace and Lorraine to the new Germany.

This caused bitter resentment in France and many people wanted revenge. From 1871–88, German foreign policy was directed by the Chancellor, Otto von Bismarck. He attempted to isolate France by building alliances and friendship treaties with other European powers. The rise of Germany changed the balance of power in Europe and led to diplomatic tension.

As European powers felt increasingly threatened by each other, so they made the following defensive alliances:

- **The Triple Alliance** was formed in 1882 between Germany, Austria–Hungary and Italy. The countries agreed to come to each other's aid if attacked by another power.

- **The Triple Entente** started as an alliance formed in 1894 between France and Russia (the Dual Entente) which said that if either country were attacked by Germany the other would go to its aid. In 1904 Britain signed the Entente Cordiale with France which resolved colonial differences. Britain then reached an agreement with Russia in 1907 and the Entente Cordiale became the Triple Entente.

Europe was now divided into two well-armed camps.

The war at a glance

Year	Western Front	Eastern Front	Other Fronts
1914	German armies advance through Belgium. **August:** Battle of Mons. **September:** Battle of the Marne. Schlieffen plan halted. **October–November:** Armies race for the sea. Trench warfare follows.	**August:** German armies victorious over Russians at Battle of Tanneberg and in **September:** Masurian Lakes.	**November:** British forces occupy Basra on the Persian Gulf as part of the war against Turkey.
1915	**April–May:** Germans use chlorine gas at the Battle of Ypres. **Autumn:** British and French offensives comes to little.	**May–September:** Huge offensive by German army in Galicia results in the Russian army retreating 300 miles and losing 1,000,000 soldiers. **September:** Russian commander Grand Duke Nicholas Nicholaievich replaced by Tsar Nicholas II.	War against Turkey – British forces advance on Baghdad but are forced back to Kut. **March:** Dardanelles campaign begins. **April:** Treaty of London promises parts of the Austrian Empire to Italy in exchange for joining the war. British troops conquer the Cameroons. South Africans invade German South West Africa. Fighting in East Africa.
1916	**February:** Battle of Verdun begins. **July:** Anglo-French forces attempt to relieve pressure on Verdun at the Battle of the Somme.	**September:** Advances by Russian General halted by 15 German divisions from the Western Front. Russian army loses another 1,000,000 men.	**January:** Dardanelles campaign halted. **April:** British troops in Kut forced to surrender. Russians launch a campaign against the Turks in Armenia. General Smuts pushes Germans back in East Africa.
1917	**April:** Failed French offensive at Chemin des Dames. **May:** Mutiny breaks out in the French ranks involving half of the army. British offensive at third Battle of Ypres (Passchendaele). No breakthrough in horrific conditions.	**February:** Tsar abdicates, replaced by a Provisional Government. **Summer:** Disastrous Galician campaign. **October:** Bolshevik revolution. **December:** Peace negotiations with Germans at the Polish town of Brest-Litovsk.	**April:** USA declares war on Germany. **October:** Italian line breaks at the Battle of Caporetto. Situation stabilised with help from British and French reinforcements. Over 300,000 troops lost. **December:** British take Jerusalem from the Turks.
1918	**March–April:** Germans launch huge offensive. Initially successful, then halted due to lack of reserves and supplies. **May–June:** German offensive in the Champagne region halted by French/American troops. **August:** Battles of the Marne and Amiens; Allies on the offensive. Germans are pushed back towards the border. **11 November:** Hostilities cease at 11 o'clock.	**March:** Treaty of Brest-Litovsk. Russians forced to sign away huge areas of land including the Baltic States, the Ukraine and Finland. Russian collapse in the East.	**Summer:** The Austro-Hungarian Empire disintegrates. **September:** British break Turkish lines in Palestine, helped by Arab forces led by T.E. Lawrence (Lawrence of Arabia). **October–November:** Italians break through at the Battle of Vitorio Veneto. **November:** Allied fleet arrives at Constantinople.

The war in the air and at sea	The British Home Front
War at sea: **August:** British and French navies blockade Central Powers. **December:** German Pacific Fleet defeated by British Fleet at the Battle of the Falkland Islands. German battleships bombard Scarborough and Hartlepool.	**August:** The Defence of the Realm Act (DORA). The government takes over the railways. **September:** Recruiting campaign begins. **December:** Union of Democratic Control set up by those opposing the war.
War at sea: **January:** Naval skirmish at Dogger Bank. Result inconclusive. German submarine campaign in the Atlantic. **May:** The liner *Lusitania* is sunk. **War in the air:** Germans try to draw the Royal Flying Corps back to Britain by bombing targets on the British mainland. Fifteen Zeppelin raids on British towns.	**May:** Coalition government replaces the Liberal government. Munitions Act gives the government power to take direct control of munitions factories. **June:** War Committee is set up. **July:** Ministry of Munitions is set up. National Registration Act Act registers men eligible for military service. **October:** British nurse Edith Cavell is executed by the Germans.
War at sea: **31 May/1 June:** Battle of Jutland. Result inconclusive **War in the air:** **April:** French introduce the Nieuport 3 and Spad 3 planes. The British unveil the Sopwith Camel. 41 Zeppelin raids against England.	**January:** Conscription is introduced. **April:** Easter Uprising in Dublin by those who want Irish Independence. **December:** Lloyd George becomes prime minister.
War at sea: Submarine war against Allied shipping intensifies. Introduction of convoy system in the second half of the year reduces losses considerably.	**February:** Bread rationed, voluntary rationing of other foods food shortages increase. Government guarantees prices of basic food. Women's Land Army created. Air raids continue against towns on the east coast.
War at sea: Repeated naval raids on the British coast. **June:** German fleet scuttled at Scapa Flow. In June 1919, the German sailors sink their own fleet when it is under guard at Scapa Flow. **November:** Following the armistice the German fleet surrenders to the British at Rosyth.	**February:** Women over 30 are given the vote for the first time. **March:** Ministry of Information created to improve morale. **April:** Meat rationing introduced. **July:** Education Act raises the school leaving age.

Digging deeper

The Assassination of Archduke Franz Ferdinand, Sarajevo, 28 June 1914

Sunday 28 June 1914 was a warm and sunny day in Sarajevo. The Bosnian city was swept clean and colourful rugs hung from the balconies in honour of Archduke Franz Ferdinand who was due to visit the city that day. Son of Emperor Franz Joseph and heir to the Austro-Hungarian Empire, Franz Ferdinand was an important visitor. The Archduke was to be accompanied by his wife, Countess Sophie, and together they were coming to inspect the Austrian army units stationed in Sarajevo.

There were some Serbs who despised the Austrian monarchy and who saw Franz Ferdinand as a good target for assassination. One group, the Bosnian Serb movement called the Black Hand, sent six potential assassins to Sarajevo. Armed with bombs and poison in case they were arrested, the young assassins waited for the Archduke's arrival on that fateful day. Their hope was that by assassinating the Archduke they might provoke a situation out of which Serbia could gain greater independence. The Archduke was warned of potential trouble in Sarajevo but decided that the visit must go ahead.

At around 10am the cavalcade of four cars swept into Sarajevo. The Archduke looked resplendent in his pale blue uniform littered with medals. As the cars carrying the royal party approached the first member of the Black Hand, he took fright and fled. The second potential assassin was far bolder; he threw his bomb at the Archduke's car but it bounced off and exploded under the next car, injuring 20 bystanders.

The Archduke was furious at his day being ruined. He demanded to be taken immediately to the local hospital in order to visit a policeman injured in the bomb attack. On the way to the hospital one of the Black Hand terrorists, Gavrilo Princip, jumped onto the car's running board and fired at close range. One bullet went through the Archduke's neck, the other hit the Countess in the stomach. The Archduke and his wife were dead.

The assassin, Princip, was arrested. Because he was only seventeen years old at the time, he was not executed but was imprisoned at the fortress of Terezin where he died in April 1918 of tuberculosis. This assassination was the trigger for war. But why should the assassination of an obscure archduke in a remote corner of eastern Europe result in a world war?

SOURCE A

The assassination of Archduke Franz Ferdinand in June 1914.

A world war

Tension developed in Europe as the countries of the two alliances built up their armed forces. The naval race between Britain and Germany was particularly important. Britain's main priority outside the country was the protection of the empire. To that end Britain needed to maintain naval superiority. However, there were people in Germany, including the kaiser (emperor), who felt that if Germany were going to become an important world power with a large empire, it would need to challenge the dominance of the British Royal Navy. In 1898 and 1900 Navy Laws were passed in Germany. These provided for the construction of a fleet to rival the Royal Navy. The British response was to design the dreadnought, a battleship that could outperform all other warships. In 1906 the battleship was launched. The response of the German government was to build its own dreadnoughts. The race was on. Between 1906 and 1914, Britain built 29 dreadnoughts; Germany built 17.

The arms race did not automatically lead to war. On many occasions the British and German governments tried to reach agreement about naval and other issues. There were attempts in 1899 and 1907 at the Hague Conferences to limit the arms race but both ended in failure. In 1912 Lord Haldane visited Berlin in what has become known as the 'Haldane Mission'. Both sides attempted to come to an agreement about German colonial expansion and the size of their respective navies. However the talks failed, mainly because some German politicians did not want to reduce the size of their navy and saw confrontation with Britain as inevitable.

The Moroccan Crisis

In addition to military rivalry, colonial rivalry also existed between all of the Great Powers – Britain, France, Russia, Germany, Austria–Hungary and Italy – and an important example of this was Morocco. In 1911 anti-French demonstrations there led to the French sending troops into the country. The Germans argued that this action broke the agreement made between France and Germany in 1909 which had stated that Morocco was to be under French control. In response they sent the gunboat *Panther* to the port of Agadir on the coast of Morocco in July 1911. These actions provoked a strong and critical response. The British Chancellor of the Exchequer, David Lloyd George, attacked the German action in a speech full of threatening language. In the face of hostility and without the full support of its Italian and Austrian allies (see page 107) the Germans backed down. They accepted the existence of French control in Morocco in return for part of French Congo. The importance of the Moroccan Crisis was that it exposed tension and suspicion between the Great Powers.

Storm clouds gather

The fear of being surrounded by hostile neighbours and fighting a war on two fronts remained at the heart of German diplomatic policy. This was particularly the case as the emperor, Kaiser Wilhelm II, increasingly listened more to his generals than ministers for advice. In December 1912 a secret war council was held in Berlin that many historians believe was a crucial turning point on the road to war. At the meeting Wilhelm correctly predicted that Austria needed to deal with the growing threat of Serbia but that any action would probably lead to war with Russia. Wilhelm believed that in such a situation Germany would have to back its ally Austria with military support.

To the German High Command the issue was not whether the war should be fought or not, but when it should be fought. In 1913 the French government of Louis Bartou passed the Three Year Law which increased military service from two years to three. It also considerably strengthened the French army. The Russians were not ready for war in 1914 but German military intelligence reported that the Russians were in the process of building railways in Poland that would be able to deliver large numbers of troops to Germany's borders. In July 1914 Germany's Chief of General Staff, General Helmut von Moltke, argued that 'We shall never again strike as well as we do now, with France's and Russia's expansion of their armies incomplete'.

The Schlieffen Plan

Moltke's views were very much influenced by the detail of the Schlieffen Plan (see below). Drawn up in 1905 by the Chief of the German General Staff, Alfred von Schlieffen, the plan mapped out how it would be possible for Germany to fight a war effectively against France and Russia at the same time. A rapid assault of France through Belgium would have the effect of knocking France out of the war in six weeks. The might of the German army would then be transported eastwards to defeat the Russian army before it had fully mobilised. The Schlieffen Plan is important in explaining why war broke out.

The July Days

This was the context in which the assassination of Archduke Franz Ferdinand took place in Sarajevo (see page 110). The events of 28 June 1914 gave the Austrians the opportunity to humiliate Serbia. However, they needed to be wary of provoking the Russians unless they had German support.

- On 5 July 1914 the kaiser gave the Austrians full support to deal with Serbia as they saw fit. This is known as the Blank Cheque and was a crucial turning point on the road to war.

The Schlieffen Plan, drawn up in 1905.

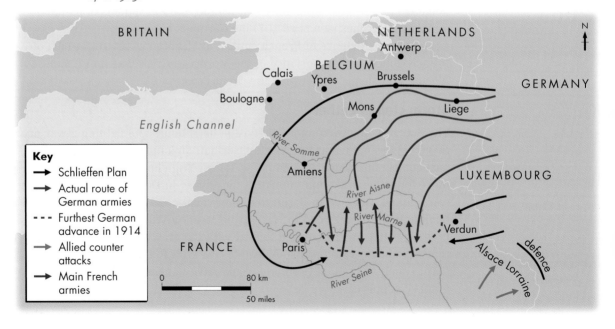

- Some members of the Austro-Hungarian government such as the Hungarian Prime Minister, Count Tisza, initially opposed provoking hostilities with Serbia. They were eventually won over by those keen on war.

- On 23 June the Austrians presented an ultimatum (a list of demands) to Serbia. Their demands included a suppression of anti-Austrian publications and organisations, arrest of Serbian officials involved in the assassination plot and collaboration of Serbia into an enquiry. The Serbs, wishing to avoid war, agreed to all points except one – they would not allow Austrian police to take part in the investigations into the criminal actions in their country.

- As tension rose, the British Foreign Secretary Sir Edward Grey proposed a conference to deal with the issue. Austria refused to talk further and declared war against Serbia on 28 July.

- The pressure on the Russian Tsar Nicholas II to act was great. His military advisers urged mobilisation to which he agreed on 30 July.

- The following day the Germans issued a twelve-hour ultimatum to Russia to reverse the decision. No answer was received and on 1 August Germany declared war on Russia.

- The Schlieffen Plan was now put into action and on 3 August Germany declared war on France. That night the German invasion of Belgium began.

British attitudes to war

The response of the British cabinet was, at first, hesitant. Britain was not obliged to join the war in support of France by the terms of the 1904 Entente Cordiale (see page 107). Indeed the Liberal cabinet was split with only the Foreign Secretary, Sir Edward Grey, and First Lord of the Admiralty, Winston Churchill, being in favour of all-out war. However, the invasion of Belgium changed the attitudes of politicians and the wider public. Many people in the cabinet were also very concerned that German success against France would result in a German-dominated Europe.

The Conservative opposition led by Andrew Bonar Law argued for British support of France and Russia as a matter of 'honour and future security'. The result was that on 4 August 1914 Britain declared war against Germany. In Parliament, the Liberal David Lloyd George argued that Britain had a 'solemn international obligation' to enter the war to defend Belgium. Europe was plunged into an uncertain future. As the British Foreign Secretary Sir Edward Grey was to comment, 'The lights are going out all over Europe … we shall not see them lit again in our lifetime.'

Question time

'The most important reason for the outbreak of the First World War was colonial rivalry.' How far do you agree with this statement?

This is an essay-writing question and you will need to think carefully about the causes of the war in order to answer it. The points below will help you structure your essay:

- **Prioritise** The question attempts to prioritise for you. However you should try to work out what you think were the most important causes of the war and be able to support your view.

- **Plan** In three lines, say what you think is the answer to the question. Your first point will directly answer the question. The next two points will map out the argument you are going to follow in your essay. You should then decide which factors you are going to put in each paragraph.

- **Write** Start with a brief introduction. Write in clear paragraphs. Try to follow your argument throughout. Remember, always try to support your argument by referring to facts and examples.

The war in 1914

Mons, Marne and the 'race to the sea'

On the night of 3 August 1914, the German army swept into Belgium. It succeeded in pushing the Belgian army and British Expeditionary Force (BEF) back after the Battle of Mons. In his belief that the French and British were on the verge of defeat, General Molkte ordered soldiers to be transferred from the Western Front to the Eastern Front. This was to prove a costly decision. At the Battle of the Marne in early September the German advance was checked. The German army withdrew from its position to a stronger defensive line north of the River Aisne. There then followed a 'race to the sea' (the North sea) in which both sides attempted to outflank their opponents but with both sides failing. A series of bitter battles, such as the first Battle of Ypres in November 1914, were fought with heavy losses but with no decisive breakthrough. The casualties of the first five months of the war were high, the French army alone losing 306,000 soldiers.

The popular belief in most countries was that the war would be over by Christmas. But by Christmas 1914 there was no end in sight. The trenches stretched from the English Channel to Switzerland as each side dug in to prevent the other getting to the coast first. This had a very important impact on the future of what was to be a war of little movement.

Digging deeper

Christmas on the front in 1914

On Christmas Day 1914, along many sectors of the front line there was an informal truce. Where the German Royal Saxon Regiment faced the Scottish Seaforth Highlanders, troops from both sides emerged from their trenches, exchanged cigarettes and other presents and played football for around an hour. The Germans won 3–2. In other sectors, troops were able to repair their trenches in full view of the enemy without being attacked.

SOURCE A

On Christmas Eve there was a lull in the fighting, no firing going on at all after 6pm. The Germans had a Christmas tree in the trenches, and Chinese lanterns all along the top of the parapet. Eventually the Germans started shouting, 'Come over, I want to speak to you'. Our chaps hardly knew how to take this but one of our 'nuts' belonging to the regiment got out of the trench and started walking towards the German lines. One of the Germans met him half way across and they shook hands and became quite friendly.

I went out myself on Christmas Day and exchanged some cigarettes for cigars, and this went on from Christmas Eve till Boxing Day without a single round being fired. The German I met had been a waiter in London and could speak our language a little. He says they didn't want to fight.

The evidence of Gunner Herbert Smith of the Royal Field Artillery, 1914.

SOURCE B

German and British troops posing together on the Western Front on Christmas Day, 1914.

In some areas the truce went on for a week. It was only broken on the command of the senior officers who became uneasy about the truce and the friendship between the troops.

The events of Christmas 1914 were not to be repeated. The generals on both sides ordered that mixing with the enemy would be severely punished. As the war dragged on, the attitudes of soldiers changed towards the enemy with much more hostility and bitterness.

On our part of the front the truce went on for a week. One of the Dublin Fusiliers was killed one day by a bullet which came over from the front of Plugstreet Wood and the Saxons immediately sent over and apologised, saying it hadn't been anything to do with them, but [the bullet] was from those so-and-so Prussians on their left. Eventually orders came through for our battery to open fire on a farm behind the German lines. We sent someone over to tell the Boches (this is French slang for the Germans) and the next morning at eleven o'clock I put twelve rounds into the farmhouse. That broke the truce on our front.

Evidence from 2nd Lieutenant Cyril Drummond of the Royal Field Artillery who witnessed the truce at Christmas 1914.

Kitchener's army

The British army was not large in comparison to the armies of the continental powers such as Germany or France. Whereas the German army had over 2 million soldiers available, the British maintained a small professional army of 248,000 soldiers with a further 190,000 colonial soldiers if needed. The difference between the British and other armies was that the British army was made up of professional soldiers.

In August 1914, the BEF set off for France. The only troops remaining in Britain were part-time soldiers known as the Territorial Force. With the high casualty rate of the army as it retreated through Belgium, more and more Territorials were asked to go to France. By Christmas 1914, 22 Territorial battalions had crossed the English Channel.

The new Secretary of State for War, Field Marshal Lord Kitchener, decided that it was necessary to recruit a new army. Men joined up with their friends and workmates in what became known as 'Pals Battalions'. Supported by an effective propaganda campaign, hundreds of thousands of civilians volunteered to join Kitchener's new army.

The reasons such a large number of soldiers joined up are many. Most felt that it was their duty to fight and joined up out of a sense of patriotism – they wanted to fight 'For King and Country'. Others looked forward to an adventure and escape from dreary employment (or indeed from unemployment). Many men were encouraged to join by their mates while others joined up fearing being left behind. The Britain that many of the volunteers lived in was a Britain of long hours and poorly-paid and boring jobs.

Investigation

What is the value to the historian of propaganda art from 1914–18?

In August 1914 men were encouraged to join Lord Kitchener's army at public rallies and meetings held in cities, towns and villages. On 5 September a picture of Lord Kitchener with the accompanying slogan 'Your Country Needs You' appeared on the front cover of the magazine *London Opinion*.

Such was the impact of the cover that the Parliamentary Recruiting Committee decided to produce the poster shown in Source F. The poster became the most recognisable propaganda image of the war and much copied. Its attraction is the simplicity of the message. Kitchener's piercing gaze is intended to draw the viewer to the poster and its message. In appealing to the patriotism of the viewer, the poster shows how important national pride was at that time.

SOURCE D

Daddy, what did *YOU* do in the Great War?

SOURCE F

BRITONS

"WANTS" YOU

JOIN YOUR COUNTRY'S ARMY!
GOD SAVE THE KING

SOURCE E

REMEMBER SCARBOROUGH!

The Germans who brag of their "CULTURE" have shown what it is made of by murdering defenceless women and children at SCARBOROUGH.

But this only strengthens

GREAT BRITAIN'S resolve to crush the

GERMAN BARBARIANS

ENLIST NOW!

The propaganda posters in Sources D to F are from 1914–18. Look at them carefully and then answer the following questions.

1. What do these posters reveal about Britain between 1914 and 1918?

2. Do these posters give the historian a reliable insight into British attitudes towards the war?

The war in 1915

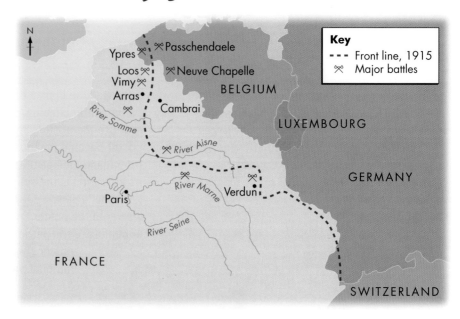

Fighting on the Western Front in 1915 was indecisive. At the end of 1914 the armies of both sides had dug trenches along a 2080 km (1300 mile) front. The French wanted to fight a war of attack to remove the Germans from French soil. The British were all too willing to assist. However, the battles of 1915 on the Western Front all resulted in large numbers of casualties for little gain.

The Germans generally took to the defensive, hoping to be able to transfer troops to the Eastern Front. But the Allies' attacks were poorly organised. Large numbers of troops were sent over the top of the trenches to fight in the open with poor support from their own artillery (gunners). Communication between units at the front line and the rear was poor. The generals were often long distances behind the lines with little real understanding of the conditions in which their soldiers were being asked to fight.

Gallipoli

In November 1914, the Ottoman Empire (Turkey) joined the war on the side of Germany. This move had been anticipated by the British government and, in particular, the First Lord of the Admiralty, Winston Churchill. His belief that Turkey could be knocked out of the war by a naval operation in the Dardanelles was shared by others, including Lord Kitchener.

The idea of a campaign in the East was opposed by the French. They believed that the war would only be won in the main theatre of war, the Western Front. However, in January 1915 the Russians appealed to their Allies for help to divert the Turks from fighting in the Caucasus mountains. The decision was made to land a force in the Dardanelles. What followed is a tale of muddle and incompetence.

In order to weaken the enemy, naval ships began bombarding Turkish positions on 19 February 1915. The next phase of the operation saw an

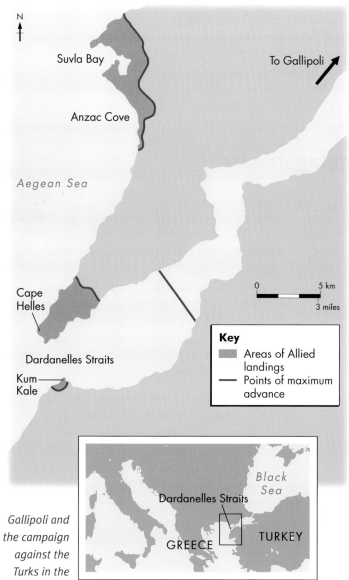

Gallipoli and the campaign against the Turks in the East.

attempt to clear mines in the Dardanelles Straits. This was tricky and not without its problems. On 18 March two British ships, *Ocean* and *Irresistible*, and the French ship *Bouvet* were sunk by mines and another seven ships were badly damaged. The attempt to dominate the Dardanelles Straits was suspended. The 65 days between the start of the Allied bombardment of Turkish positions and the landing of troops gave the Turks plenty of opportunity to strengthen their defences considerably. Their commander, the German Lipman von Sanders, deployed his six divisions of troops wisely.

The invasion

The Allied plan was to land troops on the beaches of the Gallipoli peninsular. The problem they faced was that most of the beaches were overlooked by cliffs and steeply rising ground.

On 25 April Allied troops landed. The ANZAC division (see page 120) landed at what became known as ANZAC Cove, the French landed at Kum Kale and the British landed at Cape Helles. In some places the Turkish troops were poorly organised and resistance was minimal. Elsewhere Allied troops met fierce resistance. The ANZAC troops made some headway inland on the first day, but were then forced back by Turkish troops. The high positions were held by the Turks.

On W beach at Cape Helles (otherwise known as Lancashire Landing), the Lancashire Fusiliers were cut down in the water and the sea was coloured 'absolutely crimson'. Six of the Lancashire Fusiliers were awarded the Victoria Cross for their heroism on this day. Until 4 May a fierce battle raged with the Turks losing 14,000 troops, and the ANZAC losses being around 10,000. Stalemate followed across the peninsular. The summer of 1915 was hot and conditions on the Gallipoli peninsular became very difficult. The Allied Commander General Sir Ian Hamilton, decided that the deadlock could be broken with an attack at Suvla Bay on 7 August. The attack failed after four days of bitter fighting.

The calls in Britain were now for evacuation of the peninsular. In November this was agreed by the Dardanelles Committee of the War Council.

The evacuation of the Gallipoli peninsular was everything that the offensive by the Allies had not been – orderly and well planned. Between late December and 8 January, the Allies slipped away without the Turks noticing. The Gallipoli campaign resulted in 300,000 Turkish casualties and 265,000 Allied casualties. For the Allies, Gallipoli was a failure. The Russians could still not be supplied through the Dardanelles Straits and Serbia was not relieved in any way.

Digging deeper

The ANZACs at Gallipoli

The Gallipoli campaign will be best remembered in the English-speaking world for the contribution of the soldiers from Australia and New Zealand. The greatest loss of life on the Allied side was sustained by the British, with 21,255 of their soldiers' lives lost, while 8,709 Australians and 2,701 New Zealanders also perished. The involvement of the ANZAC countries also had a far-reaching impact on their development as independent countries that were once part of the British Empire. For Australians, the Gallipoli campaign helped to define their country as distinct from the British. In the ANZAC nations, 25 April is still remembered as ANZAC Day and people from the two countries travel to visit ANZAC cove on the Gallipoli peninsula.

The myth has developed that the ANZAC troops were brave in comparison to the British troops. Yet those of the Lancashire and Dublin Fusiliers were as heroic and suffered as greatly as the ANZACs. Another myth has grown that the ANZACs were sent into battle while the uncaring English commanders 'drank tea'.

The tragedy of the ANZAC contribution in Gallipoli was that its troops came from small communities that suffered from the high casualty rates. On 7 August the Auckland and Wellington Battalions were ordered to storm Chunuk Bair, a ridge rising 350 metres above the Aegean Sea. So fierce was the fighting that the New Zealanders that survived had to dig a new trench because the old trenches were filled with the dead.

Along the coast that same day, the Australians attacked a ridge at the Nek. Wave after wave was sent over the top of the trenches and was cut down by the machine gun fire. Of the 600 who went over, 372 became casualties. Many of the Australians who died or were wounded that day came from the sparsely populated area around Perth in western Australia. Their deaths had an impact for years to come.

Carved in sandstone and placed near ANZAC Cove is a message from Mustapha Kemal (otherwise known as Kemal Ataturk) who became the president of Turkey in 1920. It is addressed to the grieving mothers from the other side of the world. The memorial reads as follows:

Those heroes that shed their blood
And lost their lives
You are now living in the soil of a friendly country
Therefore rest in peace.
There is no difference between the Johnnies
And the Mehmets to us where they lie side by side
Here in this country of ours.
You the mothers
Who sent their sons from far away countries
Wipe away your tears
Your sons are lying in our bosom
And are in peace.
After having lost their lives on this land they have become our sons as well.

The war in 1916

By the end of 1915 both sides were forced to take stock. After much discussion about the direction of the war, the generals of the Allied and German High Commands came to the same conclusion – that the war would be won or lost on the Western Front. The French commander, General Joffre, persuaded his British Allies that they should plan for an offensive in 1916 on the Somme. The newly-appointed British commander, Sir Douglas Haig, had preferred to attack in Flanders but was eventually persuaded otherwise.

Verdun

In Germany the Chief of the General Staff, General Falkenhayn, believed that the best way of forcing an end to the conflict in Germany's favour was to mount an offensive at a strategically important point of the front, inviting the French to defend with every man they had. The place he chose for the offensive has become forever linked to the slaughter and sacrifice of the war: Verdun. The plan was code-named Operation Gericht (Judgement).

On 21 February 1916 the Battle of Verdun began. Verdun was a fortified town surrounded by a series of forts designed in the seventeenth century by Louis XIV's most famous military architect, Vauban. In the face of a devastating bombardment, the French were forced to fall back to the protection of the Forts of Douaumont, Thiaumont and Vaux. On 25 February the Germans took Fort Douaumont. However, the French defence was stiffened by the appointment of General Pétain. The German attack eventually ground to a halt, but not before a staggering 700,000 French and German soldiers had been killed.

SOURCE A

Hell, *by Georges Leroux, painted in 1917–18. Leroux was a French soldier.*

The Battle of the Somme

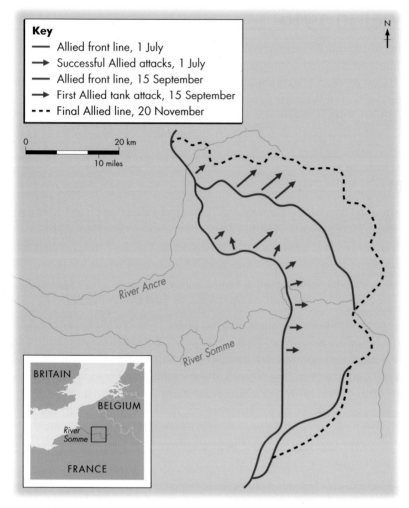

Key
— Allied front line, 1 July
→ Successful Allied attacks, 1 July
— Allied front line, 15 September
→ First Allied tank attack, 15 September
- - - Final Allied line, 20 November

0   20 km
10 miles

River Ancre

River Somme

BRITAIN

BELGIUM

River Somme

FRANCE

The Battle of the Somme, 1916.

In order to help the French, the British commander, Sir Douglas Haig, planned the long-awaited Allied offensive on the Somme. He hoped for a break through the German lines that could be exploited with the use of cavalry. The plan included a week-long bombardment to be followed by an infantry attack along a sixteen-mile front. The tale of the first day of the Battle of the Somme is one of tragedy. The deep and well-defended German defences were able to withstand Allied attacks. The battle raged fiercely throughout July 1916, with heavy casualties at places like Delville Wood and High Wood. For a gain of three miles in July 1916, the Allied armies suffered 200,000 casualties. In September 1916, a new weapon, the tank, was first used on the battlefield but with little long-term effect apart from terrorising the defending German troops.

On 19 November the offensive was brought to a halt. The German army had been weakened by the Somme campaign but so had the British army, which suffered 419,654 casualties. The loss of many of Kitchener's volunteer army was one of the most tragic stories in British military history. There is no doubt that the Somme changed attitudes in Britain for good.

Digging deeper

The first day of the Somme: 1 July 1916

1 July 1916 Preparations for the Battle of the Somme were considerable. Around 500,000 men from Kitchener's army were moved up to the front line with 100,000 horses and 455 heavy guns and howitzers (short guns for shelling at a steep angle). Deep tunnels were dug under the enemy trenches and nineteen mines were laid to be exploded just before the attack.

24 June 1916 Shelling of the German lines had begun from 1400 guns firing some 1.5 million shells over the next week. The British soldiers were told that the bombardment would cut the barbed wire in front of the German trenches and be so destructive that nothing could survive. The reality was different. The Germans were well dug into strong defensive positions. They occupied deep dugouts along the sixteen-mile front. The bombing did considerable damage to the nerves of many of the German soldiers, but most survived.

The aims of the first day of the Somme were to break the German line and roll the German army back, with the use of cavalry, under the command of General Goupz. These aims were highly optimistic. Haig's Chief Intelligence Officer, General Charteris, recognised that the battle was to be one of attrition (wearing the enemy down). The night before the battle, Haig noted that the morale of the troops was high. The Pals Battalions (see page 116) packed the communications trenches and took up their positions in the front line.

At Serre, the Pals Battalions of the 31st Division, men from the industrial towns of Bradford, Leeds, Accrington and Barnsley among others, awaited the dawn. At Theipval, the 36th Ulster Division prepared for action. In Theipval Wood, a box of grenades was dropped to the floor of the trench and was in danger of exploding. A young Ulsterman, Billy McFadzean, threw himself onto the box as it exploded. His sacrifice in protection of his comrades won him the first Victoria Cross of the day.

At 7.20 am the British bombardment intensified. Simultaneously the huge mine placed under the German trenches at Beaumont Hamel was exploded. However, the British bombardment then stopped which allowed the German defenders time to get to their machine guns. The tragedy of the day began to unfold. In front of Beaumont Hamel was Y Ravine, a deep gorge that was to be the first objective of the attacking troops. Those first over the top were slaughtered in large numbers. At 9.15am the men of the 1st Newfoundland Regiment were ordered to go over the top. Unable to reach the front line because the trenches were clogged with the dead and wounded, the Newfoundlanders emerged from the communication trenches 300 yards behind their own front line. To get into No Man's Land (the neutral area between the two enemy positions) they had to pass through gaps in the British barbed wire. The German machine gunners cut the battalion to ribbons. Of the 752 Newfoundlanders who left the trenches, 684 were either killed or wounded.

SOURCE B

Men going 'over the top' on the first day of the Somme, 1 July 1916.

Elsewhere the Pals Battalions suffered an enormous number of casualties. Some divisions did manage to reach their objectives. The men of the 36th Ulster Division ignored the orders to walk after emerging from their trenches. Instead they massed in No Man's Land and stormed the German lines as the British barrage lifted. However, they were forced to give up their gains as supporting battalions were cut to shreds. The centre of the British attack that fateful day centred around the village of La Boiselle and what was known as 'Sausage and Mash' valleys. Wave after wave of soldiers was sent over the top, bayonets glinting in the summer sun. The German machine gunners fired up and down the line. The 36th Ulster Division suffered the worst casualties of the day – around 6,000 men were either killed or wounded, most of the damage being done in the first ten minutes of the attack. As the troops had advanced, the German troops in the front line had fired coloured rockets into the sky – the signal for the German artillery to open fire.

Many officers had feared the worst. Reports from scouts revealed that the bombardment had failed to cut the German wire. Many put on a brave face nonetheless for the sake of their troops. Captain Nevill of the 8th East Surreys bought four footballs on his last leave in London. Each platoon under his command was issued with a ball. A prize was offered to the first platoon that kicked its ball to the German lines. At zero hour Nevill was seen leading his men over the top. A football was kicked high in the sky and in the direction of the German lines. Nevill was killed instantly as were most of his men.

Many other divisions suffered heavy casualties. For example, around 700 of the Accrington Pals who had joined up so enthusiastically in August 1914 were part of the 31st Division that faced the German enemy in front of the village of Serre. As the Accrington Pals emerged from the trenches they were met with a hail of machine gun fire. In less than 20 minutes, 235 had been killed and 350 wounded.

The khaki-uniformed bodies of the dead and wounded littered No Man's Land. Throughout the day fresh waves of soldiers were sent over the top, many to their deaths.

At the British army headquarters, Field Marshal Haig reacted with bitterness to the failure of his plan.

The 8th Corps had been ordered to attack Gommencourt as part of a diversionary plan. They were partially successful but 15,000 casualties were sustained during the attack. Haig's response in his diary revealed his ignorance of his casualties and of the experience of his troops. He wrote, '*The 8th Corps said they began well, but as the day progressed were forced back. I am inclined to believe from further reports that few of the 8th Corps left their trenches*'.

The first day on the Somme was a tragedy for the British army and the worst day in British military history. As the sun set over the Somme battlefield, the enormity of the catastrophe became apparent. Of the 100,000 troops who attacked that fateful morning, 20,000 had been killed and another 40,000 were wounded.

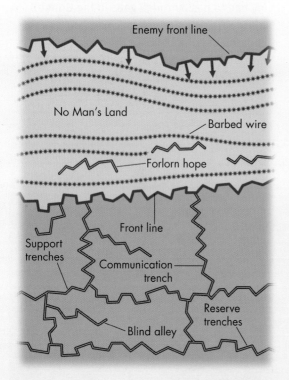

The trench system.

Question time

Source C is an extract from the novel *Birdsong* by Sebastian Faulks. It is historical fiction based on a central character, Stephen, who is a soldier in the Battle of the Somme. The author was not an eyewitness to the events he writes about. Is this still useful evidence? Discuss this with a partner and write your conclusions in your exercise book.

Discuss the following points and add more of your own.

- How do you think Faulks found out about the war?
- Does it matter if he got things wrong?

SOURCE C

The second hand of his watch moved in slow motion. Twenty-nine past. The whistle in his mouth. His foot on the ladder. He swallowed hard and blew.

He clambered out and looked around him. It was for a moment completely quiet and the bombardment ended and the German guns also stopped. Skylarks wheeled and sang high in the cloudless sky. He felt alone, as though he had stumbled on this fresh world at the instant of its creation.

Then the artillery began to lay down the first barrage and the German machine guns resumed. To his left Stephen saw men trying to emerge from the trench but being smashed by bullets before they could stand. The gaps in the wire were jammed with bodies. Behind him the men were coming up. He saw Grey run along the top of the trench, shouting encouragement.

Byrne was walking beside him at the slow pace required by their orders. Stephen glanced to his right. He could see a long wavering line of khaki, primitive dolls progressing in tense deliberate steps, going down with a silent flap of arms, replaced, falling, continuing as though walking into a gale. He tried to catch Byrne's eye but failed. The sound of machine guns was varied by the crack of snipers and the roar of the barrage ahead of them.

He saw Hunt fall to his right. Studd bent to help him and Stephen saw his head opening up bright red under machine gun bullets as his helmet fell away.

His feet pressed onwards gingerly over the broken ground. After twenty or thirty yards there came a feeling that he was floating above his body, that it had taken an automatic life of its own over which he had no power. It was as though he had become detached, in a dream, from the metal air through which his flesh was walking. In this trance there was a kind of relief, something close to hilarity.

From Birdsong (1993) *by Sebastian Faulks.*

The war at sea

The control of the sea was essential to both Britain and Germany in their attempts to win the war. In 1914 the British navy was the largest in the world. However, the arms race that had taken place before the war ensured that the German navy was a formidable enemy. On the other hand the range of fire of the new British dreadnought battleship was up to ten miles. Both fleets were sufficiently powerful to act as a deterrent to each other. To that end Admiral Tirpitz of the German High Seas Fleet and Admiral Jellicoe of the British Grand Fleet decided to keep the fleets in port.

The main reason for this reluctance to engage in battle was clear – to lose a major sea battle might well result in losing the war. This was because each side needed to maintain the supply of food and other materials coming by sea.

Submarine warfare 1915–16

Instead of challenging the British battle fleet head on, Tirpitz recommended using unrestricted submarine warfare as a means of weakening the British war effort. This meant using U-boat submarines to sink boats that were supplying the Allies. The Allies responded by imposing a naval blockade (preventing ships entering or leaving) on Germany. On 4 February 1915, the German government announced a submarine blockade of Britain.

On 7 May 1915, the US passenger ship, the *Lusitania,* was sunk by a German submarine with the loss of 1198 lives, including 139 Americans. Wary of provoking the USA into war, the Germans temporarily stopped submarine warfare by promising in September 1915 and again in May 1916 that they would not attack neutral ships. These guarantees did not end submarine warfare but limited its effectiveness.

Despite the reluctance of both the British and German fleets to engage in warfare, there were minor skirmishes which showed up some of the potential weaknesses of both sides.

- At Coronel in November 1915, two British ships were sunk by German battle cruisers.

- This was followed by the Battle of the Falkland Islands in which six German warships were sunk by the British. This showed the German High Command the danger of being dragged into open combat on the high seas.

- At Dogger Bank in January 1916 the tables were turned when the British Grand Fleet failed to do much damage to a trapped German war fleet.

The Battle of Jutland

By mid-1916 the priority for the German fleet was to break the stranglehold of the Allied blockade of Germany. Admiral von Scheer (Commander of the German High Seas Fleet) decided therefore to attempt to damage some of the British Grand Fleet by drawing it into battle. Scheer ordered a squadron of five battle cruisers to sail into the North Sea. This squadron would be followed by the main German High Seas Fleet. Their aim was to draw the British battle cruisers into a trap. However, the British intercepted messages detailing the German plan.

At 2.30pm on 31 May 1916, the two battle cruiser squadrons engaged. Very soon it became clear that the German crews were superior in manoeuvring their ships and in marksmanship. Two British ships, the *Indefatigable* and the *Queen Mary*, were sunk. By late afternoon, the German High Fleet was drawn unknowingly into a trap laid by Jellicoe. At 6.45pm the two main fleets, totalling 250 ships, clashed. Admiral Scheer quickly became aware that the German fleet was now outnumbered and outgunned and he used the descending mist to turn south and then eastwards away from Jellicoe's fleet.

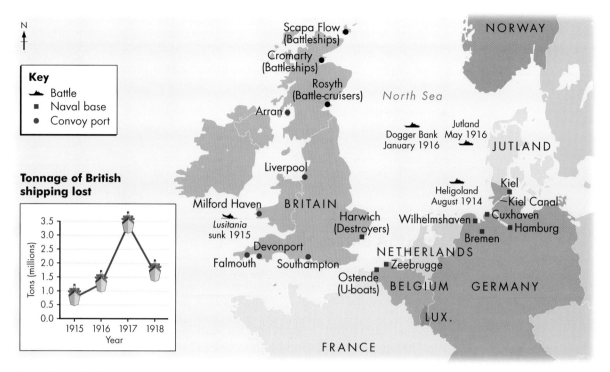

Tonnage of British shipping lost

The North Sea battles and losses in 1917.

The Germans made for the safety of their minefields at Horn's Reef and then to port at Kiel. The outcome of the Battle of Jutland was indecisive. The Royal Navy lost a greater number of ships, fourteen in total against German losses of eleven ships. However, the more important consequence was that the German battle fleet remained in port for the remainder of the war. This meant that the Allies were able to maintain their blockade of Germany which was to have such an important impact in 1918. After Jutland, the British had the upper hand at sea.

Unrestricted submarine warfare 1917–18

The stalemate of Jutland drove German military planners back to the idea of unrestricted submarine warfare. On 8 January 1917 a meeting of senior civil and military officials at Pless concluded that the only way the war could be won was if Britain was brought to its knees by a blockade. The danger of such a policy was that it could bring the USA into the war on the side of the Allies, because it was likely that its boats would be sunk as part of the U-boat campaign. The German planners believed that the war would be won 'within five months' if merchant shipping (ships bringing goods) could be sunk at the rate of 600,000 tonnes a month.

Initially the U-boats did well and in April 1917 they managed to sink 841,118 tonnes of Allied shipping. However, the British economy was able to cope with shortages through an effective system of rationing. The German U-boat fleet was not able to keep up its high rate of success for a number of reasons.

- Large numbers of U-boats were sunk by mines (20 out of the 63 U-boats were sunk by the Allies in 1917). The Germans had difficulty in replacing the number of U-boats being sunk.

- The British Prime Minister, David Lloyd George, managed to persuade the Royal Navy to adopt the convoy system, where merchant ships carrying supplies were protected by naval ships. The first convoy sailed on 10 May 1917 and the system proved to be a great success. By 1918 only one per cent of ships in convoys were lost to submarine attacks.

- The British introduced Q ships. These were armed ships disguised as merchant vessels, which deterred U-boat commanders from attacking so freely.

A more important factor in deciding the outcome of the war was the continued success of the Allied blockade of Germany. By 1918, 44 per cent of German merchant shipping was either seized or sunk by the British.

The USA enters the war

The sinking of merchant shipping did threaten seriously to reduce British supplies. However, unrestricted submarine warfare failed to bring Britain to the verge of defeat, but it did bring the USA into the war.

In January 1917, the German Foreign Minister, Herr Von Zimmermann, sent instructions to the German minister in Mexico to secretly work for an alliance against the United States. Several US ships were sunk in February and March and British intelligence deciphered the Zimmermann telegram revealing plans for an alliance against the United States. On 6 April 1917 the US President Woodrow Wilson dropped his policy of neutrality and declared war against Germany.

Naval operations in the closing year of the war were restricted to submarine and destroyer activities. The convoy system reduced the number of Allied merchant ships sunk. The Germans repeatedly raided the English coast, for example, on 26 April 1917 and 15 February 1918. To counter this threat, the British launched an attack on the German submarine base at Zeebrugge. This was followed by an attack on Ostend. Neither of these attacks was particularly successful at halting U-boat operations. The submarine threat was not reduced until the British overran the German submarine bases in Belgium in late 1918.

Question time

How did each of the following affect the direction of the war:

- the Battle of Jutland and its aftermath
- unrestricted submarine warfare?

You will need to consider the effects of these events on both Germany and the Allies.

1917 and Passchendaele

In mid-1917 the French army mutinied. The response of Field Marshal Haig to the French situation was to push for an offensive in Flanders. The main opposition to such an offensive was the British Prime Minister, David Lloyd George, who feared the effects of more British casualties on public opinion. However, Haig's plan was accepted in mid-June 1917 by the Committee on War Policy.

Haig believed that he could break through the German lines and push to the coast. If successful, he could severely weaken the German submarine offensive by taking the naval bases of Blankenberge and Ostend. Many people were worried by Haig's plan as the area of the battlefield was prone to flooding and the weather in August was often wet. In addition the German defenders were well dug in and experienced soldiers.

The Allied bombardment begins

On 22 July 1917, a huge Allied bombardment began with 2300 guns pounding German lines. Over four million shells landed in the period up to 3.50am on 31 July, when the bombardment turned into a creeping barrage. This is when the artillery aims to land its shells in front of advancing enemy soldiers. The British 2nd and 5th armies went over the top with support from the French 1st army. The attack had started before dawn and some progress was made. However, on some parts of the front the German defences were too strong. At midday the Germans counter-attacked. Almost simultaneously the heavens opened and a huge downpour turned the battlefield into a boggy mess. The rain did not stop for three days, leaving conditions virtually impossible. Haig postponed the offensive until the rain stopped on 4 August. He then ordered that the offensive be continued.

Three months of bloody fighting followed. A series of attacks which collectively became known as the Battle of Passchendaele (named after a village behind the German front lines) followed. The Allied advance was extremely slow and led to huge casualties. Around 70,000 British soldiers died in the mud of Passchendaele, with more than 170,000 wounded. Over half the British army, some 43 divisions, were involved in fighting in these appalling conditions. The initial aims of reaching the Flanders coast were long forgotten, but Haig pressed on with the campaign. Attack followed attack for three months, but for little gain and with little hope of success.

An example of the kind of assault that was launched took place on 12 October. The aim was for the New Zealand and 3rd Australian Divisions to capture the village of Passchendaele. As the soldiers moved up to the attack, the rain began to fall. The Germans were aware of the approaching assault and bombarded the Allied troops with gas shells. The mud was so deep that many shells failed to explode. As the ANZAC troops advanced they were cut down by machine gun fire. By the end of the day, 3000 New Zealanders had become casualties for no gain.

Men carrying a stretcher at the Battle of Passchendaele in 1917.

The inflexibility of Haig was shown at its worst at Passchendaele. After the destruction of the ANZACs, Haig looked to the Canadian regiments to carry on the battle. The fear of the Canadian commander, General Sir Arthur Currie, was that the battle would be very costly to his division. The rains had reduced the battlefield to little more than a swamp. Currie's fears were realised – almost 16,000 Canadians were killed or wounded in the final push for the remains of what had been Passchendaele. By now the battlefield was a scene of almost unimaginable horror. The final assault of the campaign was made on 10 November.

How useful was the campaign? The Germans did use a third of their army in the defence of their line but the British used around a half of theirs in the offensive. Another 240,000 British troops were made casualties of the war, including 70,000 dead.

Later in the year, tanks were used for the first time on a large scale by the British at the Battle of Cambrai. The British managed to advance five miles in the direction of Cambrai but were pushed back by a German counter-attack.

Digging deeper

The Passchendaele mud: 1917

The mud of Passchendaele made the soldier's fear of death even greater. Below are extracts from evidence supplied by those who experienced the horror of Passchendaele in 1917.

SOURCE B

Going up to the line for the first time my indications of the horrors to come appeared as a small lump on the side of the duckboard [wooden planking used as a walkway in the trenches]. I glanced at it, as I went past, and I saw to my horror, that it was a human hand gripping the side of the track – no trace of the owner, just a glimpse of a muddy wrist and a piece of sleeve sticking out of the mud. After that there were bodies every few yards. Some lying face downwards in the mud; others showing by the expressions fixed on their faces the sort of effort they had made to get back on the track.

Major George Wade, South Staffordshire Regiment.

SOURCE C

We fell into mud and writhed about like wasps crawling from rotten plums. The dead and wounded were piled up upon each other's backs. The second wave of soldiers coming up behind were knocked down and lay in heaving mounds. They had to lie where they were or until a stray bullet found them or they were blown to pieces. Their heart-rending cries pierced the incessant [unending] din of explosions.

This anonymous account gives a clear idea of the horror of the battle.

SOURCE D

We'd had an awful time getting the guns up the plank on to Westhoek Ridge – and that was before the worst of the mud. Three weeks later we couldn't have done it at all. It was just sheets of water coming down. It's difficult to get across that it's a sea of mud ... [As] I'd gone down from the gun position to meet the ammunition wagon coming up the supply road ... a heavy shell came over and burst very close. There were six horses pulling that wagon and they took fright at the explosion, veered right off the road and down they went into the mud. We had no possible way of getting them out. In any event they sank so fast that we had no chance even to cut them loose from the heavy wagon. We formed a chain and stretched out our arms and managed to get the drivers off, but the poor horses just sank faster and faster and drowned before our eyes. One of the drivers was absolutely incoherent [rambling] with terror. It was the thought of being drowned in that awful stuff. It's a horrible thought.

Lieutenant J. W. Naylor.

Question time

How useful to the historian is the evidence of Major Wade (Source B) and Lieutenant Naylor (Source D) in explaining the significance of Passchendaele?

Digging deeper

Visiting the battlefields

Today, many people visit the area where the battles of the First World War were fought. The Belgian town of Ypres is surrounded by around 160 British Commonwealth cemeteries, containing the graves of many thousands of British and Commonwealth soldiers who lost their lives at the front.

Menin Gate

The Menin Gate is a huge monument marking the entrance to the town through which many Allied soldiers marched on their way to the front line for the last time. At the time of the war, there was no actual gate on this site. The point was then marked by statues of lions on either side of the road (the lions now are in Canberra, Australia). The soldiers said at the time, 'Tell the last man through to bolt the Menin Gate'.

As a monument to these men and their bravery the gate that stands on the site today was built and opened in 1927. After the ceremony to open the monument in 1927, buglers from the British Army played the Last Post. A year later the local police chief came up with the idea that the Last Post should be played every evening by buglers from the Ypres Fire Service. From 11 November 1929 to the present day (with the exception of the years of the German occupation from 1940-4) the Last Post has been played at 8.00pm every day. It is a simple and most moving ceremony. On the monument are carved the names of the 55,000 men of the Commonwealth who died in the area and have no known graves. When you search the monument you can read all the different names and nationalities of those who died in and around Ypres.

If you visit the large square in the centre of the town with its magnificent Cloth Hall and St Martin's Cathedral, it is interesting to note that both buildings appear to have been built in medieval times. However, closer inspection of the dates on many of the bricks in the square reveal that they are from the twentieth century. Ypres was completely destroyed during the war and was rebuilt with reparations money in the 1920s.

Tyne Cot

The largest British cemetery in the area is called Tyne Cot. It has 11,000 burial plots and a Memorial to the Missing in honour of 35,000 soldiers with no known grave. There is a register which contains the names and details of those buried in the cemetery. Nearby is 'Hill 62' which was also known as Sanctuary Wood. It contains the only real section of trenches remaining in the Ypres area. The shell-pocked earth is still clearly visible.

SOURCE E

The Menin Gate in Ypres, Belgium.

The last year of the war: 1918

With the Russians out of the war and the USA sending ever more material to the Western Front, the German High Command decided in early 1918 to launch one last great offensive that might win the war. The German High Command had at its disposal the elite of the German army and they outnumbered the Allies. On 21 March the German army attacked the British lines at St Quentin. The British soldiers were surprised by the speed of the German attack that followed the initial bombardment by chemical weapons. Over 7000 British soldiers of the 5th Army were killed and 21,000 were taken prisoner on the first day of the German offensive. The German army advanced up to 40 miles but outran its supplies and was eventually checked.

THE SANDS RUN OUT.

The war ends

In the summer of 1918, German Field Marshal Ludendorff attempted two further offensives on the Aisne and Marne. This time, however, neither was successful and on 18 July the Allied Supreme Commander, Joffre, ordered a counter-attack. By the summer of 1918 the Americans were pouring 250,000 troops a month into France. The Allies made steady progress towards Germany with the British successfully taking the well-fortified Hindenberg Line in September 1914. As the situation deteriorated for Germany at the front and at home, members of the German High Command, including Ludendorff, began to talk about peace. On 9 November the kaiser abdicated (stepped down) and on the eleventh hour of the eleventh day of the eleventh month 1918, hostilities ceased.

The cost of the war

The war had cost the lives of around 1 million men of the British Empire, 325,000 Turks, 500,000 Italians, 1.2 million men from the Austro-Hungarian Empire, 1.7 million Frenchmen, 1.7 million Russians and 2 million Germans. One in three of all the men born in Britain and France in the years 1892–5 was killed. They were 'the lost generation' as they were frequently referred to after the war. The memorials that sprang up across Europe represented the sense of loss, but could not fail to hide the personal anguish of so many. At the end of the war around three million women were left widowed across Europe, often with the prospect of raising children alone on meagre state pensions and allowances.

A memorial to some of those killed in the First World War.

Not only were large numbers killed. Post-war Europe had to deal with a generation of survivors who had been badly wounded. A considerable number of the war wounded were permanently disabled. Over 41,000 British servicemen had a limb amputated. The mental distress and disorder suffered by many soldiers meant that around 65,000 were hospitalised. By 1938, 3800 First World War soldiers were still confined to psychiatric hospitals, unable to deal with the horrors of war that they had experienced. However these were only the tip of the iceberg. Far greater numbers suffered silently. It is impossible to measure just how much the war survivors suffered.

Life in the trenches

One of the particular features of the First World War was the use of trenches. We have a wealth of evidence of trench life. Many soldiers kept diaries in which the reality of their living conditions was graphically explained. Although letters were censored, some officers did send letters which contained details of their experiences. As historians we can also learn about trench life from memoirs such as *Goodbye to All That* (1929) by Robert Graves or *All Quiet on the Western Front* (1929) by Erich Maria Remarque. Experiences of trench life varied considerably depending on the time of year, which part of the front the soldier was on and whether or not a major attack was planned for that area. Soldiers were rotated through the trenches; the British soldier spent no longer than two weeks at any one time in the front line.

The construction of the trenches varied. Because they were on the defensive and so were not moving forwards, the Germans built far deeper trench systems. On the Somme the Germans constructed bunkers to a depth of 9 metres. These bunkers could house up to twelve soldiers who could seek refuge from the constsnt bombardment.

One of the most difficult aspects of trench life was boredom. If there was no attack, sentries were posted and the soldiers in the front line would spend their time undertaking menial tasks. Occasionally one side would send over a few shells, and raiding parties were a way of keeping the enemy on their toes. These usually took place at night and would consist of a small group of soldiers raiding the enemy's front lines, taking prisoners and gaining intelligence on the other side. At night, flares would be launched by both sides in order to spot enemy raiding parties.

While waiting in the trenches, the soldiers had to endure conditions that would test their nerves to the limit. Occasionally soldiers had to suffer horrific bombardments. The sound of a shell coming over and the crack of the explosion terrified the soldiers almost as much as the fear of being killed.

British soldiers in a trench during the Battle of the Somme in 1916.

SOURCE B

... the idea of being hit by a jagged piece of steel. You hear the whistle of the shell coming, you crouch down as low as you can, and just wait. It doesn't burst merely with a bang, it has a kind of crack with a snap in it, like the crack of a very large whip.

Writer and poet T. E. Hulme, who served in the Royal Artillery in Belgium, summed up the soldiers' concerns.

Such bombardments terrified all soldiers, experienced or new to the trenches. Many were to suffer from 'shell shock' (a nervous disorder) during and after the war.

SOURCE C

One man threw himself down on the bottom of the trench, shaking all over and crying. Another started to weep. It lasted for nearly one and a half hours and, at the end of it, parts of the trenches were all blown to pieces.

T. E. Hulme describes the effect of a sustained bombardment.

The discomforts of the trenches

Soldiers had to put up with daily discomfort. There were many complaints about the standard ration of tinned food, bully beef and jam. Often food had to be brought up to the front line and those carrying it could get lost or killed. Lice and rats were the constant companions of soldiers in the front line. Lice lived in the lining and seams of the soldiers' clothes and were virtually impossible to get rid of. Rats grew to an enormous size as a result of a plentiful supply of food – corpses.

While German soldiers often slept in dugouts with properly constructed beds, the British slept in fox holes cut into the side of the trench.

Soldiers were forbidden to take off their boots in the trenches, in case they were caught out by a surprise attack. In rain-soaked trenches, soldiers often developed 'trench foot' – a condition where their feet rotted in their boots due to lack of blood supply.

Despite the horrors of the war, most men continued to fight. The reasons are complex. Perhaps the most important explanation for why men continued to go over the top, often in the face of near certain injury and death, was that they did not want to let their friends down. Soldiers also took pride in fighting for their regiment and many spoke of a deep comradeship born in the trenches.

For others, trench war was too much. Over 300 British soldiers were shot for desertion after brief court marshals (when a soldier is tried by a military court). The families of those executed by their own side were forced to carry a shame they still have not removed today. They received no war pension and their names were not inscribed on local war memorials. The tombstones of the executed simply noted the date and the supposed reason for their execution.

Digging deeper

Soldiers of the empire

When war was declared in 1914, Britain had an empire that covered a quarter of the globe. The countries of the British Empire offered to help Britain in its hour of need. This help was of great importance to the British war effort.

In all around 40 per cent of British forces were from the empire. India alone contributed 1.3 million soldiers and labourers to the war effort. In 1914 the Indian army fought on the Western Front and in the winter that followed they held long stretches of the front line, often in horrific conditions. By the end of 1915 some battalions of the Indian army had suffered a 100 per cent casualty rate. Many Indians also worked as labourers behind the front lines. To help them in their work they brought the most effective means of carrying heavy loads with them – elephants.

The contribution of the ANZAC troops at Gallipoli and the Newfoundlanders at the Somme has been covered on pages 120 and 123. The contribution of others is less well known. Irishmen, West Indians, and South Africans all served throughout the war. Black soldiers of the King's African Rifles fought in East Africa against the Germans. The British West Indies regiment served with distinction on the Somme.

Over 200,000 soldiers from empire forces lost their lives and 600,000 were wounded. There is little doubt that Britain's ability to fight the war was considerably enhanced by this contribution.

SOURCE D

Troops from the West Indies on the Western Front in France, 1916.

Investigation

People in the First World War

Choose one of the following exercises.

1   Find out about your ancestors and their lives during the First World War.

This can be a very exciting exercise. Your aim should be to find out as much as possible about any of your family members who were alive during the 1914–18 war. You should try to find out about the lives of both men and women. It is just as interesting to discover about the lives of those on the Home Front (see pages 138–41) as those who served in the armed forces. Plan your work in the following stages:

- Prepare yourself for your research task. Arm yourself with a note-book in which you can jot down your notes. Your first exercise will be an attempt to draw a family tree.

- Talk to your mother/father/guardian. Ask them if they have any knowledge of their family history. They might have a family tree, mementoes or memories of stories told to them. Any scrap of evidence will do and you should write down everything you find out, making careful note of where it came from.

- If you are given any photographs or mementoes such as letters, do not use the originals. Instead you should photocopy them and return them to their owner.

- If possible, contact your grandparents or great-uncles and aunts. Ask them if they can help you, and then prepare some well thought out questions for them.

Write up all your information as clearly as you can. Use photocopies of photographs and mementoes to illustrate your project.

Don't be downhearted if you find out very little. In your write-up you should explain the process you went through to try to find out information.

2   Research local history.

Another exciting project is to research the history of the people of your locality. Was there, for example, a Pals Battalion from your local area?

You could start by doing the following:

- Go to your local library and ask for help or surf the Internet for information. These websites at www.heinemann.co.uk/hotlinks are a useful starting point.

- With your parent/guardian's permission you might talk to someone they know who has a good knowledge of the history of the area.

3   Research the history of a region/country in 1914–18.

You might not want to research the history of individuals but of a region or a different country. Your relatives may not have lived in Britain but in another part of the world during this period. You can try to find out some facts about the country from which your family originated. These can include the following:

- Were people from that country involved in the war? If they were, how were they involved?

- How did the war change the country?

- What were the main political changes in the country at the time?

- What was life like for the people who lived there at the beginning of the twentieth century?

Find out more facts for yourself.

The Home Front

The government responsibilities during the war were far greater than ever before. It needed to ensure that the armed forces were properly supplied and that morale remained high. To this end the Defence of the Realm Act (DORA) was passed on 8 August 1914. Under the act the government was given special powers. Anyone communicating with the enemy could be arrested.

At first the British war effort at home suffered because of the large numbers of skilled workers joining the armed forces. By the end of 1914, around 25 per cent of workers in the explosives and chemicals industries had joined up. Many also feared a drop in coal production because by July 1915 around a fifth of the nation's miners had volunteered to fight.

In May 1915, a report by *The Times* war correspondent, Colonel Charles Repington, reported that the British army was handicapped in its operations by the lack of shells. One result of the uproar was that the government, under the leadership of Prime Minister Asquith, was reorganised. Instead of being a government with members just from the Liberal Party, it became a coalition government, which means that it had members from other main political parties. The new government created a Ministry of Munitions the following July with David Lloyd George at its head. This was a new step in the move towards a more efficient war economy. The Ministry of Munitions took control of factory production and the manufacture of all war-related materials. In October 1917, the ministry had control of 143 national factories. In the first year of the war, Britain was producing 50 planes a month. By the last year of the war that figure had risen to 2700 a month.

Conscription

Such were the losses of men in battle in 1915 that the government felt it must try to find ways of encouraging people to join up, rather than rely on them doing so voluntarily. As the reality of war became widely known, so the numbers joining up of their own accord decreased. In 1915, the government introduced the Derby Scheme. Under this scheme single men were encouraged to 'attest' – to promise to serve whenever they were asked. However only 1,150,000 men attested out of a possible 2,179,000.

To the government, the case for conscription – forcing certain groups to join the army – was now far clearer. In January 1916, the government introduced the Compulsory Military Service Bill. All single men between the ages of 18 and 41 were liable to be called up for service. The only groups that were exempted were workers such as miners who were essential for the war effort.

The introduction of conscription made the lives of conscientious objectors much harder. These are people who refused to fight because it went against their conscience or personal beliefs. Two groups had been set up in 1914 to oppose the war; the British Neutrality League and the British Neutrality Committee. After 1916 a new group, the Non-Conscription Fellowship, was created. Members were conscientious objectors who refused to fight but

were prepared to help with the war effort. Many of this group found their way to the front line as stretcher-bearers. In all, around 7700 served in Britain and 3300 served in non-combatant groups. However other 'conchies' (the slang term for conscientious objectors) refused to have anything to do with the war. They were punished by imprisonment and their treatment in prison was harsh. In June 1916, the philosopher and leading pacifist spokesman, Bertrand Russell, was prosecuted for writing and issuing an anti-conscription pamphlet.

Women and the war

One of the most important issues in Britain in the years leading up to the war was the debate over the right of women to vote (see pages 99–103). The war led to a temporary end to this debate. The suffragette leaders, Emmeline and Christabel Pankhurst, decided to suspend their campaign until the end of the war and instead campaigned with other women demanding the 'right to serve'. There was still a lot of resistance to women working because many people still felt that the woman's place was in the home. Many trade unions were also against women doing skilled factory work and they thought they would lower standards and would ultimately take men's jobs in the factories.

However, from the start of the war women worked in munitions factories. The increase in numbers was dramatic. In 1914 there were 125 women working in the Woolwich Arsenal; by 1917 this figure had increased to 28,000. Munitions work could be dangerous. The explosive TNT used in many weapons caused skin to go yellow. As a result of their appearance, munitions workers were nicknamed 'canaries'. Even worse was the danger of explosions. In 1917 there was huge explosion at the munitions works at Silvertown in East London that killed twelve women workers.

Attitudes changed towards women workers with the creation of the Munitions Ministry in 1915 and the introduction of conscription for men in 1916. Agreements were made with the trade unions that the introduction of women into men's work would not reduce men's pay. Some employers tried to avoid replacing a skilled man directly with a woman. Instead the job might be given to an unskilled man or a small group of women.

It was only in the national factories, which were run by the Ministry of Munitions, that women were promised close to equal pay.

The extent of women working in men's jobs, outside war-related jobs, should not be exaggerated. The percentage of women going out to work rose by around 5 per cent. As before, many married women did not go out to work and the number of married female munitions workers was still relatively small. At the end of the war women were quickly dismissed. It was only in clerical work (such as typing) that women tended to keep their new jobs. Women failed to gain equal pay or equality in the workplace despite the role they had played.

Digging deeper

To what extent were women's lives changed by the First World War?

Just as the lives of many men were altered by serving at the front line, so many women's lives were changed by their experiences during the war.

SOURCE B

[The sick] were in a terrible state, all suffering from dysentery and enteric [both serious infections of the intestine]. Their insides had simply turned to water, and all they had been able to do for them on shore was to tie their trousers tight round their legs with pieces of string … All we could do was strip them off, clean them up and then put them to bed … It was pitiful to see them, so weak, and blood and water pouring out of them.

Nurse Sister Mary Fitzgibb gives an account of the state of the troops she had to deal with.

SOURCE C

Women certainly gained in confidence during the war and a new self-pride was displayed in the growing use of cosmetics and in dress reform. The Land Army had helped lead the way here. As a contemporary song put it,

Dainty skirts and delicate blouses
Aren't much use for pigs and cows-es.

Not only were trousers worn for the first time but skirts became much shorter.

By the historian Trevor May, 1987.

SOURCE D

We think that a woman's place is in the home, looking after the home, husband and family and if she is a young woman she ought to be learning something better than pit bank work [work at a coal mine].

John Wadsworth, General Secretary of the Yorkshire Miner's Association writing in Yorkshire Evening Post, *June 1916.*

SOURCE E

With one firm the men are paid full time during a Zeppelin raid while the women are not. At another firm the women were employed part on shell and part on fuse making. They were paid as fuse makers only. This was women's work so they were paid lower wages.

From Southampton Times, *1919.*

SOURCE F

It has been found necessary to restrict, and in some cases to stop unemployment benefit to [female] ex-munitions workers in Sheffield. Three hundred women who have refused to accept work in domestic service have been suspended from all benefit.

From Morning Post, *April 1919.*

SOURCE G

It would have been utterly impossible for us to have won the war had it not been for the skill, enthusiasm and industry which women of this country have thrown into the war.

From a speech made by Prime Minister David Lloyd George at the end of the war in 1918.

SOURCE H

Women workers were recruited not from those previously unoccupied, but rather from those who had already been in paid labour elsewhere in the economy. Thus it is best to regard with considerable scepticism [doubt] the many statements made during the war about its 'revolutionary' effects on women's work.

By the historian Jay Winter, 1988.

SOURCE I

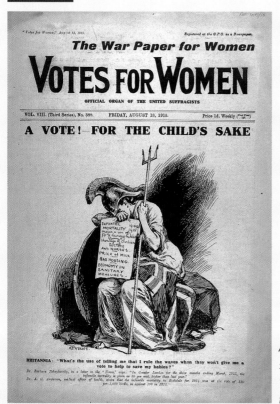

BRITANNIA: "What's the use of telling me that I rule the waves when they won't give me a vote to help to save my babies?"

SOURCE J

The worse case I saw – and it still haunts me – was of a man being carried past us. It was at night, and in the dim light I thought that his face was covered with black cloth. But as he came nearer, I was horrified to realise that the whole lower half of his face had been blown off and what had appeared to be a black cloth was a huge gaping hole. That was the only time that I nearly fainted on the platform, but fortunately I was able to pull myself together. It was the most frightful sight, because he couldn't be covered up at all.

Claire Tisdall recounting her experience one evening during the Somme campaign.

Question time

1   'The First World War changed the lives of British women for good.' How far do Sources B to J confirm this statement?

To answer the question you will need to sort the sources into two broad groups:

- those that point to long-term major changes
- those that point to little change.

2   How useful are each of the sources? To answer this question you should consider the following:

- how likely is it that the author or artist has accurate knowledge of the situation
- what is the purpose of the source?

A cartoon from the cover of Votes for Women, *August 1915. The picture shows Britannia above the slogan 'What's the use of telling me that I rule the waves when they won't give me a vote to help save my babies'.*

How the war has been remembered

The First World War had a huge impact on British and European culture. Even the English language was altered to include terms like 'going over the top'. The most important and lasting impact on our understanding of the war has come through the work of a collection of poets and writers. Two of the most significant are Wilfred Owen and Siegfried Sassoon. Owen and Sassoon experienced the true horror of trench warfare at first hand. Both were treated for nervous breakdowns. Owen could face no more after he was posted to a forward position and had to look at the scattered remains of a killed fellow officer for a number of days without relief. Owen was killed in action a week before the end of the war in 1918.

Although soldiers' letters were censored by officers, they still give historians an excellent picture of the views, hopes and fears of the front line soldiers. Many letters contain information about the routine life of soldiers. Source A is just one example.

SOURCE A

My Darling Wife

Another night has passed and another morning come and I am still in trenches and in good health. Although all day and night on Monday it rained steadily yet Tuesday (yesterday) morning broke fair and fine and we had a nice day except underneath everything was mud and slosh. We were employed all the morning and afternoon in putting down boards along the trenches and have greatly improved it for walking.

Just a few words about your last parcel. I don't often mention everything, but I do appreciate the rag you send me, it is so very useful. The piece this week is lovely and I make a very shrewd guess that, when I am using it as a tablecloth, it was not always used for that purpose but once formed part of my lady's – 'Oh dear, oh dear', what am I saying? – nevertheless it is grand to wrap my bread in and keep my food clean and nice. Cigarettes – capital [excellent] but don't send any more until I ask you to. Toffee, condensed milk, candles, rice and potted meat: the toffee, milk, rice and one candle have all gone. The little pat of butter is always welcome, and the bread dodge I think is an improvement on buying expensive cakes. Please discontinue sending tea, sugar, salt for a bit, Darling, as I have plenty.

If you require new clothes in the way of overcoat or mac or gloves or anything in fact for the winter, don't let your self go short will you. Just take it from the cash and note it in the book as I told you, so that we can see how the cash is made up for the sake of keeping proper accounts. Now I will answer the other letters later. I'm afraid I twaddle a lot but never mind.

I remain ever your own devoted

Bert

Adapted from a letter by Rifleman Bert Bailey of the 11th Battalion, Rifle Brigade.

This contrasts very much with the image given of the war in much of the poetry written during and after it. Source B is one of Owen's most famous poems, *Dulce et Decorum Est*. In the poem Owen is describing a gas attack and its aftermath.

SOURCE B

Bent double, like old beggars under sacks,
Knock-kneed, coughing like hags, we cursed through sludge,
Till on the haunting flares we turned our backs
And towards our distant rest began to trudge.
Men marched asleep. Many had lost their boots
But limped on, blood-shod. All went lame; all blind;
Drunk with fatigue; deaf even to the hoots
Of tired, outstripped Five-Nines that dropped behind.

Gas! GAS! Quick, boys! – An ecstasy of fumbling,
Fitting the clumsy helmets just in time;
But someone still was yelling out and stumbling,
And flound'ring like a man in fire or lime …
Dim, through the misty panes and thick green light,
As under a green sea, I saw him drowning.

In all my dreams, before my helpless sight,
He plunges at me, guttering, choking, drowning,

If in some smothering dreams you too could pace
Behind the wagon that we flung him in,
And watch the white eyes writhing in his face,
His hanging face, like a devil's sick of sin;
If you could hear, at every jolt, the blood
Come gargling from the froth-corrupted lungs,
Obscene as cancer, bitter as the cud
Of vile, incurable sores on innocent tongues, –
My friend, you would not tell with such high zest
To children ardent for some desperate glory,
The old Lie: Dulce et decorum est
Pro patria mori.

Dulce et Decorum Est *by Wilfred Owen.*

Art

During and after the war, artists attempted to represent the horror and brutality of the experience. Many artists visited the front line and were struck by the sights they saw. The painting on page 144 is the work of John Singer Sargent. He visited the front line in France in July 1918. While there he came across a scene that was to leave a deep impression on him.

Outside a dressing station were hundreds of wounded soldiers who were victims of a German mustard gas attack. In his painting Sargent shows the aftermath of the attack. The soldiers in the foreground lie waiting for attention. The main focus is the line of soldiers shuffling along.

SOURCE C

Gassed by John Singer Sargent, painted in 1918.

At the front an orderly attempts to guide the soldiers but the rest of the gassed men have to fend for themselves. Towards the back, one of the line breaks to vomit on the ground. In the background men play football with the confidence of movement now so lacking among the soldiers. Both columns of men walk as in a funeral procession. Sargent paints the sun setting in the background which heralds the coming darkness.

Question time

Study Sources A to C.

1   What impression of the war does each source give?

2   Both Wilfred Owen and Bert Bailey fought in the trenches. Why do you think they gave such different impressions of the war?

3   Which source would be more useful to an historian researching the war?

4   What does *Dulce et decorum est pro patria mori* mean? Why does Wilfred Owen call it 'the old Lie'? Do you agree?

5   Find other poems written by poets such as Owen, Sassoon, Edward Thomas, Edmund Blunden or Rupert Brooke. Chose *one* of the poems you have found and try to explain its meaning.

6   Compare the painting *Gassed* (Source C) with the poem *Dulce et Decorum Est* (Source B). What are the similarities and differences in these sources?

7   If soldiers' letters were censored, do you think they are still useful pieces of evidence? Explain your answer.

4 Assessment section

Look at the sources below and then answer the questions that follow.

A cigarette card depicting a scene from the First World War.

SOURCE B

The crucial point here is that men fought because they did not mind fighting. For most soldiers, to kill and risk being killed was much less intolerable than we generally assume ... Even the most famous war writers provide evidence that murder and death were not the things soldiers disliked about the war.

From The Pity of War *(1998) by Niall Ferguson.*

SOURCE C

After firing once Kendle looked at us with a lively smile; a second later he fell sideways. A blotchy mark showed where the bullet had hit him just above the eyes ... After an awareness that he was killed, all feelings tightened and contracted to a singled intention – 'to settle that sniper' on the other side of the valley. If I had stopped to think, I shouldn't have gone at all. As it was I discarded my tin hat and equipment, slung a bag of bombs across my shoulder, abruptly informed Fernby that I was going to find out who was there ... Just before I arrived at the top [of the opposite slope] I slowed up and threw my two bombs. Then I rushed the bank vaguely expecting some sort of scuffle with my imagined enemy. I had lost my temper with the man who shot Kendle; quite unexpectedly, I found myself looking down into a well conducted trench with a great many Germans in it.

From the novel The Complete Memoirs of George Sherston *(1937) by Siegfried Sassoon. The novel is autobiographical and describes many of Sassoon's experiences as an officer on the Western Front.*

SOURCE D

We always judged a new officer by the way he conducted himself in a trench, and if he had guts we always respected him. The two new officers soon won our respect. One of them was called Mr Fletcher, and all the men in B swore that he was not only the bravest man in France, but had more brains than all the Battalion officers put together. One morning when we were in the line he was informed that he had been awarded the Distinguished Service Order, and it happened that only a few minutes after he took a sharp quick look over the parapet and got sniped through the head. During the whole of the war I never saw men so cut up over an officer's death as in this case.

Extract from Old Soldiers Never Die *(1933) by Frank Richards. Richards served as a soldier throughout the war.*

SOURCE E

The salient [land jutting out] was a dead loss. From the tactical side it was sheer murder. You had this Ypres–Yser Canal and you got the strangest feeling when you crossed it. You'd almost abandon hope. And as you got further out you got this awful smell of death. You could literally smell it. It was just a complete abomination of desolation. I wept when I came into the salient.

The evidence of 2nd Lieutenant H. L. Birks, Tank Corps, writing about Passchendaele in 1917.

1 Compare Sources A and C with Sources B and D. What are the similarities and differences between them?

2 Study Sources B and E. How do these interpretations differ?

3 Which of the sources do you consider most useful and which do you consider least useful to an historian studying soldier's lives in the First World War? Explain why you have come to your conclusion.

4 Study all the sources. What impression do they give you about the attitudes of soldiers to the war? Remember to refer to the sources when answering this question.

5 Why did the Allies win the war in 1918?

6 'Lions led by donkeys'. To what extent do you think that this is an accurate description of the British army on the Western Front from 1914–18?

Creative writing

In this chapter you have read an extract from *Birdsong* by Sebastian Faulks. It describes the experiences of a character called Stephen. Your task is to write a story about a character from the First World War. It is important that your story is based on a historical event that happened. Try to use as much information from the chapter, including the pictures, so your story is as accurate as possible.

Debate

To undertake this debate you need to get into groups. In Source B on page 145 the historian Niall Ferguson claims that 'men fought because they did not mind fighting'. Indeed Ferguson's idea is backed up by other historians who claim that the First World War was not such a bad experience for those who survived. Their argument is based around the idea that life for many soldiers before the war was harsh and many easily adapted to war conditions.

In your groups you are to debate or write an argument about this proposal:

The First World War should be seen as a horrific experience for all soldiers who took part in it.

Further reading

Sebastian Faulks *Birdsong* (Vintage, 1994)

Martin Middlebrook *First Day on the Somme* (Penguin, 2001)

Erich Marie Remarque *All Quiet on the Western Front* (Heinemann, 1970)

The Second World War 1939–45

To most of those who lived through it, the First World War was supposed to be the 'war to end all wars', but only 21 years later, in 1939, another world war broke out that was to become a 'total' war, affecting those fighting as well as civilians on a scale never seen before.

Why did war break out in 1939?

At the Treaty of Versailles in 1919, which agreed the peace terms after the First World War, the League of Nations was set up. It was to be an organisation to which all countries of the world would eventually belong and which would keep peace in the world. The League did help in many areas after the war, for example, with the settlement of minor disputes and the resettlement of refugees. However, it was weakened by the fact that three of the world's more powerful countries – the USA, the Soviet Union and Germany – were not members at the start. The two leading members of the League, Britain and France, followed foreign policies based on their own interests, not that of the League.

The League did not have an army to enforce its decisions and so larger countries could ignore its directives. An example of this was in 1936 when Italy, led by Benito Mussolini, invaded Abyssinia (now Ethiopia). The League of Nations objected but could do little to stop Mussolini. The weakness of the League meant that there was still no international body powerful enough to intervene and prevent war.

German foreign policy 1935–9

In 1933, the leader of the Nationalist Socialist (Nazi) Party, Adolf Hitler, was appointed Chancellor of Germany. Hitler had fought in the First World War and was very bitter about Germany's defeat in 1918. The policies he followed over the next six years were one of the main reasons why war broke out in 1939.

Destruction of the Treaty of Versailles
At the end of the First World War, Germany was punished at the Treaty of Versailles by the victorious powers – France, Britain and the USA. Hitler, the Nazis and many Germans believed that the Treaty of Versailles was unfair.

- Germany lost land including West Prussia, Posen and Alsace-Lorraine.

- Germany was forbidden to unite with Austria, a fellow German-speaking country.

- Germany had to accept the blame for starting the war and pay reparations (compensation) to the Allies.

- Germany's army was reduced to only 100,000 soldiers.

Hitler made the destruction of the Treaty of Versailles one of his main foreign policy aims. In 1935, Germany left the League of Nations (which it had joined in 1926) and in the same year Hitler started increasing the numbers of soldiers in the German army through conscription. The Treaty of Versailles had insisted that the area known as the Rhineland (see map) remained de-militarised – there were to be no German soldiers based there. In 1936, Hitler ordered troops into the Rhineland. There was no military response from Britain and France which suggested to Hitler that they would no longer insist on the Treaty of Versailles being upheld.

Lebensraum

The gaining of *Lebensraum* (living space) was one of Hitler's main ideas. Hitler believed that the German people were superior to all others. As part of this belief, he argued that the German people should have more space to the east in what was Poland and the Soviet Union.

Hitler, anti-communism and anti-Semitism

Hitler and the Nazis hated communists and Jews (hatred of Jews is known as anti-Semitism). As the Soviet Union was the main communist country in Europe, Hitler believed that Germany would eventually have to fight the Soviet Union for supremacy in Europe. He also believed that the Jews were responsible for all the problems that beset Germany and that a war which would remove them from Europe would have to be fought.

Land lost by Germany as a result of the Treaty of Versailles in 1919.

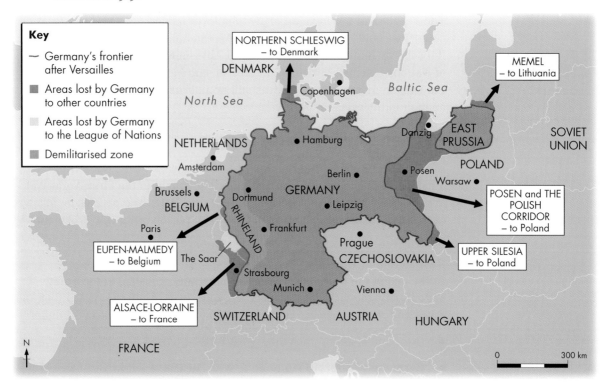

The war at a glance

Year	Europe	Africa and the East
1939	**September:** Poland overrun by Germany and the Soviet Union. **November:** Soviet Union invade Finland.	
1940	**March:** Finland surrenders to Soviet forces. **April:** Germany overruns Denmark and Norway. **May:** Germany overruns Belgium, the Netherlands, Luxembourg and invades France. Allied troops evacuated from Dunkirk beaches.	**September:** Japan occupies French colonies in Asia. **August:** Italian troops invade British territory. **December:** British counter-attack.
1941	**April:** Germany invades Yugoslavia and Greece. **May:** Germany invades Crete. **22 June:** Operation Barbarossa. Germany and Allies invade the Soviet Union. **End October:** German forces reach outskirts of Moscow.	**7 December:** Japanese airforce bombs US fleet at Pearl Harbor. **25 December:** Japanese forces capture Hong Kong. In Africa, British advances reversed by German army.
1942	**Summer:** German offensive pushes towards the oil rich Caucusus region. **September:** Soviet Union launches an offensive at Stalingrad.	**January:** Philippines are overrun. **February:** Singapore falls. Over 60,000 Allied troops surrender. **March:** Japan occupies Rangoon, the capital of British-held Burma. In North Africa, Axis forces defeated by Allied troops at El Alamein. **November:** Allied forces land in North Africa (Operation Torch).
1943	**January:** Leningrad relieved. **2 February:** German forces at Stalingrad surrender. **July:** German army defeated at the large-scale tank battle at Kursk. **July:** Allied troops invade Sicily. **September:** Allied troops invade mainland Italy.	Allied forces attack Japanese troops in the South Pacific.
1944	**6 June:** D-Day. Invasion of mainland Europe by Allied forces. **September:** British forces attempt to shorten the war with a failed parachute drop at Arnhem. **December:** German forces attempt to counterattack at the Battle of the Bulge.	Allied troops roll back Japanese forces.. **August:** Guam and the Philippines recaptured.
1945	**March:** USA crosses the Rhine at Remagen. **April:** German resistance broken at the Rhine. **May:** Battle for Berlin as Russian forces fight their way into the capital.	American forces suffer 20,000 casualties at the Battle of Iwo Jima. **April:** Americans invade the island of Okinawa only 300 miles from mainland Japan.

Year	Diplomatic changes	The war in the air and at sea
1939	**3 September:** Britain and France declare war on Germany. **28 September:** Germany and Russia arrange to divide Poland between them.	**September:** Britain announces a naval blockade of Germany. **December:** German battleship *Graf Spee* sunk in the South Atlantic.
1940	**10 May:** Neville Chamberlain resigns as Prime Minister. Replaced by Winston Churchill. **10 June:** Italy declares war on France and Britain. **22 June:** France and Germany sign an armistice. **27 September:** Italy, Germany and Japan sign pact.	**May:** German submarines operate from bases in France and attack ships in the Atlantic supplying Britain. **November:** Italian fleet badly damaged at Tarranto. **July–October:** Battle of Britain.
1941	**March:** Americans start Lend-Lease programme to provide help to Britain. **8 December:** USA declares war against Japan. **11 December:** Germany and Italy declare war on USA.	**May:** German battleship *Bismarck* sunk by the Royal Navy. **December:** The battle in the Atlantic between German U-boats and allied convoys result in the sinking of up to 500,000 tons of allied shipping in one month.
1942	**June:** Churchill goes to Washington to discuss the future of the war effort. **August:** Churchill goes to Moscow to discuss ways of helping the Soviet Union.	**May:** Battles between US and Japanese navies at Coral Sea. **June:** Battle of Midway. **November:** Solomon Islands. Japanese navy in the Pacific destroyed. In the Atlantic 5.4million tons of Allied shipping is sunk.
1943	**January:** Casablanca Conference. Roosevelt and Churchill agree to aim for unconditional surrender of Axis forces. **July:** Mussolini sacked as Prime Minister of Italy. **September:** Italy surrenders to the Allies. **Nov-Jan:** German forces seize a number of Italian cities.	Allies gain the upper hand in the Battle of Atlantic.
1944	**November-December:** Tehran Conference. Roosevelt, Churchill and Stalin meet in Tehran to discuss war operations.	Allied bombing campaign of Germany intensified.
1945	**February:** Yalta Conference – Allies make plans for the division of Germany. **April:** F. D. Roosevelt dies; replaced by Harry Truman. Mussolini captured and executed. Hitler commits suicide. **April-June:** San Francisco conference sets up the United Nations. **7 May:** Germany surrenders unconditionally. **July-August:** Potsdam Conference discusses future of Europe. **14 August:** Japan surrenders.	**May-August:** Air campaign against Japan. **6 August:** Atomic bomb dropped on Hiroshima. The following week a second atomic bomb is dropped on Nagasaki.

Anschluss and appeasement

As an Austrian, Hitler always hoped for the unification of his homeland with the rest of Germany. In 1938 he saw his dream realised as he ordered German troops into Austria and formed an *Anschluss* (union) between the two countries. Hitler then turned his ambitions to Czechoslovakia, as three million German-speakers (Sudeten Germans) lived there who wanted union with Germany. The Czechoslovaks turned to Britain and France for protection, but their response was to hand over the area in which the Sudeten Germans lived to Germany.

The decision by the British and French governments to allow the Germans part of Czechoslovakia was the result of a policy known as appeasement (giving in to someone's demands to keep them happy). The British politician most closely associated with this policy was Neville Chamberlain, who became prime minister in 1937. The huge loss of life during the First World War meant that many people supported the idea of avoiding war at all cost. The economic depression of the 1930s had left neither Britain nor France in a position to fight a war. Only in 1935 did they start to re-arm.

Declaration of War, September 1939

In March 1939 Hitler ordered the invasion of the rest of Czechoslovakia. This went beyond any restoration of lands lost at Versailles. It was clear that appeasement had failed. Hitler's next step was to take the port of Danzig in Poland which had been lost at Versailles.

Britain and France changed their policy and warned Germany that if Poland was invaded then they would go to war with Germany. Hitler did not take this seriously and went ahead with plans for invasion.

Hitler's territorial gains before September 1939.

In August he made an agreement with the Soviet Union (the Nazi-Soviet Pact) which detailed how Poland would be divided up. This surprised the whole world because the Nazis and the Soviets were thought to be enemies. However, the Soviet leader, Josef Stalin, wanted to build up his forces because he feared a German attack, so he signed the agreement to buy time. Hitler ordered the invasion of Poland on 31 August. When German troops crossed the Polish frontier on 1 September, Chamberlain, with the support of France, issued an ultimatum to Germany to withdraw. At 11.15 am on 3 September, he made this radio broadcast to the British people:

This morning the British ambassador in Berlin handed the German government a final note saying that, unless we heard from them by eleven o'clock that they were prepared at once to withdraw their troops from Poland, a state of war would exist between us. I have to tell you now that no such undertaking has been received and that consequently, this country is at war with Germany.

France declared war against Germany on the same day.

Hitler's domination

The fall of Poland and Norway 1939–40

By 17 September 1939, Russian troops had invaded eastern Poland, as had been secretly agreed in the Nazi-Soviet Pact. Faced with war on two fronts, Poland was defeated. By the end of September, it had ceased to exist. The Russians had taken one half and the Germans the other. British and French guarantees had amounted to nothing. The key to Germany's success over Poland was *Blitzkrieg*, meaning 'lightning war'. This new military strategy involved the use of aircraft as well as troops to rapidly crush the opposing forces and tanks.

After the defeat of Poland in September 1939, there was a period of relative calm in western Europe. This was shattered in April 1940 by the renewal of *Blitzkrieg* by Germany in an invasion of neutral Norway. Norway and Sweden supplied more than half of Germany's iron ore, so they were vital for the production of weapons. Despite British and French help, Norway was soon defeated. Germany had guaranteed its supplies of iron ore and could now use the Norwegian fjords as ideal bases for U-boats.

Chamberlain had considered occupying Norway before Hitler invaded so as to cut off Germany's iron ore supplies, but he had hesitated. He was worried about world opinion if Britain invaded a neutral country. Where Chamberlain had hesitated, Winston Churchill had urged decisive action. The mood in the country was changing; the air raids, petrol rationing and gas masks reminded people that Britain was indeed engaged in a war. More decisive leadership was needed. Chamberlain resigned on 10 May 1940 and Winston Churchill was elected by Parliament to become prime minister. He declared that he had 'nothing to offer except blood, sweat and tears'.

Digging deeper

Churchill as war leader

Winston Churchill was 65 years old when he became prime minister and head of the wartime coalition government. However, his wartime role was to make him one of the great figures of the twentieth century. There are many different opinions of Churchill as you will see from these sources.

SOURCE A

At the Foreign Office and in the war cabinet I shared responsibility under the prime minister until the end of 1940, through the days which preceded, witnessed and followed the collapse of France and Belgium and the miracle of Dunkirk. The main burden of all this fell upon Churchill, and inspired him to give leadership to the British people, matchless and unforgettable ...

From the memoirs of Lord Halifax, who was Foreign Secretary until the end of 1940. The memoirs were published in 1957.

SOURCE B

From first to last, his part in winning the war was greater than any man's – British, American or Russian. He was fertile in resource, inexhaustible in argument, and a spur and stimulus to bold action of any kind. As prime minister, Churchill oversaw every department of the country's life and moulded it into an instrument of total war. This gigantic man fired the whole nation with his passionate indignation [justified anger], pugnacity [readiness to fight], impatience and refusal to admit defeat ... Without him there would have been no triumph.

The historian, Arthur Bryant, writing in 1959.

SOURCE C

6 Oct. 1943: It is quite clear in my mind that with the commitments we have in Italy we should not undertake serious operations in the Aegean ... By 3.25 pm determined to go for Rhodes without looking at the effects on Italy. I had a heated argument with him.

7 Oct. 1943: Another one and a half hour's battle with PM [Churchill] to hold on to what I think is right. The same arguments brought up again and again.

19 Jan 1944: In all his plans, he lives from hand to mouth; he can never grasp a whole plan – selects individual pieces of the vast jigsaw puzzle and concentrates on it at the expense of all others.

29 Mar 1945: I feel that I can't stick another moment with him and would give almost anything never to see him again.

From the diary of Field Marshal Lord Alanbrooke, Chief of Imperial General Staff from 1941–6 commenting on his relationship with Churchill.

SOURCE D

Then came the catastrophes of May and June 1940 when France collapsed and Italy entered the war. In that appalling crisis, the first need was to build up the defences of Britain, and the second to provide for the defence of the Mediterranean area. Those two needs were difficult to meet simultaneously. Churchill's boldest and greatest action was seen in the risks he took to strengthen the defences of Egypt before Britain itself was secure against invasion ... The outcome reflected on Churchill's judgement ...

The opinion of a military historian, Sir Basil Liddell Hart, written in the 1970s.

SOURCE E

Surveying the situation in July 1945 it was hard to argue that Britain had won in any sense save that of avoiding defeat. He had destroyed the awful tyranny of Hitler, but what had risen in its place?

At the end of the war Churchill was, once again, faced with what looked like an attempt by one power (USSR) to dominate Europe, an odd result for so much expenditure of treasure and manpower.

Churchill stood for the British Empire, for British independence and for an anti-Socialist vision of Britain. By July 1945 the first of these was on the skids, the second was dependant solely on America and the third had just vanished in a Labour election victory.

From Churchill: The End of Glory *(1993) by historian John Charmley.*

SOURCE F

Until more than halfway through the war, the British Empire could boast of no great triumph … In 1942 Churchill was fighting for his political life as discontent swelled at home over Britain's lack of military success, and it took Montgomery's victory at El Alamein in November to secure the prime minister's position for the rest of the war.

Written by Angus Calder in The Myth of the Blitz *(1991).*

 Question time

Study Sources A to F.

1   Which sources are positive about Churchill and which are less positive?

2   Why do the sources differ in their viewpoint? Your answer should look at the situation and purpose of the source:

- When did the author write the source?

- What was the circumstance in which the source was written?

- Why did the author write the source?

The fall of France 1940

On 10 May 1940, the same day that Churchill became prime minister, Hitler ordered the invasion of Luxembourg, Holland and Belgium. His main objective was the defeat of France and revenge for German defeat in the First World War. *Blitzkrieg* tactics were once more successfully employed. Holland and Belgium soon fell and Hitler then turned his attention to France.

He avoided the Maginot Line (a line of defensive fortifications built in the 1930s along the Franco–German border) by attacking through the Ardennes Forest using tank divisions commanded by Erwin Rommel. On 12 May the Germans crossed the French border. The British and French troops had been pushed back from Belgium and were encircled in the French town of Dunkirk. Hitler stopped the advance of his tanks. His intention was to destroy the British army on the beaches of Dunkirk using the German Air Force (the Luftwaffe). Between 24 May and 4 June 1940, the British mounted a desperate operation to rescue the stranded troops, using ships of the Royal Navy as well as any small private vessels that were seaworthy. The British government hailed this as a great triumph. In reality it had been a crushing defeat, although 330,000 Allied troops were evacuated and ferried

Key

- Battle of Britain Aug–Oct 1940
- London Blitz Sept–Oct 1940
- Towns bombed by the Luftwaffe

N

0   100 km
50 miles

SCOTLAND

Wick
Aberdeen
Dundee
Edinburgh
Glasgow

North Sea

NORTHERN IRELAND

Belfast

Newcastle
Sunderland
Middlesbrough

Barrow

Irish Sea

Leeds
York
Hull
Manchester
Liverpool
Sheffield
Lincoln
Burton
Nottingham
Great Yarmouth
Norwich
Lowestoft
Birmingham
Coventry
Ipswich

WALES

ENGLAND

Harwich

Pembroke
Swansea
Cardiff
Bristol
Reading
London
Chatham
Bath
Aldershot
Canterbury
Southampton
Brighton
Dover
Exeter
Weymouth
Portsmouth
Newhaven
Portland
Plymouth
Falmouth

English Channel

back to Britain. Paris was captured by the German forces on 14 June and on 22 June the French signed an armistice [truce] with the occupying Germans. Britain now stood alone and prepared itself for the prospect of a Nazi invasion.

The Battle of Britain July–October 1940

Having established control over France, Hitler drew up plans for the invasion of Britain, called Operation Sealion. The first stage of the plan was the destruction of the Royal Air Force which would then leave Royal Navy ships at the mercy of German U-boats and torpedo boats. The fight for control of the skies over the Channel began in July 1940. The battle was to rage from July to October, during which time the Luftwaffe lost 1733 planes and the Royal Air Force 915 planes.

The different phases of the Battle of Britain in 1940.

Investigation

The Battle of Britain

The Internet is a good starting point for further research and investigation about the Battle of Britain. The website for this investigation at www.heinemann.co.uk/hotlinks contains photographs of the event and a useful interactive calendar.

By clicking onto dates on the calendar which are recorded in blue, you can find out, for that day, details about the number of aircraft involved in fighting, the number shot down, the number of casualties and information about the extent and location of damage caused by bombing.

Use the information from the website to complete the following task:

In pairs, choose a date from each of the following periods of the Battle of Britain:

- 10 July to 7 August
- 8 August to 23 August
- 24 August to 6 September
- 7 September to 14 September
- 15 September to 17 September.

1. Download information about particular dates during each of the five phases of the battle outlined above.

2. Produce a series of press releases informing the British people about what is happening. Remember that censorship would influence what you would be able to say. Think of phrases to use that will get past the censor who will not allow anything that gives an impression of bad news.

Digging deeper

The peace mission of Rudolf Hess

After October 1940, the only obstacle in the way of Hitler's domination of western Europe was Britain. Some historians believe that Hitler had been genuinely surprised when Britain had stuck to its pledge to go to war if he invaded Poland. Perhaps he thought that a policy of appeasement would be adopted once more, and that, when the threat of war approached, Britain would abandon Poland.

After the German failure to establish air superiority in the Battle of Britain, the idea of a truce with Britain began to be discussed in Nazi circles. Whether Hitler was party to these discussions is unclear. Also unclear is the question of whether he had prior knowledge of the peace mission of Rudolf Hess. This was one of the most bizarre events of the whole war.

In May 1941 Rudolf Hess, Hitler's deputy *führer* (leader) from 1934, flew from Germany and crash landed in Scotland, where he demanded to see the 14th Duke of Hamilton, whom he claimed to have met at the 1936 Berlin Olympics. His mission, he said, was to arrange peace between Britain and Germany so that, together, they could wage war against the Soviet Union.

There is no doubt that the Duke had attended the Olympics, but he subsequently claimed he had never met Hess. Churchill refused to meet Hess, who was imprisoned for the remainder of the war. Hitler claimed to have no knowledge of Hess's plans. In 1946, Hess was sentenced to life imprisonment at the Nuremberg war trials. He spent the rest of his life in Spandau Prison, Berlin, before allegedly committing suicide in 1987.

This event is shrouded in mystery, and some awkward questions remain unanswered. Why did Hess believe he would be welcome in Britain at such a time? Why did he think Britain would support his peace plan? What part did Britain's Secret Intelligence Service (SIS) play in the plot? Why are Foreign Office files on Hess still closed?

It has never been established how Hess's plane managed to crash land near Glasgow without being attacked by British air defences.

A former RAF flight mechanic, Francis MacCormack, claimed that two Aldergrove-based Czech pilots came within seconds of shooting Hess's plane down. He said, 'I remember the excursion well. I was in the crew room in Aldergrove, at the time when they said that two pilots had gone up on a scramble. Later, we got the commentary that they were coming back, and that their target had turned back over Scotland. We didn't realise, until a day or two later, that it had been Hess. When it was announced that he had landed in Scotland, we knew then that it must have been him. My own personal opinion now is that our people knew that Hess was coming. When you reflect on it, how on earth was a person like Hess allowed to come over the country, over northern England and over the borders without being intercepted?'

Dr Peter Waddell, a university lecturer from East Kilbride, went further. He examined a map, printed on silk and carried by Hess on the flight, which came into the possession of the Home Guard. It was a standard issue for British Secret Intelligence Service Agents. Waddell claims that the man who died at Spandau was not the real Hess at all, but a double, or 'doppelganger', planted by the SIS after the execution of the real Hess, whom they had captured in Scandinavia.

Using evidence from the records of Dr Hugh Thomas, the British military surgeon who examined Hess at Spandau, Waddell claimed that the real Hess had been shot through the lung in the First World War and was scarred for life on his chest, front and back. 'Yet at Buchanan Castle Military Hospital on 13 May, the man showed no scars whatsoever. The real Hess had a large gap between his front teeth. The published 1941 dental plan of the man shows no sign of that gap. The man in Spandau on his death in 1987 showed no body scars or internal scar tissue on X-ray. He could not possibly be Rudolf Hess.'

Even Hess's death is something of a mystery. Using a length of electrical extension cord Hess, a frail old man of 93, hanged himself in the garden of Spandau on 17 August 1987. But why should a man who had survived for 40 years in an Allied-controlled prison commit suicide when an international campaign for his release was gathering momentum? Howard Jones, a Scotland Yard detective at the time, thought there was enough evidence to suggest that Hess had been murdered, and he sent a report to the Director of Public Prosecutions (DPP) in which he said so. The DPP did not agree and nothing happened. There was a motive for Hess's murder; once free, he might have spoken out and told the 'real' story of why he crash-landed in Glasgow, and may have implicated the SIS and senior government officials in the plot. Perhaps the truth will never be revealed.

Activity time

You are investigating the mystery of Rudolf Hess. What questions would you want to ask, and how would you set about finding an answer to these questions?

North Africa

German victories in western Europe made the Italian leader, Benito Mussolini, believe that the war was virtually over, and on 10 June 1940 Italy declared war on Britain and France. Mussolini's aim was to claim a huge north African empire by invading British Somaliland and Egypt. At first the Italians pushed the British army back, but a subsequent naval defeat meant that Mussolini was unable to keep his forces in Africa well supplied.

Early in 1941, Hitler decided to help Italy. He sent General Rommel and four German divisions to Africa (the Afrika Korps). By May 1942, Rommel had pushed the British back to the port of Tobruk, which fell in a single day. Eighty thousand British prisoners were taken. Just as in western Europe, Hitler's troops in Africa seemed to be invincible.

Operation Barbarossa

On 22 June 1941, the Nazis launched their attack on the Soviet Union. This was code-named 'Operation Barbarossa' and involved an army of 3 million men, 3600 tanks and 1800 planes.

The aims of the campaign were to destroy communism, create *Lebensraum* (see page 148) and enslave the supposedly inferior Slav race (many Russians were Slavs). Hitler also wanted the vast wheat fields of the Ukraine as a source of food for his people, and the oil fields of the Caucasus could be used to supply fuel for the war effort.

Hitler anticipated an easy victory and the Soviets were totally unprepared. After only three days of fighting, almost the entire Soviet air force had been destroyed. By mid-July, 400,000 Soviets had been captured and the important city of Leningrad was under siege. However, by the time winter arrived in late October 1941, the Soviet armies had not been completely defeated. The German armies got to within 60 kilometres of Moscow, but a Soviet counter-attack halted the advance until after the winter.

The Pacific

In the 1930s, large parts of south-east Asia were controlled by the British, French and Dutch. The USA was also becoming a strong military force in

The war in North Africa

the Pacific, as was Japan. With its government dominated by army officers, the Japanese embarked on a policy of expansion in Asia from the early 1930s. In 1931, Japan attacked Manchuria and in 1937, the rest of China.

Pearl Harbor and beyond

The US people had tried to stay out of a European war. They had maintained their isolation, even though their sympathies were with Britain. The US President, Franklin D. Roosevelt, considered himself a friend of the British, and the USA had lent and sold vast quantities of military equipment to Britain, but Americans had little appetite for war, either in Europe or against the Japanese in the Pacific region.

The Japanese, however, believed that their only real potential rival to supremacy in Asia and the Pacific was the USA. Therefore the Japanese military decided to strike a blow against the US fleet in its base at Pearl Harbor in Hawaii on 7 December 1941.

The US Navy was taken by surprise – over 2400 men were killed, five battleships were sunk and three were put out of action. The USA declared war against Japan the next day. However the impact of this declaration was

SOURCE G

The USS West Virginia, burning after the bombing of Pearl Harbor, December 1941.

not immediate. By May 1942, Japan had gained control of the British colonies of Malaya, Singapore, Burma and Hong Kong. It also had control of the Philippines and two US bases at Guam and Wake Island. Singapore was a significant loss for Britain, as were the 80,000 troops taken prisoner.

Pearl Harbour can be seen as a major turning point in the war. The German attack on the Soviet Union had faltered. British resistance in North Africa had not been broken, and Britain was isolated but not beaten. Now the USA had entered the conflict with its huge pool of resources and manpower. The tide was turning.

Digging deeper

Roosevelt's reactions to Pearl Harbor

Despite the obvious danger of German and Japanese aggression, most Americans were not prepared to commit the USA to war. By December 1941, the US President, Franklin D. Roosevelt, believed that the Japanese threat in the Pacific was such that the USA should join the war. However, he knew that it would be very difficult to persuade the US Congress (government) to agree to a declaration of war. The importance of Pearl Harbor was that it put the blame for starting the war between Japan and the USA on the Japanese. The following sources describe the reaction of Roosevelt to Pearl Harbor.

SOURCE H

While I was sitting at lunch, the president called me up on the telephone and in a rather excited voice to ask me, 'Have you heard the news?' I said, 'Well, I have heard the telegrams which have been coming in about the Japanese advances in the Gulf of Siam.' He said, 'Oh, no, I don't mean that. They have attacked Hawaii. They are bombing Hawaii.' I thought that the Japanese had solved the issue of whether the USA should go to war or not by attacking us directly in Hawaii.

From the diary of the US Secretary of War, William Stimson, 7 December 1941.

SOURCE I

Roosevelt always realised that Japan would jump on us at the first possible moment. Hence his great relief at the method Japan had used. In spite of the disaster at Pearl Harbor and the blitz warfare with the Japanese during the first few weeks, it turned the US people in favour of war against Japan.

Adapted from a diary extract by Harry Hopkins, January 1942.

SOURCE J

Our two nations are now full comrades-in-arms. The courage which your people have shown in two long years of war inspires us as we join the struggle. The forces which have plunged the world in war, however strong, cannot beat free peoples fighting in a just cause.

Roosevelt writing to the British King George VI, December 1941.

SOURCE K

We are all in the same boat now. This certainly simplifies things.

Roosevelt speaking to Winston Churchill on 8 December 1941.

SOURCE L

Roosevelt's pride in the navy was so terrific that he was having physical difficulty in getting out the words that he knew that the navy was caught by surprise. I remember that twice he said to the minister responsible for the navy, 'Find out for God's sake, why those ships were tied up in rows'.

It was obvious to me that Roosevelt was having a dreadful time just accepting the idea that the navy could be caught unawares.

Frances Perkins, Minister of Labor in Roosevelt's government, describing the president's reaction to the attack.

Question time

Study Sources H to L.

1 Write down a list of sentences to explain Roosevelt's reaction.

2 Back up each sentence with at least *one* quote from the sources.

Here is an example:

Roosevelt was relieved at the attack on Pearl Harbor because it led to greater support for war. It turned the US people in favour of war against Japan (Source I).

The Home Front

When Neville Chamberlain announced on 3 September 1939 that Britain was at war with Germany, it came as no great surprise to most British people, and preparations for war were intensified.

In Britain, attack from the air was feared and heavy casualties, especially in large, densely populated cities like London, were anticipated. From 1 January 1938, it was the responsibility of local authorities to set up Air Raid Precautions (ARP) schemes. The government also created the Auxiliary

ARP wardens in London during the Second World War.

Fire Service. Throughout the war these services were on the front line of what became known as the civil defence.

ARP wardens

As part of the ARP scheme, wardens were recruited. As the war approached the government feared that Britain might be attacked with gas. The ARP wardens were given the responsibility of distributing 38 million gas masks. This was just one of many responsibilities. On Friday 1 September, two days before the start of war, the black-out was enforced by ARP wardens for the first time. To avoid helping enemy aircraft, all lights that could be seen from the sky were to be turned off or covered. The fact that cars were now not permitted to use headlights led to around 3000 deaths in road accidents. Given that there was a period of calm from September 1939 to May 1940 (the so-called 'phoney war'), the preparations for attack on Britain were met with increasing cynicism by some people.

The ARP services recruited from a broad cross-section of society and by the end of the war, over one million men and women had volunteered to serve. They were to play an important role as the bombing of Britain began. It was the responsibility of the ARP warden to report air raid damage, warn people about unexploded bombs and seal off affected areas. They would often provide immediate help in bombed areas until the emergency services could arrive.

National Fire Service

The National Fire Service (which incorporated the Auxiliary Fire Service) consisted of 39 fire-fighting forces in 1942. In all, around 400,000 people joined the National Fire Service during the war. As the bombing of Britain started, red fire engines were replaced by wartime grey engines and tin helmets were issued to the firemen. Many fire brigades also had fire boats, especially in London, where fire teams worked valiantly to control fires on the docksides and streets in the heart of London's East End during the Blitz in 1940.

Casualty Service

Around 240,000 people volunteered to join the Casualty Service during the war. First aid parties would attend the scene of an incident, dealing with minor injuries on the spot and sending more serious cases back to first aid posts, each with a doctor and trained nurses. The most serious cases were sent to a casualty clearing hospital. The medical services also controlled the emergency mortuaries which dealt with the vast numbers of fatalities caused by air attacks.

During the war 2379 civil defence workers were killed, or were 'missing, believed killed'. A further 4459 were injured and detained in hospital. Their work was crucial in maintaining morale on the Home Front (the war effort in Britain), especially when facing the consequences of the bombing campaigns.

Digging deeper

The Home Guard

The Local Defence Volunteers (LDV) were formed in 1940 to help in the defence of Britain against German invasion. About 500,000 men were recruited and equipped with British, Canadian and US weapons. They hastily built whatever defences they could, including trenches and concrete gun emplacements (or 'pill boxes').

The LDV were also expected to fight the Germans if they invaded, but some questioned whether they would be able to perform this task. Many of the volunteers were over 40 years old, the age limit for army service, and few had weapons or even uniforms.

In July 1940, the government renamed the LDV the Home Guard. Behind their backs, many people commented that LDV stood for Look, Dive and Vanish. Reading the following sources will help you make up your own mind about the Home Guard.

SOURCE C

Over a million men enrolled [in the Home Guard] by the summer of 1940. This provided a welcome activity for veterans of the First World War. It had less value as a fighting force. There were few rifles to spare for it until the late summer, and even when these were issued, there was no ammunition. The Home Guards harassed innocent citizens for their identity cards; put up primitive road-blocks, the traces of which may delight future archaeologists; and sometimes made bombs out of petrol tins. In a serious invasion, its members would presumably have been massacred if they had managed to assemble at all. Their spirit was willing though their equipment was scanty.

From English History 1914–1945 *(1965)*
by A. J. P. Taylor.

SOURCE B

A Home Guard roadblock in Findon, West Sussex, June 1940.

SOURCE D

Their value to the defence of Great Britain was unquestionable. Apart from weapons and equipment, the army's greatest need throughout the summer was for training; and training was impossible while there were 5000 miles of coast to watch ... road blocks to man, and bridges to protect ... For all these duties the Home Guard was available. Had it not been, an almost intolerable strain would have been placed on the Home Forces.

From Invasion 1940 *(1958) by Peter Fleming.*

SOURCE E

Friends laughed at me because during the war my dad joined the Home Guard. At the start it was called the Local Defence Volunteers. My mum called it the 'Look, Dive and Vanish Brigade'. My friend Gillian's father was a dispatch rider in Italy. That was terribly glamorous.

From a modern history book.

SOURCE F

I was woken up in the early hours of the morning by the tolling of a church bell, and a shrill voice shouting below my bedroom window, 'Invasion, sir, invasion!' In rushed a Home Guard in a state of great excitement. 'They are landing on the beach, sir, there are hundreds of them!' A moment or two later we were peeping over the top of a sandhill not far from the beach ... There were hundreds of them but they were not Germans. 'You silly man,' I said, 'don't you know what those are? They are stakes placed on the beach to stop German aeroplanes landing at low tide.'

The commander of a Home Guard unit, quoted in The Home Front: An Anthology of Personal Experience 1938–45 *(1981) by Norman Longmate.*

 Question time

Study Sources B to F.

To what extent was the Home Guard useful to the British war effort?

Evacuation

The threat to the civilian population from bombing meant that large numbers of people were evacuated from the cities in the first years of the war. Around 2 million people made their own arrangements for evacuation, staying with friends and relatives. Just under 1.5 million people were evacuated by the government. Many of these came from poor working class families. The government made much of this event, allowing press photographers to take pictures of happy mothers and children enjoying themselves in the safety of their country retreats. The reality of evacuation for a significant number of families was very different.

SOURCE G

Dear Mum,

I hope you are well. I don't like the man's face. I don't like the lady's face much. Perhaps it will look better in daylight. I like the dog's face best.

From a postcard of a recently-evacuated child writing to his mother in 1939.

The evacuation process was a huge operation, co-ordinated by the National Federation of Women's Institutes. Women and children packed their belongings into a suitcase and made their way to the nearest railway station. They had a label which showed their name and home address. Since many of the children had not travelled on a train before, their journey often proved bewildering. When they reached their destinations, they were taken to reception centres like the local school, church or village hall. They crowded together and waited their turn to be chosen by 'host families'. Local people received an allowance for taking in evacuees. They got paid 10 shillings and six pence (52.5p) for the first child, and 8 shillings (40p) for each subsequent evacuee they took in. This was to pay for food and other essentials. Once chosen by host families, the evacuees were taken to their new homes.

Most evacuees found a warm and affectionate welcome, although not all enjoyed such good fortune. There were reports of evacuees being forced to do heavy and menial work, and of being deprived of any benefits of the allowance that their host family had been paid. A few even complained that they were not allowed out of their rooms by their host families. The experience of evacuation varied according to individual circumstances.

Many in the countryside were shocked by the bad language and lack of manners of their guests. One lady who told off a five-year-old for swearing was told, 'I'll tell my Dad about you and he'll come and knock your bleeding block off!'.

The National Federation of Women's Institutes received 1700 complaints from host families, which they published in a report. Complaints included taking in children who had head lice, skin diseases and who were prone to bed-wetting. Some evacuees only had the clothes that they had travelled in. A number had never washed regularly, and having a bath was a new experience. There were also occasional problems of conflict between local children and the evacuees in local schools, and in some areas, school was opened for local children in the morning and evacuees in the afternoon.

Rationing

Much of Britain's food supplies came from overseas, and German U-boats had been effective in preventing supply ships from bringing their cargo into Britain. As a result, food was often in short supply. To counteract the possible effects on public morale of lengthening food queues in shops, the government introduced rationing on food in January 1940. The aim of rationing was to ensure that food was shared out equally, rather than being bought up by the rich.

Everyone was issued with a ration book, and men, women and children had to register with shopkeepers to make sure that they got their ration every week. The amount of food people could buy varied (see below) and more and more food was rationed as the war went on. Recipes were issued by the Ministry of Food to help housewives make food go a long way. Many recipes included vegetables. Woolton Pie, named after Lord Woolton, the Minister of Food, was very popular in wartime Britain.

WOOLTON PIE

Briefly boil the following:

INGREDIENTS
A bunch of carrots
Chopped swede
Diced parsnips
Potatoes

METHOD
Cover with a white sauce and pastry, and cook until pastry is golden.

Average weekly adult ration during wartime	
Milk	6 glasses
Eggs	1 per fortnight
Meat	500g
Butter or margarine	300g approx.
Sugar	2 teacups
Edible oil	$\frac{1}{2}$ teacup
Tea	just under 1 teacup of dry tea leaves
Cheese	30g, increased to 225g later in the war
Jam	$1\frac{1}{2}$ teacups

There was some variation in the amount of food people were allowed, for example, workers in heavy industry got a little more. For most people, however, the average weekly adult ration in Britain during the war was as shown on the left.

Home-grown fruit, vegetables and bread were not rationed. As a result, many people began to grow fruit and vegetables in their gardens and allotments. People also kept hens and geese.

As the war progressed, goods other than food began to be rationed, including clothes from June 1941. The government wanted to shut down clothes factories and use the 450,000 workers in the production of munitions. The Ministry of Food and the Board of Trade thesrefore encouraged the country to 'Make Do and Mend'. Old woollen clothing was unpicked by volunteers and re-knitted into warm clothing for the British troops. Nylon parachute material was sold for underwear. Sheets were patched or turned into bandages. Envelopes were re-used and newspapers were recycled. Even scrap food was collected in bins on street corners and taken to farms to feed the pigs.

you never know who's listening!

CARELESS TALK COSTS LIVES

Most people co-operated with the rationing system. However, a black market also sprang up where people could buy goods or food 'under the counter' from traders or local shop keepers.

How did the government keep up morale?

The government was keen to ensure that it had the full backing of the British people during the war. Two government organisations controlled the flow of wartime information made available to the public.

- The Censorship Bureau banned all press photographs showing wounded soldiers, dead air raid victims, or houses destroyed by bombs.

- The Ministry of Information produced propaganda – it distributed official news and information about the war – that it wanted the British public to hear.

There were leaflets, films and radio broadcasts. In particular, there were many government poster campaigns. Campaign slogans were simple and easy to remember: 'Careless Talk Costs Lives' (Source I), 'Dig For Victory', 'Your Britain – Fight For It Now!' are amongst the more famous ones.

Entertainment was used to keep up morale. Some sports continued and films, music and dancing were all popular. The Entertainments National Service Association (ENSA) was formed to bring entertainment into people's homes through the radio. It soon became more popularly known as 'Every Night Something Awful'. To keep factory workers' spirits high, in June 1940 the BBC introduced a radio programme called *Music While You Work* which proved to be very popular.

Winston Churchill's speeches were broadcast on the radio to encourage people to support the war effort and to make them feel their contributions were valued. His speeches seemed to sum up the 'bulldog spirit' of stubborn courage and did much to maintain morale, even during Britain's darkest days. His words during the Battle of Britain, 'Never before in the field of human conflict has so much been owed by so many to so few', helped convince the public that victory was possible.

Digging deeper

Britain and the Blitz

The Blitz on Britain's cities began on 7 September 1940. It marked the end of the Battle of Britain and the beginning of Hitler's attempt to bomb Britain into submission. At this point in the war it was vital that the government maintained the support of the public. This meant that reports from the time had to minimise the extent of the damage and maximise the impression that the public was prepared to put up with such adversity in the cause of defeating Hitler.

The bombing of British cities was to leave a trail of death and devastation. Apart from London, a number of industrial cities were destroyed including Coventry which was attacked on the night of 14 November 1940. The centre of the city was gutted and 554 people were killed in one night. In 1942 German bombers turned their attention to historic towns and cities such as Canterbury and Exeter in reprisal for the attack on the medieval German town of Lubeck. Towards the end of the war the Germans attacked targets in the south of England with V1 and V2 rockets. In all some 60,000 civilians were killed in German raids.

SOURCE J

East London paused for a moment yesterday to lick its wounds after what had been planned as a night of terror. But it carried on.

From The Daily Herald *9 September 1940.*

SOURCE K

Fire-bombs used in the raids last night caused a huge blaze and firestorm, sucking in cold air like a gale. Tremendous heat was generated, causing the fire to spread rapidly ... The flames were so large and their heat so great as to blister the paint on fire boats on the opposite side of the Thames, 300 yards away.

From a report by the Chief of the London Fire Brigade, September 1940.

SOURCE L

The whole story of the last weekend has been one of unplanned panic. The newspaper versions of life going on normally are grotesque. There was no bread, no milk and no telephones. There is no humour or laughter.

From a report by local officials on conditions in London, September 1940.

SOURCE M

The church was a popular shelter so it was full when the bomb fell. The bomb had burst in the middle of the shelterers, mostly women and small children. The scene resembled a massacre, with bodies, limbs, blood and flesh mingled with little hats, coats and shoes. The people were literally blown to pieces. The work of the ARP services was magnificent – by nine o'clock all the casualties were out. After a heavy raid there was the task of piecing the bodies back together in preparation for burial. The stench was the worst thing about it – that, and having to realise that these frightful pieces of flesh had once been living breathing people. There were always odd limbs that did not fit, and there were too many legs. Unless we kept a very firm grip on ourselves, nausea and sickness were inevitable.

From an account of the Blitz by an ARP member, 14 September 1940.

SOURCE N

What warmth! What courage! What determination! People singing in public shelters. Women's Voluntary Service girls serving hot drinks to fire fighters during raids. Everyone secretly delighted with the privilege of holding up Hitler. Certain of beating him.

From a letter from Humphrey Jennings to his wife, October 1940.

SOURCE O

Morrison shelters proved their worth over and over again. Countless families escaped uninjured, although their shelters were completely buried in debris. Police officers and rescue workers regularly report how people emerged smiling and safe from the wreckage of their homes. The speed and efficiency of the rescue workers made a very favourable and reassuring impression throughout the district.

From an Exeter newspaper in May 1942. Exeter was very badly hit by bombs during the war.

SOURCE P

People met in the air raid shelters, in the tubes [London Underground] at night, or they queued for spam [processed meat] or whatever it was that they could get hold of, one egg a week. Everybody lost their inhibitions [shyness] about talking to their next door neighbours. When the raids were over they used to celebrate in the early morning, and this was the spirit that I think a lot of people hoped would continue after the war.

From Now The War Is Over *(1985) by P Addison.*

SOURCE R

People would rush to get to the tubes, almost knock you over to get down the escalator, because people were getting panic-stricken to get down there, to get out of the noise, to get out of the devastation. We lived like rats underground. You'd queue for hours to get a good spot on the platform – you'd want to avoid the cold, smelly, draughty parts. People spread newspapers on the floor or left bundles on the floor to show it was their territory, and somebody might come and kick that away and that would lead to arguments over who should be there. Sometimes you'd get people squaring up and fighting.

From a book about the Blitz written in 1990.

Question time

Study Sources J to R.

Write two contrasting reports about the Blitz:

- The version from the Ministry of Propaganda showing that people were coping.

- The version from an historian who believes that morale was poor during the Blitz.

SOURCE Q

A photograph, posed for propaganda purposes, showing a milkman delivering among the ruins of a bombed city.

Activity time

You have been asked to set up a classroom exhibition to show what life was like on the Home Front in the Second World War. What items would you include? Explain why you have selected these items.

The tide turns

Up to May 1942, the Axis powers (Germany, Italy and Japan) were winning the war.

- In western Europe, France had surrendered and only Britain remained defiant against the German armed forces.

- In North Africa, Rommel had captured Tobruk.

- In the Soviet Union, Leningrad was under siege and the German army was only 96 kilometres (60 miles) away from Moscow.

- In the Pacific, Japan controlled vast areas of territory, including Singapore and two US bases.

On the surface, victory seemed a real possibility for the Axis powers. However, the tide was beginning to turn:

- German forces in Russia were already over-stretched and were unprepared for the winter that was coming.

- The entry of the USA into the war in December 1941 tipped the scales in favour of the Allies.

From June 1942, the Axis powers suffered a series of defeats from which, ultimately, they were unable to recover. The year 1942 was a turning point in the war as a whole.

North Africa

The Axis advance was halted in July 1942, and an attempt by Rommel to break through Allied lines in September ended in defeat. The Allies won a major victory in October 1942 at El Alamein in Egypt. Rommel's Afrika Korps was heavily outnumbered by British and New Zealand forces and were chased out of Egypt. This was a very important turn of events – it led to the expulsion of Axis forces from North Africa, the surrender of the Germans and Italians at Tunisia in May 1943, and preparations for an Allied invasion of Italy.

Eastern Europe

During the spring of 1942, the Soviet Union had launched a series of offensives with the aim of recapturing territory they had previously lost. When these failed, the Germans went back on the offensive. They reached Stalingrad by the end of August and although they virtually destroyed the city, they could not force the Soviet Union to surrender.

Digging deeper

The Battle of Stalingrad, 1942–3

Stalingrad was the key battle of the Second World War. If the Germans had managed to capture the city, they would have been able to break through to the oil-rich Caucasus Mountains to the south of the Soviet Union. By mid-October the German Sixth Army, under the command of General Paulus, had captured more than half the city. On 14 October 1942, Paulus launched an offensive to break the resistance of Russian troops who were holding out in two factories. The Germans failed to dislodge them.

The Russian leader, Stalin ordered his generals to launch a counter-attack, and by 23 November the German Sixth Army was completely encircled. Unless they withdrew, they would surely face complete destruction. Paulus sent a telegram to Hitler.

> Our ammunition and petrol supplies are running out. Several batteries and anti-tank units have none left. Supplies not expected to reach them in time. Army heading for disaster if it does not succeed, within very short time, in pulling together all its strength to deal knock out blow against enemy now assailing [attacking] it in south and west. For this it is essential to withdraw all our divisions from Stalingrad and northern front.

On 24 November, Hitler replied,

> The Sixth Army is temporarily surrounded by Russian forces … The army must be persuaded that I shall do all in my power to supply it adequately and to disengage it when the time is convenient. I know the valiant Sixth Army and its Commander-in-Chief and that every man shall do his duty.

The German situation became desperate. Temperatures dropped to –30°C and the German bread ration was cut to just 50 grammes a day. Starving soldiers killed their horses and fed on the meat. Later still, they dug up the frozen carcasses so that they could eat the bones. Paulus's men could not break through Soviet lines and relief from outside the encirclement did not arrive. On 8 January 1943, the Soviets delivered an ultimatum demanding the German

SOURCE A

A German tank stuck in a snow drift at Stalingrad in 1942, next to the bodies of dead Russian soldiers. A troop of Russian soldiers is passing by.

surrender. Hitler told Paulus that 'surrender is forbidden'. On 22 January, two weeks into the final Soviet offensive, Paulus sent another telegram to Hitler informing him that the Sixth Army had little option but to surrender. His men had no ammunition, food was running out, and more than 12,000 wounded troops were receiving no medical aid. Paulus asked for an immediate reply, but none came.

On 31 January, Hitler promoted Paulus to the rank of Field Marshal. No German Field Marshal had ever surrendered and Hitler urged Paulus to commit suicide rather than face humiliation. He did not. He was captured soon after and the last troops surrendered on 2 February. A total of 22 German divisions had been destroyed during the battle and 800,000 German soldiers were killed.

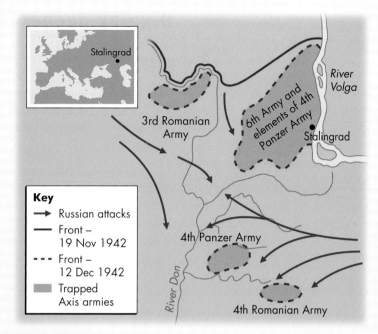

The Battle of Stalingrad, 1942.

From 1942 onwards, the Axis powers were in retreat on every front. The tide had turned in favour of the Allies, and slowly but surely, victory for them appeared to be getting nearer.

Western Europe

As the Soviets were forcing the Germans into retreat, Britain and the USA opened a second front in western Europe by crossing the English Channel and invading France. On 6 June 1944, Operation Overlord began. This was D-Day, when Allied troops landed on the beaches in Normandy. Five beaches in Normandy were chosen for the landings from the sea. The US troops landed on Utah and Omaha beaches and faced fierce opposition before breaking the German resistance. British and Canadian forces landed on the beaches code-named Sword and Juno where German resistance was far lighter.

From D-Day onwards the Germans faced a war on two fronts. The Soviet armies were steadily advancing in the east and British and US forces were advancing in the west. On 25 August 1944 the Allies liberated Paris from the Germans. In September, they liberated Belgium. There was, however, strong resistance from the German troops. Over 7000 British paratroopers were either killed or captured after the unsuccessful attempt to seize strategically important bridges across the River Rhine at Arnhem. In December 1944, Hitler launched his final offensive in the Ardennes, known as the Battle of the Bulge. This held up the final invasion of Germany by six weeks. During this time, the British and US air forces launched massive bombing raids on key German cities.

Digging deeper

The Allied bombing of Germany

From 1942 onwards, British Air Marshal Arthur Harris took over 'Bomber Command'. He had an unshakeable belief in the potential of bombing raids to break enemy resolve. His motto was 'the bomber will always get through'.

As a result, bombing raids on German cities intensified. British and US bombers took part in 'area bombing', where whole areas of cities were singled out and bombed to destruction with no effort made to avoid residential or civilian areas. In 1942 British and US bombers dropped about 72,000 tonnes of bombs on Germany. By 1944, this figure had spiralled to 1.6 million tonnes.

One of the cities devastated by bombing was Hamburg. A number of attacks in July and August 1943 destroyed 55 to 60 per cent of the city, did damage to an area of 48 square kilometres (30 square miles), and completely burned out 20 square kilometres (12.5 square miles). In all 300,000 houses were destroyed and perhaps as many as 42,000 people were killed.

In February 1945, British and US bombers attacked the city of Dresden. The death toll at Dresden will never be known as the city was packed with refugees at the time. However, nearly 40,000 were officially identified and a further 20,000 suspected as having been killed. The bombing of Berlin was a regular event in the last year of the war. It caused considerable damage to buildings but did not destroy the morale of Berliners as had been hoped.

SOURCE B

February 1944: I feel a growing sense of wild vitality within myself, and of sorrow too. Is that what the British are trying to achieve by attacking civilians? At any rate they are not softening us up ... The disaster which hits the Nazis and anti-Nazis alike is welding the people together. After every raid special rations are issued – cigarettes, coffee, meat. If the British think they are going to undermine our morale they are barking up the wrong tree.

Written by journalist Ursala von Kardorff in her diary, at the time of the raids on Germany.

SOURCE C

The ruins of Dresden after Allied bombing in February 1945.

Fighting in the Pacific

On 4 June 1942, the Japanese attacked the US base at Midway Island in the Pacific Ocean. Although outnumbered, the Americans had cracked the Japanese code and were expecting the attack. In the battle that followed, the Japanese fleet had to withdraw and it never regained the offensive. The Battle of Midway is regarded as a vital turning point in the war in the Pacific.

In order to begin the recapture of Pacific islands held by Japan, the Americans launched a new strategy called 'island hopping'. This meant taking key islands

I was overwhelmed with work. Wounded were everywhere. Some men had one foot or leg off, others had both off; some were dying, some dead ... I called for stretcher bearers to get the more seriously wounded to the sick bay where they could receive treatment, but the passageways had been blocked off due to the bomb hits. So we gave more morphine, covered the patients with blankets, and did the best we could. Many patients went rapidly into shock ... Blood was everywhere.

Joseph Pollard, a medical officer on board the warship Yorktown, *writing at the time of the Battle of Midway in 1942.*

We have used the bomb against those who have attacked us without warning at Pearl Harbor, against those who have starved and beaten and executed American prisoners of war, against those who have abandoned all pretence of obeying international laws of warfare. We have used it in order to shorten the agony of war, in order to save the lives of thousands and thousands of young Americans.

President Truman, speaking in a radio address, justifying the use of the atomic bomb on 9 August 1945.

and building bases from which to attack mainland Japan itself. The aim was to surround Japanese strongholds and cut off supplies. This new strategy appeared to work, but the rate of progress was slow. The Japanese defended their strongholds fanatically. On the small island of Iwo Jima, the Americans lost 20,000 men between 19 February and 17 March 1945.

Throughout 1945 the US air force launched a massive bombing campaign against Japan. Secretly, US and British scientists had been developing nuclear weapons during the war. On 6 August 1945 President Truman took the decision to drop the newly-developed atomic bomb on the city of Hiroshima. Almost 100,000 people were killed instantly and another 60,000 died later from burns, radiation, or other wounds. The city was devastated. Still Japan did not surrender. On 9 August 1945 a second atomic bomb was dropped on Nagasaki, killing 40,000 civilians. Five days later, the Japanese offer of surrender was accepted.

The end of the war

From January 1945, Hitler lost touch with what was happening at each front line. He was living in a concrete bunker underneath the chancellery building in Berlin. By 29 April 1945, the Russians had reached the outskirts of Berlin, and British and US forces were closing in on the western outskirts of the city. Berlin was already in ruins after months of heavy Allied bombing. German citizens were left to fend for themselves in the face of the relentless Russian advance. People camped out among the ruins of their former houses with no facilities of any kind, apparently 'scavenging like animals' in order to survive. The war was lost.

- On 30 April 1945 Hitler committed suicide.

- On 2 May 1945 Berlin surrendered.

- On 7 May 1945, General Jodl signed the unconditional surrender of the German forces.

- On 8 May 1945 Von Keitel surrendered to the Russians.

In Britain on 8 May 1945, crowds of people celebrated VE Day (Victory in Europe Day). People danced and celebrated in huge street parties.

A poster from the Second World War.

SOURCE B

Working in a factory was not fun. To be shut in [the factory] for hours on end, with not even a window to see daylight, was grim. The noise was terrific and at night when you shut your eyes to sleep all the noise would start again in your head. Night shift was the worst of all ... I think boredom was our worst enemy.

A factory girl from Andover, talking about her experiences in 1941.

SOURCE C

As in the First World War, women took a much more active role in industrial and agricultural life once war broke out. Factories and food production were kept going by women's 'war work'. In Britain, Churchill commented that 'this war effort could not have been achieved if women had not marched forward in their millions'.

From a modern history textbook, published in 2001.

1   Look at Source A. What impression does this source give of women's work during the Second World War?

2   Look at Source B. How does the impression of factory work in Source A differ from the impression given in Sources A and C?

3   Why do these impressions differ?

4   'During the Second World War the British people had to make considerable sacrifices.' Comment on this statement, using all the sources and your own knowledge. You should comment on the following areas – women's work, evacuation, bombing and rationing.

Creative writing

Many young children had their world turned upside down by war. You might try to read *Carrie's War* (1973) by Nina Bawden, which is the story of a child who is evacuated.

Your task is to write a story about the experiences of a child during the Second World War.

Turning point

For this exercise you should work in pairs.

There are a number of important turning points during the war. A turning point is a critical moment which changes the course of history. What do you think are the three most important turning points of the Second World War?

Place your three turning points in order of importance. For each one you should try to do the following:

●   describe the event

●   explain why it was so important as a turning point.

You might be asked to explain your decision in front of the class. In order to prepare for this, you and your partner must first have discussed your work in depth.

Research – what was life like during the war?

As part of your studies, it would be useful to try to interview someone who was alive during the war. Look back to the rules about doing this in the chapter on the First World War (page 137). However it should be easier to find information because there are still many people alive who remember the years of the Second World War.

The person you are writing to may not have lived in Britain but in another part of the world. This will be very useful as you can compare the information they give you with that of the people who lived in Britain. Here are some guidelines to help you with your research:

●   Write to a relative or elderly person who you think might have information about life during the war.

●   In your letter ask them a series of questions which will help you find out about life in wartime.

●   If it is possible, and you have the permission of your teacher/guardian/parent, you might undertake an interview. If you do this, it is best if you can interview them with a tape recorder so you are not writing down too much during the interview.

There are also some websites you might contact which will give you a chance to read about the experiences of those who lived through the war. There is an example of a website you might contact at

www.heinemann.co.uk/hotlinks

Further reading

M. Arnold-Foster *The World at War* (Thames-Methuen, 1983)

N. Kelly *The Second World War* (Heinemann, 1989)

A. and A. Pike *The Home Front in Britain 1939–1945* (Tressell, 1985)

K. Shephard *International Relations 1919–1939* (Stanley Thornes, 1998)

6 The Holocaust

Anti-Semitism – the hatred of Jews – in Europe has a long history. In the Middle Ages, Jews were wrongly blamed for all the ills of society, including the Black Death of 1348–9. In several countries, they were stripped of their rights, and medieval German chronicles contain illustrations of Jews being burned to death in public.

Whilst many countries gave full rights to Jews during the nineteenth and early twentieth centuries, there was still much anti-Semitism in Germany before the creation of the Weimar Republic in 1918. When the German stock market crashed in 1873, the Jews were blamed for it. A large amount of anti-Jewish literature was widely circulated at this time. One prominent German wrote that in Berlin, '... they [the Jews] actually control the whole city government'. In 1879, a German academic wrote, 'The Jews are our national misfortune'. After the creation of the Weimar Republic, full democratic rights were extended to previously disenfranchised groups (those who did not have the vote). These included the Jews. They were given full citizenship and were employed in all areas of work, especially in the professions like law, medicine, as academics in universities and in the civil service. It must also be remembered that not all Germans or political parties were anti-Semitic. Parties such as the Social Democrats were not anti-Semitic, and by the 1930s the German Jewry was highly integrated into society and intermarriage between Germans and Jews was high.

But between 1933 and 1945, with the rise of Hitler and Nazism (see pages 147–51), all this was reversed and the Jews were systematically victimised. Whilst the Weimar period was one of general advancement for Jews in Germany, it is true to say that the Nazi policy of persecution after 1933 was more in line with Germany's anti-Semitic past. In times of hardship and crisis, the Jewish people were used as scapegoats.

Digging deeper

Hitler's anti-Semitic views before 1933

While Hitler and the Nazis only started to put their anti-Semitic views into practice when Hitler came to power in 1933, it is important to look at how Hitler's views developed.

Hitler's extreme views about the Jews were widely known as he had made them public in his autobiography, *Mein Kampf*, which became a best-seller after its publication in 1924.

> **SOURCE A**
>
> Was there any shady undertaking, any form of foulness, especially in cultural life, in which at least one Jew did not participate? On putting the probing knife carefully to that kind of abscess, one immediately discovered, like a maggot in a putrescent [rotting] body, a little Jew, who was often blinded by the sudden light.
>
> *From Mein Kampf (1924) by Adolf Hitler.*

SOURCE B

The black-haired Jewish youth waits for hours on end, satanically [like a devil] glaring at and spying on the unsuspicious girl whom he plans to seduce, adulterating [corrupting] her blood and removing her from the bosom of her own people ... The Jews were responsible for bringing Negroes into the Rhineland with the ultimate idea of bastardising the white race which they hate ... [this is] the nightmare vision of the seduction of hundreds of thousands of girls by repulsive, crooked-legged Jew bastards.

From Mein Kampf *(1924) by Adolf Hitler.*

SOURCE C

Hitler's anti-Semitism bore no relation to facts, it was pure fantasy: to read these pages is to enter the world of the insane, a world peopled by hideous and distorted shadows. The Jew is no longer a human being, he has become a mythical figure, a grimacing, leering devil invested with infernal [hellish] powers ... The Jew is everywhere, responsible for everything – the modernism in art and music Hitler disliked; pornography and prostitution; the anti-national criticism of the press; the exploitation of the masses ... not least for his own failure to get on.

Alan Bullock, an historian describing Mein Kampf *in 1962.*

SOURCE D

Adolf Hitler was ... the one most obsessed with hatred and fear of the Jews ... he believed that they were the source of all evil, misfortune and tragedy ... the demonic hosts whom he had been given a divine mission to destroy. There is little doubt that *Kristallnacht* [public acts of violence towards the Jews on 9 November 1938] and much worse was in Hitler's mind long before he came to power ...

Gordon Craig, an historian, describing Hitler's views in 1981.

Question time

1   Draw a spider diagram on 'Hitler's views about the Jews'. Try to include all the characteristics Hitler believed the Jews possessed.

2   Compare your spider diagram to the opening section of this chapter which contains other people's views about the Jews. Are there any similarities and differences?

Persecution of the Jews 1933–8

Once Hitler came to power as Chancellor of Germany in January 1933, he immediately set out to persecute the Jewish people of Germany in a number of ways. Most historians accept the facts of what happened in these years, but they still dispute what Hitler's long-term intentions were. Some are in no doubt that Hitler had a long-term plan to destroy the Jewish race.

SOURCE A

Even Hitler did not seem to have extermination in mind when he came to power. *Mein Kampf* does not mention concentration camps. Indeed, there does not seem to have been a clear plan. Hitler hoped many Jews would leave Germany voluntarily, and solve his problems for him ...

From a modern history textbook, published in 1996.

SOURCE B

*An anti-jewish cartoon,
from a children's book.*

Within days of taking power in 1933, Hitler called for a boycott (ban) of all Jewish businesses. Nazi newspapers printed progressively more extreme anti-Jewish propaganda. In April 1933, Jews were forced to give up their jobs in the civil service and from September of the same year, they were not allowed to inherit land. In schools, too, drastic changes were made (see page 181).

By 1935, Jews had been banned from parks, swimming baths and restaurants. They had had their citizenship removed and also their right to vote. The Nuremberg Laws written in 1935 forbade marriages and sexual relations between Jews and non-Jews. Since the death of President Hindenburg in 1934, Hitler had been feeling more confident about his personal ability to take more extreme measures against the Jews. Nevertheless, he still exercised some restraint during this period. The Olympic Games were held in Berlin in 1936 and persecution against the Jews was reduced while there were so many foreign visitors to the capital.

After the Olympics, Hitler stepped up the persecution against the Jews. In 1938, Jews had to register their property and Jewish doctors, dentists and lawyers were prevented from treating or representing non-Jews. From October 1938, Jews had to have a red 'J' stamped on their passports. However, none of this could prepare the Jews for what was to happen one month later – *Kristallnacht* (night of broken glass).

Digging deeper

Kristallnacht

Kristallnacht refers to the public acts of violence committed against the Jews all over Germany on the night of 9 November 1938. This night saw the smashing up of 8000 Jewish shops and businesses; the burning of 267 synagogues; the murder of 91 Jews; the arrest of 40,000 Jews and their imprisonment in concentration camps; and the smashing of glass to the value of 24 million marks.

Hitler commented that this was the revenge of the people for the killing of a diplomat in Paris by a Jew two days earlier, but also revenge for the years of 'parasitic' activities of Jews feeding off the honest toil of ordinary German citizens. Was this a spontaneous uprising, or was it all planned in advance by the Nazis?

SOURCE C

In the autumn of 1938 Hitler was concentrating on foreign policy. He went to the trouble of reminding the Nazi Party that further persecution of the Jews would not be welcome. At this time, Josef Goebbels, Chief of Propaganda, was desperate to restore his position of favour with Hitler. The *Führer* disapproved of Goebbels' affair with a famous actress. The chance Goebbels was waiting for came when a German diplomat was murdered in Paris by a Jewish youth. Goebbels made sure that the Party newspapers gave massive coverage to the 'Jewish outrage'. He dashed to Munich and urged Hitler to allow a spontaneous reprisal. Hitler said that the 'SA should be allowed its last fling'. The reprisals began.

A British historian, writing in 1991.

SOURCE D

The murder in Paris of Herr Von Rath led in Germany today to scenes of systematic plunder and destruction which have seldom had their equal in a civilised country since the Middle Ages. In every part of the Reich, synagogues were set on fire or dynamited, Jewish shops smashed and ransacked, and individual Jews arrested or hounded by bands of young Nazis through the streets ... But destruction and looting did not begin in earnest until this afternoon. A large cafe in the Kurfurstendamm had been plundered of its bottles of wines and spirits and these were being gleefully thrown at what remained of the windows ... The active participants in this display were youths and little boys of the Hitler Youth – the only uniformed body which I actually saw taking part in this destruction ... During the entire day, hardly a policeman was to be seen in the streets where the 'purge' was in progress, save those few who were directing traffic. In no case, so far as can be learned, did the police dare to interfere with the demonstrators.

Report written by the Berlin correspondent of The Times, *November 1938.*

SOURCE E

The shattering of shop windows, looting of stores and dwellings of Jews ... was hailed subsequently in the Nazi press as 'a spontaneous wave of righteous indignation throughout Germany'... On the contrary, in viewing the ruins ... all of the local crowds observed were obviously benumbed over what had happened and aghast over the unprecedented fury of the Nazi acts.

Statement by the American Consul in Leipzig, 21 November 1938.

SOURCE F

Attention: Chiefs or Deputies. This telex must be delivered at once in the fastest possible manner.

1   Operations against Jews, in particular against their synagogues, will commence very soon throughout Germany. There must be no interference. However, arrangements should be made, in consultation with the General Police, to prevent looting and other excesses.

2   Any vital archival material that might be in the synagogues must be secured by the fastest possible means.

3   Preparations must be made for the arrest of from 20,000 to 30,000 Jews within the Reich. In particular, affluent Jews are to be selected. Further directives will be forthcoming during the course of the night.

4   Should Jews be found in the possession of weapons during the impending operations, the most severe measures must be taken ... The State Police must under all circumstances maintain control of the operations by taking appropriate measures ...

Gestapo II Muller.

This telex is classified 'Secret'.

Telex message of 9 November 1938 from the Secret State Police (Gestapo) Office, Department II, to all regional and local commands of the State Police, relating to the preparation of the attacks against Jews.

OPPRESSION AND SUPPRESSION

Nazi Bully. "My will is the will of Germany!"

A cartoon about Kristallnacht *from* Punch, *30 November 1938.*

Anti-Jewish persecution had already reached its height in Germany in the spring and summer of 1938. In June, finance offices and police stations were instructed to draw up lists of wealthy Jews. On 9 June, the Munich synagogue was destroyed. Six days later, 1500 Jewish people with a police record were arrested and sent to concentration camps. In August, the Nuremberg synagogue was destroyed. About this time, a 'small camp area' consisting of 18 huts was built at Sachsenhausen concentration camp. According to the official Memorial Centre Leaflet, these huts were 'built before the pogrom [attacks against Jews] of November 1938 to accommodate Jewish inmates' – clear evidence that the Nazis had anticipated the event. Finally, in October, all Jewish passports were stamped with a 'J', and over 15,000 'stateless' Polish Jews (many of whom had lived in Germany for decades) were forcibly expelled and sent to Poland. The events of *Kristallnacht*, therefore, had been anticipated and planned for well in advance. It is a nonsense to say it was a spontaneous uprising.

An historian writing in January 2001.

Investigation

Study Sources C to H carefully.

With a partner, prepare a talk to be given to the rest of your class. It will need to last about ten minutes and will investigate whether *Kristallnacht* was planned or spontaneous.

In your talk, you will need to do the following.

- Give factual details of what actually happened on 9–10 November 1938. This will involve sorting out facts from opinion in the sources. Try to find further resources about this event so that you can cross-check your facts widely.

- Find evidence which supports the idea that *Kristallnacht* was spontaneous and was participated in by different sections of the German public. You will need to be able to say where this evidence has come from.

- Find evidence which supports the idea that *Kristallnacht* was planned by the Nazis and was carried out largely by members of the SA and the Hitler Youth. You will again need to be able to say where this evidence has come from.

- Give your opinions about the quality of the evidence you have looked at. How have the authors got hold of their information? Were any of them eye-witnesses? When were the sources published and is this significant? How far can you trust the sources to be telling the truth?

- Reach a conclusion where you sum up your findings and respond to the original question. Remember that it is fine to conclude that it is difficult to give a final verdict for one side or the other.

Digging deeper

What were schools like for Jewish children in Nazi Germany? Did indoctrination work?

Young people were especially important to Hitler. If the German Empire was to last 1000 years (as Hitler boasted it would), then the hearts and minds of the young had to be won over. Hitler's aim was to indoctrinate [teach a strong set of beliefs] to children to believe in the superiority of the Aryan. It was his view that the so-called 'pure Germans' [Aryans] were the master race.

In schools, the Nazis controlled teachers and influenced what children were taught. Ninety-seven per cent of teachers joined the Nazi Teachers' Association, and those who remained non-members found it increasingly difficult to get work in schools. Members attended special camps which focused on methods of indoctrination. The Nazis reorganised the curriculum so that certain subjects were given special emphasis. Physical education was seen as very important in building physical fitness and a disciplined attitude. History lessons focused on the glorious achievements of the Nazis, the evils of communism, and the sinister ways of the Jews. Biology was transformed into 'racial science' in which pupils were taught how to classify racial types by their physical appearance.

It is often assumed that life for Jewish children in such schools must have been completely intolerable. Indeed, there is evidence to show how Jews were humiliated in front of their classes. Karl Hartland, the son of a Jewish banker, published a book in 1988 called *A Boy in Your Situation* in which he looked back to his school days. His account tells of the threats and intimidation he faced; several of his teachers said unpleasant things to him in front of the whole class, or excluded him from activities that were offered to the other boys, but denied him because he was a Jew. He said that the happiest day of his school life was the day when Jewish children were excluded from schools altogether (in 1938). Such evidence suggests that it was the Nazi intention to marginalise [push to the side] Jewish children as part of the overall policy of racial indoctrination.

However, according to others, Hitler's success was limited.

SOURCE I

German children being examined for suitable Aryan characteristics.

SOURCE J

It would be wrong, however, to think that all young Germans were brainwashed and believed everything they were taught. Plenty did not ... In spite of all the Nazis' best efforts through their National Curriculum ... Nazi education had no universal effects on young Germans.

From a history book published in 1997.

The persecution of the Jews in Germany 1933–8

Write an essay with the following title: 'The persecution of the Jews in Germany 1933–8 – did Hitler have a master plan?'

To plan your essay, you will need to decide what Hitler's intentions were when he came to power. If you believe he had a master plan, you will need to find evidence of:

- his consistent hatred of the Jews over the period as a whole
- whether his policies in the 1930s were a logical extension of his views as expressed before 1933
- whether the actual changes each policy made to the lives of the Jews was simply the next step on from Hitler's previous policy.

If you believe Hitler did not have a master plan, but that he just reacted to circumstances, you will need to find evidence that:

- there is a direct relationship between harsh anti-Jewish policies leading to persecution and how strong Hitler felt his position was in Germany
- the level of persecution also depended on whether or not Hitler's policies would provoke an adverse reaction from foreign governments.

Decide which picture best fits the evidence and then write up your findings, making sure you back up your views with facts and evidence. You will need to use resources in your school library and the Internet.

Year	Hitler's political position
1933	**30 Jan:** Hitler is appointed chancellor but few other Nazis in new government and no overall majority in Reichstag. **27 Feb:** Reichstag burned down. Hitler blames this on communists. Communists banned from Reichstag. **23 Mar:** Elections see increase in Nazi share of votes but no overall majority. Hitler passes Enabling Law allowing him to make laws for next four years without Reichstag approval. **May:** Trade unions banned and replaced by Nazi-run German Labour Front. **14 July:** All political parties except Nazi party banned.
1934	**30 June:** 'The Night of the Long Knives.' SS men arrest and murder Ernst Rohm and other SA leaders. **Aug:** President Hindenburg dies. Hitler takes title of 'führer' and becomes Head of State. All members of armed forces have to swear unconditional oath of obedience to Hitler.
1935	Creation of SS elite force with over 200,000 full members. Specialist SS units set up to look after the internal security of Germany, guard concentration camps and hunt down enemies of Nazis.
1936	Hitler places Gestapo and all of Germany's regular police forces under the control of SS Chief Heinrich Himmler.
1937	
1938	Hitler takes control of the army.

Diplomatic developments	Policies towards the Jews
Oct: Hitler takes Germany out of the Disarmament Conference. Begins to re-arm in secret against the terms of the Treaty of Versailles. **18 Oct:** Germany withdraws from the League of Nations.	**1 Apr:** Boycott of all Jewish places of business by SA and SS throughout Germany. **7 Apr:** Law to 'Restore Professional Bureaucracy' leads to sacking of 'non-Aryan' officials. **14 July:** Law to take citizenship away from those Jews who had obtained it in 1918. **22 Sep:** Exclusion of Jewish artists and all Jews active in the cultural sector. **4 Oct:** Exclusion of Jewish editors.
Jan: Hitler has plans to occupy Austria. **17 Feb:** France, Britain and Italy sign joint declaration guaranteeing Austria's independence. **25 July:** Attempt by Austrian Nazis to seize power in Austria fails. Mussolini is furious and orders his Italian troops to Austrian front, promising to support Austrian independence.	Local councils ban Jews from public spaces such as parks, playing fields and swimming pools. Anti-Jewish propaganda increases.
Jan: Plebiscite in Saar coalfield returns big majority in favour of re-integrating Saar into Germany. **16 Mar:** German government passes law making conscription into armed forces compulsory, defying terms of Treaty of Versailles. **11 Apr:** Stresa Front signed between Britain, France and Italy to guarantee the terms of the Treaty of Versailles.	**Summer:** Prominent public anti-Jewish signs on the increase in Germany. **15 Sep:** Nuremberg Laws passed. 'Reich Law on German Citizenship' means only those of German blood can be citizens. Also 'Law for the Protection of German Blood and Honour' forbids marriage or sexual relations between Jews and Germans.
7 Mar: German troops sent in to re-militarize the Rhineland in defiance of Treaty of Versailles. Britain and France do nothing to stop Hitler. **Summer:** Olympic Games held in Berlin. Visitors, VIPs, press and radio representatives come from all over the world. **Oct:** Germany and Italy sign the Rome-Berlin Axis in which they promise to help each other. **Nov:** Germany, Japan and Italy sign the Anti-Comintern Pact.	Professional activities of Jews are banned or are put under restriction. This includes vets, dentists, nurses, accountants, surveyors and teachers. Qualifications of Jewish doctors are cancelled. Hitler generally reduces the amount of persecution against the Jews during this period, for example, some Jews are selected to represent Germany in the Olympics.
May: Neville Chamberlain becomes British prime minister. He follows appeasement policy even more vigorously.	**12 June:** Secret directive by Heydrich ordering that protective custody must be given to all 'defilers of race'.
12 Mar: Nazis take over in Austria and the *Anschluss* (union) is achieved in defiance of Treaty of Versailles. Britain and France do nothing except to protest. **29 Sep:** Munich Conference gives Hitler permission to reoccupy the area of Czechoslovakia known as the Sudetenland. No-one seems able or willing to prevent Hitler's deliberate attempts to reverse the terms of the Treaty of Versailles.	**26 Apr:** Law forcing Jews to register all assets above 5000 Reichsmarks. **June:** Finance offices and police stations draw up lists of wealthy Jews. **9 June:** Destruction of the Munich synagogue. **10 Aug:** Destruction of the Nuremberg synagogue. **17 Aug:** Law forces Jewish people to adopt the mandatory first names of 'Israel' and 'Sara'. **5 Oct:** All passports of Jews are stamped with a 'J'. **28 Oct:** Expulsion of over 15,000 originally Polish Jews to Poland, many of whom had lived in Germany for decades. **10 Nov:** *Kristallnacht* sees widespread destruction of synagogues, businesses and apartments. At least 26,000 Jews arrested and maltreated. **12 Nov:** Jews no longer allowed to run shops and business. **15 Nov:** Jewish children excluded from schools and universities. **3 Dec:** Jews forced to give up driving licences.

The Final Solution

The Final Solution was the name given to the Nazi policy of mass extermination of Jews in specially built 'death camps' in the Second World War. It did not officially begin until 1942, after the Wannsee Conference of that year, when high ranking members of the Nazi Party met to work out the details of how the exterminations would take place.

Whether Hitler had always planned this policy from the outset of his political career has been the subject of debate, as you have seen in the last investigation (see pages 182–3). However, it is clear from his writings in *Mein Kampf* that his hostility towards the Jews was such that he would take any opportunity to 'punish' them for the 'crimes' he believed they had committed. After 1933, his opportunities to persecute the Jews increased. He proceeded with caution, but his intentions never wavered.

The events of *Kristallnacht* in November 1938 had already demonstrated that anti-Semitism in Germany was becoming increasingly violent. In January 1939, Hitler told the Czechoslovakian foreign minister, 'We are going to destroy the Jews. They are not going to get away with what they did on 9 November 1918. The day of reckoning has come.' This was a reference to his view that the Jews had been responsible for 'stabbing the army in the back' by calling for a ceasefire at the end of the First World War. Hitler believed that Germany could have gone on to win the war. A week later, in a speech in the Reichstag, he declared that if international Jewry once more plunged the world into war, 'then the consequence will be ... the destruction of the Jewish race in Europe'.

In the first two years of the war, the German army had some spectacular military successes (see Chapter 5). Each new territorial conquest brought more Jews into the German Reich; there were three million Jews in Poland alone when it was taken over by the Germans (see page 152). New conquests brought new anti-Jewish policies. One new policy was the creation of ghettos, especially in Polish cities (see pages 192–4). Another policy was the Final Solution – the systematic extermination of the Jews, which developed in two phases.

Phase One: 1939–41

After the beginning of the Second World War, Nazi leaders became much less worried about what the rest of the world thought about their anti-Jewish policies. By the summer of 1940, Germany dominated the major countries of western, northern and eastern Europe. There seemed to be nothing holding Hitler back from introducing more severe anti-Semitic measures.

Jews were sent to labour camps to work, and discussions began among high-ranking Nazis about how to dispose of them permanently. Some of their policies included forced sterilisation and working Jews to their death. When Hitler invaded Russia in 1941, the German army was accompanied by 3000 men in the *Einsatzgruppen* (Special Action Groups). These men were given the job of killing Jews. How did they do this?

- They rounded up large groups of Jews and forced them to dig mass graves in remote parts of the occupied territories.

- They forced men, women and children to line up along the edge of the grave.

- They then shot them in the head, and the bodies fell into the grave.

SOURCE A

All around and beneath her she could hear strange sounds, groaning, choking and sobbing. Many of the people were not dead yet. Then she heard people walking near her, actually on the bodies. They were Germans who had climbed down and were taking things from the dead and occasionally firing at those who showed signs of life.

Dina Pronicheva, a survivor of the Final Solution.

Members of the *Einsatzgruppen* had been specially selected to do this, but even so, many had to be given large quantities of alcohol to enable them to complete their task. Some of the intended victims of these killings miraculously survived and were later able to describe their ordeal.

SOURCE B

A Ukranian Jew being executed by the Einsatzgruppen in 1942.

Even in such desperate circumstances, people made every effort to cling on to their lives. Although this was meant to be a secret operation, photographs were taken and they did get into circulation, particularly after the war was over (Source B). By the end of 1941, half a million Jews had been killed.

Phase Two: 1942–5

From 1942–5, anti-Jewish action was stepped up. In January 1942, at the Wannsee Conference, SS Officer, Reinhard Heydrich, was given the task of organising the murder of all Jews still alive in Europe. The Conference set out detailed Nazi plans for 'the Final Solution to the Jewish problem'. From then until the end of the war, 4.5 million Jews were rounded up, deported, and exterminated, either in specially built death camps, or specially adapted concentration camps.

It was not just Jews who were subjected to Nazi terror and extermination. Since 1933, disabled people (including children), gypsies and homosexuals had been persecuted as they also offended Nazi racial laws.

The location of death camps and concentration camps where the mass murder of Jews took place during the Second World War.

The Final Solution was a grim and shocking affair. Jews were rounded up from the ghettos or from their houses in the occupied territories in eastern Europe. They were led to believe that they were going to be settled into new homes and made to work. Specially constructed railway lines, as well as existing public railway networks, were used to take them directly to the camps. These had been specially built at Chelmno, Belzec, Maidenek, Sobibor, Treblinka and Auschwitz.

Journeys usually took place on cattle trains, with each wagon being overloaded with people. There was nowhere to sit inside the wagons, the doors of which were sealed for the entire journey. A bucket was provided as a toilet. Journeys could last several days or even weeks, and it has been estimated that some 320,000 Jews died before they ever reached the camps.

Arriving at the death camps – the selection process

Upon arrival at the camps, families were separated on the railway platform. SS officers, armed with truncheons, made men stand on one side and women and children on the other.

Those that were too old, weak or sick to work were taken to the specially constructed gas chambers. These could kill up to 2000 people at once. They were told that they were to have showers and were instructed to undress and make a careful note of where they had left their clothes. They were directed into what they assumed was a bath house. Once inside, the doors were sealed and the guards poured poisonous gas crystals through vents in the ceiling. 'Zyklon B', or cyanide, was used at Auschwitz.

About one third died straight away. The rest began to scream and struggle for air, but within minutes, all had died. Those who were not sent to the gas chambers had their heads shaved and their clothing removed. They were tattooed with a number and this was now their only identity. They were forced to work and fed on starvation rations until they were of no further use to the SS. Sleeping quarters were cramped and unhygienic. Occasionally, 'tenthling' occurred: one out of every ten people was randomly selected and sent for extermination or to a medical section for experimentation (often for operations without anaesthetic). Survivors of these experiments were often shot.

Digging deeper

The role of the SS

Historians have described the extermination of the Jews as an 'industry' of exploitation and destruction. It was the job of the SS to organise and manage that industry. The SS was an élite group of committed Nazis. There were specialist units which dealt fiercely with all aspects of policing the Nazi State. Without the SS, this particular industry would have ground to a halt. How did they see their role?

SOURCE E

Since December 1941 ... 97,000 Jews have been processed using three vans without any faults developing in the vehicles. The well known explosion in Chelmno must be treated as a special case. It was caused by faulty practice ... Further operational experience hitherto indicates that the following technical alterations are appropriate ...

2   The vans are normally loaded with 9–10 people per square metre. With the large Saurer special vans this is not possible ... A reduction in the load area seems desirable ... The difficulty referred to cannot be overcome by reducing the size of the load, for a reduction in the numbers will necessitate a longer period of operation ...

3   The connecting hoses between the exhaust and the van frequently rust through because they are corroded inside by the liquids which fall on them. To prevent this the connecting piece must be moved so that the gas is fed from the top downwards. This will prevent liquids flowing in ...

6   The lighting must be better protected against damage than hitherto ... when the rear door is closed and therefore when it becomes dark, the cargo presses hard towards the door ... It makes it difficult to latch the door.

Letter to SS Obersturmbahnführer, Walter Rauff, 5 June 1942.

SOURCE F

III Transport

It is advisable to concentrate Jews to be evacuated prior to their transportation. Transports will always be assembled at a strength of 1000 each ... Each person must take the following items:

- travel rations for approximately five days
- 1 suitcase or knapsack each with items of equipment, namely:
  1 pair of sturdy work boots
  2 pairs of socks
  2 shirts
  2 pairs of underpants
  1 pair of overalls
  2 woollen blankets
  2 sets of bedlinen
  1 dinner pail
  1 drinking cup
  1 spoon
  1 pullover.

The following items may not be taken:
- stocks and bonds, foreign currency, savings deposit books
- valuables of any sort (except for a wedding ring)
- pets
- ration cards.

Before the transports leave, searches must be made for arms, ammunition, explosives, poison, foreign currency, jewellery ...

When Jews file change-of-address cards prior to leaving, the forms in the registration offices must not list the final destination but merely 'Moved – address unknown'.

Guidelines for the technical implementation of the evacuation of Jews to the east (Auschwitz), Reich Security Main Office, Berlin, 20 February 1943.

After the gas chambers

Prisoners had to collect the bodies from the gas chambers after they had died. Hair was steam cleaned and used to fill mattresses. Fat from the bodies was used to make soap, and bones were used to make fertilisers. Even the gums were extracted so that the gold fillings could be removed from the teeth. Shoes and clothing were carefully boxed according to size and sent back to Germany. In some camps, purses and lampshades were made from the skin of dead bodies; these were then used by SS officers as gifts for their wives at home.

It was a carefully planned industry of exploitation. At the end of it all, the bodies were burned in special ovens that had been designed and manufactured by German industries.

The liberation of the camps

Towards the end of the war, as the Soviet troops pushed German troops westwards and back into Germany (see Chapter 5), one by one, the camps in the east were liberated. The SS tried, where they could, to march the survivors on to camps nearer the centre of Germany, and they did their best to destroy the evidence of the camps as they closed them down.

SOURCE G

Victims of Buchenwald concentration camp, liberated by the US army, April 1945.

When the camps were liberated, Allied soldiers found only those who had been too weak to be marched away, or those that had hidden. They also found piles of dead bodies in mass graves, or huge heaps of ashes and bone fragments. They occasionally found the bodies of SS guards who had been lynched by the camp inmates as soon as the Allies had entered the camps. It was the last act of defiance of a people subjected to a frightening regime of torture and terror.

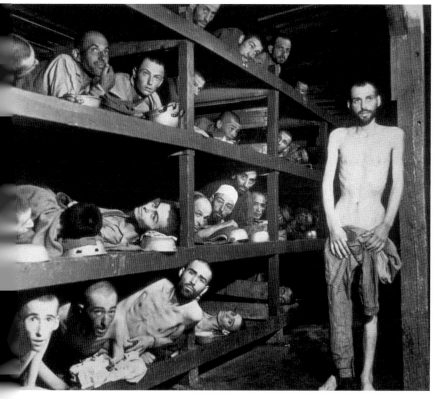

The Nazis almost succeeded in wiping out all the Jews in the territories they had occupied during the war. It is difficult to establish the actual number of Jews murdered due to the secrecy with which the Final Solution was carried out. It is thought to be around 6 million.

Those who had survived were cared for in hospitals until they were well enough to be moved. Many had lost their relatives, homes, possessions and other property. Their gradual rehabilitation into 'normal' civilian life was a long and difficult process. Their survival – and their battle to tell the truth about what happened to them – means we have evidence today of what Churchill described as 'The most horrible crime ever committed in the whole history of the world'.

After the war, 21 senior Nazis were put on trial at Nuremberg for war crimes. Three of them – Himmler, Goebbels and Goering – committed suicide and eleven others were hanged. Rudolf Hoess, the commandant at Auschwitz, went into hiding but was tracked down in 1946, put on trial in Poland, and sentenced to life imprisonment. Some Nazi war criminals undoubtedly escaped before the end of the war and created a new life for themselves, with a new identity in a foreign country.

Investigation

The Final Solution

Write an essay about the Final Solution. Divide your essay into the following sections:

- how the Jews were transported to the camps
- what happened on arrival at the camps
- how the Jews were killed
- what happened to the bodies
- what happened to the survivors.

You will need to do your own wider reading and research. You could look at books in your school library, in your local library and on the Internet.

Digging deeper

Why wasn't more done to stop the Holocaust?

Historians have often posed questions like, 'Why didn't the German people do more to stop the Holocaust?' and 'Why didn't the Allies take steps to end the killings?'

It has sometimes been argued that inaction on the part of the German people and the Allies can be partly explained by the secrecy of the whole operation. After the war was over, many

Germans claimed they had not been aware of what was going on. The Nazis controlled the press and the radio and the details of the arrangements for the 'Final Solution' were kept secret.

SOURCE H

... it seems impossible that six million people could completely disappear without anyone suspecting that they were being murdered. Ordinary Germans witnessed the transportation of Jews which was often timetabled and supervised by civil servants and policemen. Respectable German companies took orders for the poison gas for the murders and the ovens which were used to destroy many of the bodies. German and Swiss banks helped the Nazis to empty millions of marks from the victims' bank accounts and may even have helped to reprocess the gold from dental fillings.

From Challenge and Change: A Modern World Study after 1900 *(2000) by Philip Ingram.*

SOURCE I

I remember being told by a German officer that we were engaged in genocide [mass killing of a race]. First of all I didn't believe him. In fact, I was ready to turn him in to the Gestapo. And secondly, it simply didn't sink in, it didn't make any sense. We needed these people for slave labour.

A former member of the Hitler Youth recalling how he found out about the extermination of the Jews.

SOURCE J

People have often asked me what I knew about the extermination of the Jews. As armaments minister I really only concerned myself with armaments and was isolated from what else was going on. But that is really only an excuse. I did not know exactly what was going on at the camps, but I could have worked it out from the little I did know. I should have done. No apologies are possible.

Albert Speer, Hitler's architect and armaments minister, describing what he knew about the extermination of the Jews in a book he wrote after the war.

SOURCE K

Beyond sheer ignorance it seems that indifference [not caring] and fear were to blame for inactivity. The whole point of political terror is that individuals, however well meaning, are intimidated [frightened] into accepting atrocities and passing them by.

The historian Stuart Miller, writing in Mastering Modern European History *(1997).*

SOURCE L

The British and US governments were receiving information about what was happening at Auschwitz from 1942 onwards. Winston Churchill ordered that a plan be drawn up to see if the gassings could be stopped by bombing the railway lines and gas chambers there. Nothing was done. There were several reasons for this. First, it was argued that bombing Auschwitz could cost the lives of British pilots, even though pilots often flew over Auschwitz on their way to bomb other targets. Secondly, many people could not believe what they heard – it seemed too dreadful to be true. Thirdly, there were many other things that had to be done to win the war at the time, which seemed more important.

The British historian, Martin Gilbert, writing in 1981.

 ## Question time

Refer to Sources H to L.

1   How much did German people know about the Final Solution?

2   How much did the Allies know about the Final Solution?

3   Why didn't (a) German people and (b) the Allies do more to stop the Holocaust?

The Warsaw ghetto

After the war began in 1939, Jews in countries conquered by the Germans began to suffer at the hands of the Nazis. Hitler established ghettos in German-occupied countries, particularly Poland. Ghettos were areas of towns or cities which were walled off and from which Jews were not allowed to leave. For the Nazis, 'ghettoisation' meant concentrating large numbers of Jews conveniently in one place, ready to be transported to the death camps to be exterminated. After that, each ghetto would be 'liquidated', meaning that all evidence of its existence would be destroyed.

On 12 October 1940, the Nazis announced that 'Jewish residential quarters' were to be set up in Warsaw. This ghetto consisted of only a tiny proportion of the land of the whole city (about 2.4 per cent), yet into it would be crammed some 450,000 Jews (about 33 per cent of the entire population of the city). The ghetto was divided into two sections, the Small Ghetto at the southern end and the Large Ghetto in the north.

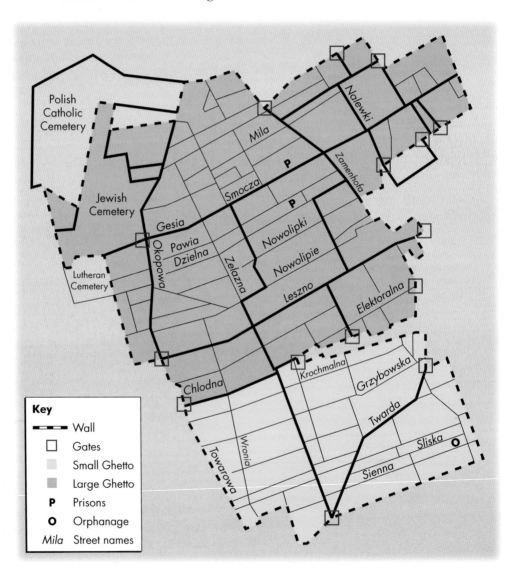

The Warsaw ghetto, 1940.

Living in the ghetto

Since the ghetto was a holding-place before transportation to the camps, it did not matter to the Nazis how many Jews died there. Cut off from the outside world, they were left to face their plight alone. A Jewish Council (of leaders from the Jewish community) was responsible for housing and sanitation. Food and coal were sent in and manufactured products were sent out. The food supply allowed by the Nazis consisted mainly of grain and vegetables. Food rationing in Poland as a whole had begun in December 1939, but by May 1940, the daily bread ration for Jews was cut to 200 grammes, whereas for other Poles it was 570 grammes. In the ghetto, it was difficult for Jews to obtain their daily allowances, meagre as they were. Western Poland had been incorporated into the German Reich, and this area, rich in agriculture, was no longer allowed to supply foodstuffs to any territory outside the Reich. Warsaw and the ghetto were outside the limits.

Some black market (illegally bought and sold) food, smuggled into the ghetto, was sold at high prices. Hans Frank, the Nazi governor of the area, predicted that they were condemning 1.2 million Jews to death by starvation in the ghetto. Wage levels were pegged back there while prices were increased by 27 times from their level in 1940. Most Jews could not find paid work, so they had to rely solely on the inadequate rations provided.

Digging deeper

How did the Jews survive in the ghetto?

The daily food ration for the Jews in the ghetto only provided about 200 calories (a healthy adult male today needs around 2500 calories). The Jewish Council made some attempts to increase the daily ration, without success. Provision of food by social welfare agencies, direct smuggling from other parts of Warsaw, increased production of food, and the operation of a black market all contributed to the heroic struggle for survival. Despite these measures, severe hunger soon gripped the inhabitants. The commissioner of the ghetto reported on 26 September 1941 that the death toll was worsening month by month due to the shortage of food and the spread of typhus.

In such desperate conditions, desperate measures were needed. In order to survive, Jews ate what they could. Horse meat was seen as a treat when it was available; when it was not, some people were reduced to eating horse blood mixed with salt and pepper and spread on bread. A doctor collected the blood from cows, secretly slaughtered in the ghetto, mixed it with onions and a small amount of fat, and fed it to patients.

People of all ages died in the streets, in shelters, in homes and in hospitals. Ghetto residents became used to the sight of corpses. Families often removed bodies from their homes onto the street after removing all evidence of identity, hoping to be able to use the extra ration card for a few days more if it were not known that the person was dead. In refugee shelters, mothers hid dead children under beds for days so that they could, for a time at least, gain a larger food ration.

The instinct to survive was strong, yet there are also many examples of self-sacrifice. Some people stretched the midday meal of soup by watering it down so that neighbours and others who had no food could share it.

In hospitals, doctors and nurses got extra rations, unlike other hospital employees. They had a meeting and decided to reduce their personal allowance in order to share the extra amongst all hospital staff.

That they survived at all was due to the fact that many Jews refused to allow the Nazis to break their spirit. The residents of the ghetto set up a secret, well organised and popular medical school which lasted for 15 months. This demonstrates that, at least until the summer of 1942, Warsaw's Jews believed that they would survive the war.

Although the birth rate inevitably fell drastically, some babies were born in the ghetto. This often occurred without anaesthetic and in unhygienic conditions. Many of the newborn did not survive, but their arrival gave hope. On seeing two pregnant Jewish women in the ghetto, one diarist commented, 'If in today's dark and pitiless times a Jewish woman can gather enough courage to bring a new Jewish being into the world and rear him, this is great heroism and daring ... At least symbolically these nameless Jewish heroines do not allow the total extinction of the Jews and of Jewry'. One baby who survived became part of a plan devised by the parents for escape. A doctor friend injected the baby with drugs to make it appear dead. They took it, weeping, to the Jewish cemetery. There, they bribed someone to bury the empty casket and took the chance to escape over the cemetery wall. They survived. Charles Roland concludes, 'We are tough and resilient and enormously adaptable under pressure. Not all of us, but enough so that it matters ... [in the ghetto] the human spirit, the humane instinct, revealed itself as still existent. The Warsaw ghetto story is replete with instances, large and small, of self-sacrifice and of dedication to others in the face of bleakness and terror'.

From the ghetto to the camps

Transportation of the Jews from the ghetto to Treblinka Extermination Camp began on 22 July 1942, when the ghetto was surrounded by Ukrainian and Latvian soldiers in Nazi SS uniforms.

Selected Jews were to report to a collection point near a railway siding, from which point they would be transported to the east on crowded freight trains. The chairman of the Warsaw Jewish Council was ordered to deliver 6000 Jews a day, 7 days a week. He committed suicide rather than co-operate with the Nazis.

On 23 July, the first transportation began. The deportations continued and soon only 45,000 of the 450,000 original Jews remained in the ghetto.

The Jewish resistance movement

A handful of Jews had escaped from Treblinka and were able to reveal the truth that the deportations were not trips to labour camps in serene rural settings, but one-way trips to gas chambers. As a result, an organised underground resistance movement, called the Jewish Combat Organisation (ZOB), was formed in the ghetto.

ZOB had no weapons or training at first, but had about 1000 members and was led by determined resistance fighters like Mordechai Anielewicz. Born in 1919 into a poor family living in Warsaw, Anielewicz had already become a full-time underground (secret) activist by 1940. He was instrumental in getting a small number of weapons for the organisation, and building bunkers throughout the ghetto.

*Members of the Polish
Underground Movement,
a resistance group.*

On 18 January 1943, SS troops surrounded the ghetto and marched in.
Anielewicz took command in what became a major street battle which
lasted for three days. Fifty German soldiers were killed or wounded and
although ZOB casualties were high, the Germans retreated and ZOB earned
respect. More importantly, it also gained 49 more revolvers, 50 grenades
and some explosives from the Polish underground movement. Anielewicz
knew that the retreat would be temporary and intensive preparations were
made for the next stage.

Total destruction

On 19 April 1943, 2000 German soldiers marched into the ghetto with tanks
and artillery. ZOB responded with grenades and home-made bombs. They
blew up a tank and drove the Nazis back. At first, ZOB had the upper hand
and the Germans suffered losses. The Nazis then began to burn down ghetto
buildings block by block, and cut off the water and electricity supplies. ZOB
held out for three weeks but on 8 May, its headquarters were surrounded
and its members committed suicide. During the fighting, 30,000 Jews were
rounded up and deported to Treblinka. Sporadic fighting continued until
16 May, but by then the ghetto had been burned to the ground.

The Warsaw ghetto

Find out more about the Warsaw ghetto by using the Internet.
Some of the best websites are listed at www.heinemann.co.uk/hotlinks

Prepare a report on aspects of life in the ghetto to include:

- living conditions and rationing
- transportation to Treblinka
- methods of surviving in the ghetto
- collaboration and resistance
- the Warsaw ghetto uprising
- monuments and memorial sites in the ghetto today.

Who said 'no' to genocide?

Many images of the Holocaust leave us with the impression that it was a crime committed by an all-powerful regime on a helpless people. Unable to resist, Jews went to their deaths bravely, but with a sense of their fate being unavoidable. With the benefit of hindsight, we might think if only others had done more. If, for example, the Allies had intervened, or if Germans and other individuals had made the effort, then genocide might have been stopped.

This impression is misleading on two counts. First, some Germans and other individuals *did* try to resist the Holocaust by helping to protect the Jews, or by trying to make the details of the Holocaust known to the wider world community. Second, many Jews themselves resisted, as in the Warsaw ghetto.

Resistance by people outside Germany

A small number of people rescued Jews from within German-occupied Europe. Individual members of the Christian Churches risked imprisonment and death by hiding thousands of Jewish children in religious institutions or with willing families.

Father Jacques de Jésus

Father Jacques de Jésus turned the boys' school in Avon (France), into a refuge for Jews and young men seeking to avoid forced labour in Germany. In January 1943, he took in three Jewish boys under false names, hid a fourth Jewish boy as a worker at the school, sheltered the father of one of the boys with a local villager, and placed the Jewish botanist, Lucien Weil, on the school's staff.

The Gestapo was informed of Father Jacques' activities and they seized him and the three Jewish students on 15 January 1944. Weil, his mother and sister were arrested at their home on the same day. On 3 February 1944, German authorities deported the boys and the Weil family to Auschwitz, where they died. Father Jacques himself was imprisoned in several Nazi camps before he was liberated by the US army at Mauthausen in May 1945. He had TB (tuberculosis, a disease of the lungs) and weighed only 75 pounds (34 kilogrammes). He died several weeks later.

Jan Karski

Perhaps even more remarkable is the story of Jan Karski, a young Catholic member of the Polish underground resistance. He was asked by Jews in the Warsaw ghetto to tell Allied leaders about the Jew's plight. He decided he needed to see their living conditions for himself. In 1942 he twice toured the ghetto disguised as a Jew. He even entered a camp near Belzec dressed as a Ukrainian guard. He met with top Allied officials, including President Roosevelt, telling them of Hitler's extermination policy. He asked them to formally condemn the genocide and to save Jews by issuing blank visas and passports. He was met with disbelief or rejection. Allied leaders told him that helping the Jews was impossible and that nothing should get in the way of the war effort. To the Allies, the genocide was a 'side issue'.

Oskar Schindler.

Oskar Schindler

There were many others who tried to help the Jews. Oskar Schindler was one of them. He operated a number of firms dealing with the manufacture of enamel kitchenware products in 1939. These firms had previously been owned by Jews, and he operated one of them directly for the Nazis. He later established his own factory just outside Krakow in Poland, in which he employed mainly Jewish workers, protecting them from deportation from the ghetto there. He used his connections with high-ranking Nazi officials to set up a branch of the Plaszow camp (to which the Krakow Jews were being transported) in his factory for some 900 Jewish workers. Under this cover, these workers were spared the horrors of the Plaszow camp. His work has been immortalised in the film *Schindler's List*.

Frank Foley

Frank Foley, who was the Passport Control Officer in Berlin from the 1930s, was in a position to control the issuing of visas to Britain and the British Empire (including Palestine). He helped thousands of Jews to escape from Germany. He risked his own life trying to save Jews threatened with death by the Nazis. He remains relatively unknown because his job in Berlin was a cover for his activities as a British spy working for MI6 (the British intelligence agency). He was liable to be arrested at any time. Yet he went into concentration camps to get Jews out, hid them in his own home, helped them to get forged passports and ignored strict government limits by providing them with visas for Palestine. One Jewish aid worker estimates that he saved tens of thousands of Jews from the Holocaust.

Who supported the Jews inside Germany?

While many people within Germany sided with the Nazis, a small, but important minority did not.

Martin Niemoller

A number of Protestant ministers, including Martin Niemoller, formed an alternative Confessional Church because they disliked the attitudes of the German Christians and the Reich Church. These ministers often spoke out consistently in their sermons about the worst excesses of the Nazi regime, especially the treatment of Jews and other minorities. Niemoller was sent to a concentration camp in 1938. He continued to speak out but survived, and was liberated from Dachau in 1945.

Paul Schneider

Pastor Paul Schneider was arrested in 1934 for making anti-Nazi speeches. He was sent to Buchenwald concentration camp in 1937, but still managed to smuggle letters out. He was whipped and tortured, fed on the most basic rations and forced into solitary confinement. He was dressed in rags and crawling with lice. He continued to preach and defy the authorities. He was kept in the camp for two years, but died at Buchenwald in 1939.

Max Josef Metzger

The Catholic theologian, Max Josef Metzger, formed the religious group Una Sancta in 1939. He had already been arrested in 1934 for writing anti-Nazi publications, and was arrested again and taken to the Gestapo prison on Prinz-Albrecht Strasse 8 where he stayed until 11 September 1943. He maintained contacts with other sympathetic Church leaders until his execution in Brandenburg penitentiary on 17 April 1944.

Dietrich Bonhoeffer

Dietrich Bonhoeffer, a Protestant theologian, believed Christians should resist Hitler and help the victims of Nazi persecution. In 1937, he was banned from preaching and his training college was closed by the Gestapo. He turned increasingly to political forms of resistance, joined an underground resistance group and worked with individuals in the military opposition. He helped devise a plan code-named Operation Seven, which aimed to help small numbers of Jews to escape from Germany on the pretence that they were needed for propaganda work in Switzerland. Bonhoeffer also became involved in plots to assassinate Hitler. In 1942, Bonhoeffer was arrested and placed in solitary confinement. He was mistreated, given dirty blankets, denied washing facilities and placed on starvation rations. In 1944, he was transferred to a concentration camp where he continued to preach the word of God in defiance of the SS. On 8 April 1945 he was sentenced to death after a trial at Flossenburg concentration camp. He was hanged at dawn the next day.

Resistance by the Jews

Many Jews resisted the Nazis in the face of overwhelming odds. We have already read about the brave resistance in the Warsaw ghetto. Some Jews who escaped capture fought in partisan groups (groups of people who attacked the Nazis from within Nazi-held territory). They hid in forests, got hold of weapons however they could, and attacked the Germans at every opportunity. There was also a remarkable amount of resistance in the concentration and death camps. To resist here was like committing suicide, but many sacrificed their lives to try to weaken the Nazis.

Resistance in the camps

Mala Zimetbaum, a Jewish woman, stole a SS uniform and secret documents telling of the Nazi slaughter. She then escaped from Auschwitz. She was caught, sent back and paraded in front of the other prisoners. She slashed her wrists with a razor and screamed: 'Don't be afraid girls! Their end is near. I am certain of this. I know. I was free.'

The Nazis beat her, then burned her alive. Her courage inspired further revolts at Auschwitz and the crematorium was subsequently blown up. In October 1943, an unidentified Jewish woman arrived among a transport of Jewish women to Auschwitz. As she was being led to the gas chamber, she drew a pistol and shot two SS guards. Immediately, the other women also resisted. They were executed by SS reinforcements.

Escape from the camps

Another form of resistance at Auschwitz was escape. A total of 667 prisoners escaped from Auschwitz, 297 of whom found refuge in neutral countries. Amongst them were two Slovakian Jews, Alfred Weczler and Rudolf Vrba who escaped on 7 April 1944. They provided the first eye-witness report of the camp to the western world. They set off the chain of events which led to the Nuremberg Trials after the war, in which leading Nazi war criminals were brought to justice.

Planned uprising at Treblinka

At Treblinka Death Camp, about 80 kilometres north-east of Poland, 100 prisoners planned an uprising in 1943. They made a key to open the lock of the ammunition store and stole weapons and other items like axes and wire cutters. The uprising began half an hour early when someone shot and killed an SS guard. Eight hundred people participated – half were killed and the other half escaped to the forest where three hundred more were killed. The remaining 100 were recaptured, ordered to dismantle the extermination ovens and then they were murdered. The uprising had failed. The Germans destroyed all evidence of the camp and created a farm on the land.

Sobibor

At Sobibor, another camp designed to exterminate Polish Jews, a plot was hatched to launch a mass escape. On 14 October 1943, the SS guards in the killing area were to be killed with hatchets and the prisoners would walk to roll call as if nothing had happened. They then hoped to march through the main gates accompanied by the sonderkommando (a group of prisoners whose job was to dispose of the bodies of murdered Jews) as usual, on their way to their day's labour. The Ukrainian guards in the watch tower would be killed with machine guns stolen from the SS and therefore the main gates would be left unguarded.

Unfortunately, on the day of the escape, one SS guard escaped from the killing area and an indiscriminate barrage of shooting began. Out of 600 people, 300 were able to break out of the camp through hailing bullets and exploding land mines. A hundred escaped to the forest and avoided capture. Almost 20 per cent of the prisoners survived and 48 soldiers were killed. The film *Escape From Sobibor* tells this remarkable story.

Digging deeper

Survival

Hitler concentrated his attacks on the European Jews. It has been estimated that six million out of the total of eight million European Jews were exterminated. In Europe Jews resisted the Holocaust with the few means at their disposal. In the ghettos and the camps, Jews plotted escapes, forged passports and papers and passed news through the underground. Few escaped, but more importantly, the Jews remained Jewish. They studied with rabbis (Jewish religious leaders) in secret and commemorated Jewish holidays. To survive one more day in the camps was to defy the Nazi Holocaust. Even though six million Jews were eventually exterminated, the testimonies (accounts) of those who survived prove that the Jewish race was not destroyed.

Judith Jaegermann

One such testimony is the remarkable story of Judith Jaegermann. She lived in Karlsbad, Germany, where her parents owned a restaurant. With persecution against the Jews intensifying from 1937, the Jaegermanns fled to Prague in Czechoslovakia, where they had to wear the yellow Star of David. In Prague, there was a curfew for Jews after 8pm, and there were many public signs on walls showing how unwelcome the Jews were. In 1941, Judith and her family were moved to a place called Theresienstadt, where she was separated from her mother and father and transferred to a children's home. She caught scarlet fever and had to be placed in quarantine. Sixteen months later, the whole family was sent to Auschwitz.

On arrival at the camp, they were shaved as was usual for new arrivals, and her father was separated from the rest of the family. They were driven into the barracks where they slept on beds without mattresses, squeezed together in the freezing cold, not knowing what the next minute would bring.

Judith's survival at Auschwitz demonstrates how Jews resisted death by bending camp rules and taking risks in order to obtain food or escape punishments. She tells of how her father, imprisoned in another part of the camp, risked his life by bringing them boiled potatoes from the kitchens where he cooked for the SS, before running back to his barracks to avoid capture. Judith also comments that the ordeal was too much for some who threw themselves onto the high tension wires that surrounded the camp and died instantly. Remarkably, Judith, her mother and her sister managed to stay together and escape selection for the gas chambers. Whenever they were called into line for selection, they stuck by each other and rubbed their cheeks to make themselves look healthier and capable of work, so the Nazis would spare them.

Eventually, as the war dragged on and the German armies were pushed back into Germany itself (see Chapter 5), the Nazis began to transport Jews back from Auschwitz to camps inside Germany. Judith's family were transported to Hamburg. Conditions were very unhygienic and disease was rife. Judith contracted a high fever but returned to work out of sheer dread of being 'liquidated'. She suffered in silence until her fever cleared up on its own.

Judith even suffered at the hands of the Allies, who by this time were bombing Hamburg. The camp in which the Jews were imprisoned was blown up and she was re-housed in another camp in the city. Judith was badly burned, and her mother fed her with extra potato peel she had found. She was discovered, and the camp commandant beat her with a revolver. She could not work for several weeks and her head was badly swollen.

Judith was later evacuated with her mother to Belsen. At this camp, there was absolutely nothing to eat and no water; she described it as total chaos. She was there for approximately two weeks without eating or drinking, until one morning they were told they were free. No one could move because they had no strength left. The British, who liberated the camp, were so shocked by what they saw that they did all they could to get food to the people. The starving Jews often died after eating because their bodies, not used to food any more, rejected it. Judith, her sister and mother, could not eat because they had contracted typhoid fever.

Gradually, their leg muscles strengthened and they began to walk again and, in time, they were repatriated to Prague. Judith ends her testimony by saying:

> My terrible traumatic memories will never leave me. Everything is still very much alive in me. My dearest Mama will always stay sacred to me. God bless her memory. She was my guardian angel during the most horrible times.

That was how Judith survived. The togetherness of her family and their personal faith kept them going. So it was for other Jews in the camps. They were the resistance. Without them, the Holocaust might well be an untold story. Their testimonies are a permanent record of man's inhumanity towards fellow man and should serve as a warning that it must never happen again.

Question time

Write three essays on the following topics:

1   Should the Holocaust be taught in schools? Some argue that it is too shocking a story to be taught and that it would be better to let the memory of this event fade into history. Do you agree?

2   Should we accept concentration camp survivors' testimonies at face value? There was collaboration with the Nazis as well as resistance inside the camps. Would any survivor want to admit that their survival may have depended (at least partly) on collaboration?

3   Should the Nazis who were involved in running the concentration camps be hunted down and prosecuted, even though they are now old men and women? As it all happened so long ago, should we forget and move on?

You may like to do some further research before you write your essay. There are many good articles, including the testimonies of survivors, on the Internet. The websites listed at www.heinemann.co.uk/hotlinks may be useful to you.

The memory of the Holocaust

Several organisations exist today with the purpose of keeping the memory of the Holocaust alive. In Britain, 27 January has become an annual Holocaust Memorial Day, to coincide with the anniversary of the liberation of the extermination camp at Auschwitz. Why is such an effort made to keep this memory alive? Since the time of the Final Solution, there have always been people ready to cover up the extermination programme. Heinrich Himmler, the SS leader, believed it should be kept secret. Speaking to SS officers in 1943 he said:

Among ourselves we can talk openly about it, though we will never speak a word of it in public ... I am speaking about the evacuation of the Jews, the extermination of the Jewish people ... That is a page of glory in our history that never has been, and never will be written.

No one spoke openly in Nazi circles about extermination at the time of the Holocaust. Other terms like 'resettled', 'evacuated' or 'deported' were used instead. In 1941 Himmler's deputy, Heydrich, ordered that the killing of Jews should be photographed or filmed only by officials, and that the results should be a state secret. Even the Allies sometimes played their part in shielding the public from the details of the Holocaust.

When Belsen was liberated in 1945, the British government sent a special army film unit to make a film that could be shown in British cinemas. It was banned from general release after censors decided its contents were too shocking and depressing for the public to witness. Whatever the horror, it is essential that the memory of the Holocaust be kept alive.

Assessment section

Why, where, when and how did the Final Solution take place?

It is difficult to explain why the Final Solution took place. However it is important that we, as historians, try to explain these events. Your school might have one of the following videos which may help:

The World at War – episode 20 *Genocide*
The People's Century – episode *Master Race*
The Nazis, A Warning from History – episode 4 *The Road to Treblinka*

The assignment is divided into four sections.

Why? This is the most important part of the answer. You need to identify and explain the long- and short-term reasons for the Final Solution. Here are some examples to help you:

- long-term – anti-Semitism in Germany, Hitler's ideas on race

- short-term – the impact of war, the role of the SS.

Where? This part of the question asks you to identify the areas of German held territory in which the Final Solution took place. To answer this section you might wish to draw a map or simply describe where the Final Solution occurred.

When and How? In this part of the answer you need to describe the different stages of anti-Semitism in Nazi Germany. There are a number of stages that you could identify:

1933–9	1939–45
Identification and separation	Ghettos
Propaganda against the Jews	Shooting
Violence against the Jews	Planned extermination

You should make sure that, as part of this description, you use dates. This will ensure that you adequately answer the 'when' part of the question. Alternatively you can draw up a separate timeline.

Planning. Before you answer this question you should plan your answer. The best way to do this is to write out your two or three main points of argument. Then you should identify what you are going to put in each paragraph. This is how to structure your answer.

- Introduction – in this paragraph you should introduce your main ideas without going into detail.

- First paragraph – you should explain your main point.

- Following paragraphs – you should explain your other points.

- Conclusion – keep this short and re-state your main argument.

Further reading

M. Gilbert *The Holocaust* (Harper Collins, 1987)

G. Lacey and K. Shepherd *Germany 1918–1945* (John Murray, 1997)

C. Martin (ed.) *The Diary of Anne Frank* (Longman, 1989)

G. Turgel *I Light a Candle* (Frank Cass, 1995)

Conflict and reconciliation: a world study after 1900

The twentieth century was marked by conflict around the world. This conflict included not just wars between countries but wars within countries. This chapter discusses three bitter conflicts of the twentieth century:

- South Africa
- The Middle East
- Ireland.

Conflict in South Africa

For hundreds of years black African civilisations and culture flourished in southern Africa. One of the most remarkable civilisations was the kingdom of Zimbabwe which grew rich on trade and the spoils of war. However, by 1914 South Africa had become a part of the British Empire and the land and political system were dominated by white settlers. The different aims, claims and values of the various groups in South Africa were at the heart of the conflict that was to last the whole of the twentieth century.

The European settlers

In the seventeenth century, the southern tip of Africa known as the Cape was a Dutch colony and the first European settlers in South Africa were Dutch. Throughout the eighteenth century, Dutch settlers, or Boers as they were called, moved inland in search of farmland. By 1760 they had reached the Orange River.

After 1815, the Cape became a British colony and British settlers began to arrive in South Africa. The British government's friendly attitude towards the black South Africans disgusted many of the Boer settlers. From 1835–7 the Boers moved to the north and east of the Orange River, in what they called The Great Trek, in order to escape from British rule. They settled in areas of the country that came to be known as the Transvaal and Natal. One of the consequences of this settlement was that they came into conflict with one of the great black African tribes, the Zulus, whose land they wanted to take.

From the middle of the nineteenth century, the Boer and British settlers attempted to increase their influence over territory in southern Africa. From the 1850s, the Boers ruled the Transvaal, calling it the South African Republic. They also ruled the neighbouring Orange Free State. The Boers fought a series of wars of conquest against local tribes. In the 1850s a tribe called the Kaffirs were reduced in population by two-thirds and in the 1860s, the Boers took the considerable lands of the Basutos.

Key
▦ Modern South Africa

ANGOLA   ZAMBIA   MALAWI

NAMIBIA   ZIMBABWE   MOZAMBIQUE

BOTSWANA

TRANSVAAL
Johannesburg
SWAZILAND

ORANGE
FREE   NATAL
Atlantic   STATE   Durban   Indian
Ocean   Ocean
CAPE COLONY
LESOTHO
Cape Town   0   800 km
400 miles

N
↑

Southern Africa as it is today.

Throughout the 1870s, the South African Republic also had an uneasy relationship with the British. Many members of the British government in South Africa wanted to bring the different provinces together under one government. The Boers fought bitterly against this move. They feared that the British would destroy their culture just as they themselves had attempted to destroy the culture of many of the black African tribes. In 1877, the South African Republic was taken over by the British, but the Boers responded with violence. A compromise was reached between British and Boers in 1881, when the Treaty of Pretoria gave the South African Republic semi-independence but under the general control of the British.

The Boer war and its aftermath

The Treaty of Pretoria did not settle the matter and eventually in 1899 the Boer War broke out between the British and Boer settlers and lasted three bitter years. At the end of the war the defeated Boers had to accept being part of the British Empire. As part of the British plans for the country, the different provinces such as Natal and the Transvaal were united into one country by the South Africa Act of 1910. Despite this political unity the European settlers were deeply divided over their views on the future of South Africa.

- **The South African Party**, led by General Louis Botha, represented those who wanted Boers to be treated equally with British settlers. They believed that South Africa should control its own affairs within the British Empire. None of the leaders of the South African Party supported rights for black or Asian South Africans. This party led the first government of South Africa from 1910 onwards.

- **The Unionist Party**, led by Sir Leander Starr Jameson, wanted to maintain the strongest links possible with the British Empire.

- **The Nationalist Party**, led by General Hertzog, wanted a separate nation for the Boers. During the First World War they sympathised with Germany. Their policies against black South Africans were the most racist, arguing that they should lose all land and rights, such as the right to vote.

By 1914, the government of South Africa was dominated by the Boers. The native Africans had lost their rights and land. The conflict of the twentieth century was based on the struggle of black Africans to regain these rights and land and to end discrimination against them.

The distribution of South African tribes.

Black and Asian South Africans

Black Africans made up the majority of the population in South Africa, although by 1914 they had seen their land taken from them in a series of wars with the European settlers. In 1857, the Xhosas rose up to fight for their land, as did the Zulus. The Basutos lost huge areas of land in a war in 1865–6. The Zulus also fought a bitter campaign against the Boers and British and in 1879 the Zulu king, Cetschwayo, was forced to surrender to the British.

In the 1880s, there were a number of organisations founded by black South Africans to promote their cause. For example, an African press was started in 1884. Black South Africans frequently rebelled against the white settlers, as in Natal in 1906, but attempts to push back the influence of the settlers were in vain. A number of educated black South Africans decided that they needed to have their own political organisation to represent their interests. In 1912 the South African Native National Congress (SANNC) was formed to fight for the rights of the black people in South Africa. In 1913 the South African Land Act restricted black people to owning land in the poorest seven per cent of the country.

It was not only the black South Africans who were to face racial discrimination (unfair treatment based on skin colour). From the 1860s, large numbers of workers were brought to South Africa from India to work on the country's sugar plantations. Other Indians were attracted by the economic opportunities South Africa had to offer and also emigrated there. This immigration worried some of South Africa's white population, and after the Boer War, the South African government began to discriminate against them, treating them differently from white people. Asian people and people of mixed race were termed 'coloured'. Immigration Laws were passed in 1907 and 1913 which restricted the number of Asians allowed into the country. The 1913 law also tried to limit freedom of movement of Asians in South Africa. These moves led to a campaign against discrimination led by a young lawyer, Mahatma Gandhi, but like many Indians he recognised that they would not find freedom in South Africa. In 1914 Gandhi left the country for India in disgust at the growing racial discrimination.

Discrimination 1918–48

Many Boers did not want to be part of the British Empire. The British had treated them badly during the Boer War and had imprisoned 120,000 Boer farmers and their families in concentration camps. In 1924 the nationalist General Hertzog became prime minister. He wanted to cut links with Britain in 1926 but accepted that South Africa should have dominion status.

This would make South Africa self-governing within the empire. Hertzog attracted the support of the South African Party for his policies and the two combined in 1934 as the United Party. This union did not please all Boers because some of them wanted to have complete independence from Britain. A group of nationalists led by D.F. Malan formed the National Party with the aim of creating a South Africa, independent from Britain, with even more racist policies towards black South Africans. Afrikaans, the language spoken by Boers, became South Africa's official language.

After the First World War, there were further changes in the lives of the majority of black people. Deprived of land, they were forced to leave their tribes and homelands. The racist land laws limited their choices.

- In 1926 Hertzog introduced a law that prevented black South Africans from doing skilled work.

- His government followed this with the 1927 Immorality Act that made marriage between black and white people illegal. Most black South Africans were forced to live in reservations and to take up unskilled work.

The need for labour meant that large numbers of the black community were drawn to the mines and factories of South Africa. In areas such as the Witwatersrand gold mines, black South Africans were forced to live in settlements called townships. These townships sprang up outside cities like Johannesburg. One township, Soweto, was to become infamous 40 years later (see pages 210–12). By 1939 the physical separation of black and white people in South Africa had become established.

The period between the First and Second World Wars saw the further development of the idea of limiting political rights of certain groups in South African society. In 1936 the South African government finally removed the rights of the black South Africans in the Cape to vote in elections, with the Representation of Natives Act. Instead it set up a separate election for the black voters of the Cape, in which they could elect three Europeans to represent them. A council for black South Africans was also set up but it was to have no power. This move reduced the ability of black South Africans to represent their interests. In 1946 the Indian Representation Act limited the voting rights of a range of coloured people.

The regime of apartheid

Establishing a divided society

The election of 1948 produced a surprise victory for the National Party, led by Malan. Although they did not get the largest number of votes, they received the largest number of seats. Prime Minister Malan immediately introduced the policy of apartheid to keep the races apart. Between 1948 and 1959 a system was put in place which was based on discrimination, brutality and racial hatred.

The aim of apartheid was to keep political and economic power for the white minority in the country. However, many of the policies of apartheid were not new. They built on the divisions that had been created when South Africa was part of the British Empire.

The following laws enshrined the main features of apartheid.

- **Prohibition of Mixed Marriages Act 1949** This law reinforced the earlier Immorality Act which said that people of different races could not marry.

- **Suppression of Communism Act 1950** This was used to ban all opposition to apartheid. The government labelled all of its enemies as communists, which made it easier to attack them.

- **Population Registration Act 1950** All South Africans were put into three different racial categories: black, white and coloured. This was important because jobs, education, housing, health, benefits and standard of living all depended on which racial group a South African was placed in.

- **Group Areas Act 1950** Every town was carved into separate 'group areas', sorting people by racial categories.

- **Passbook Act 1952** Every black South African was to be placed on a national register and had to carry an identity card. They could be stopped at any time and have these cards checked.

SOURCE A

Signs of apartheid in 1950s South Africa.

- **Bantu Education Act 1953** This set out that black South Africans were to have their own schools. They received a low level of education, and were not taught English or Afrikaans. This was intended to prevent black children from getting skilled jobs and to keep black people 'in their place'.

- **Separate Amenities Act 1953** This law meant that different races were segregated in public: on public transport, in shops, hospitals and parks. They were even to have their own separate ambulances.

- **Extension of University Education Act 1959** This expelled all non-white students from the universities of Cape Town and the Witwatersrand.

- **Bantu Self Government Act 1959** Black South Africans were forced to live in so-called 'Bantustans' where they had limited self-government, in that the white South African government could overrule decisions taken by a Bantustan government. Bantustans were to be the homelands for all black South Africans.

Organised opposition to apartheid

Despite the strength of the government, the policy of apartheid ran into opposition in South Africa. There were two main organisations with the aim of destroying apartheid. In the 1950s they embarked on a policy of demonstrations but with little success. The two groups were:

- **African National Congress (ANC)** This group had been established in 1912 as the SANNC (see page 206), and was an organisation with a mainly black membership, but it included members of all races in the fight against apartheid. In the 1950s it held a number of demonstrations including the Defiance Campaign of 1952. As part of this campaign, ANC members ignored the 'white only' signs and attempted to get arrested. In aiming to do so, they hoped to bring attention to their cause. To an extent they were successful – by the end of 1952 the membership of the ANC had risen from 7000 to 100,000.

- **Pan African Congress (PAC)** Set up in 1959 the PAC was a black-only organisation committed to removing the white-only government.

The Sharpeville Massacre 1960

In March 1960 a demonstration against the Passbook Act was held in a township called Sharpeville. At the end of the demonstration a crowd of unarmed supporters of the PAC surrounded the police station. The police opened fire, killing 63 of the demonstrators. Many of the dead were shot in the back. The Sharpeville Massacre led to uproar abroad.

The government attempted to clamp down further on any opposition at home by banning both the ANC and the PAC. In 1961 the ANC formed a military wing, Umkhonto we Sizwe (MK or 'Spear of the Nation'). The leader of the MK was Nelson Mandela (see pages 213–14). Its aim was to attack white-owned property but to avoid attacks on individuals. This mattered little to the white authorities who saw Mandela as a dangerous enemy. In 1962 Mandela was arrested. Two years later he was tried and sentenced to life imprisonment.

Continued strengthening of apartheid

Although their leaders were either in prison or in exile, opposition to the apartheid regime continued. However, from the early 1960s, the South African Prime Minister H. Verwoerd and his successor, J.B. Vorster, introduced a new form of apartheid. The black South Africans were made 'citizens' of the homelands such as the Transkei. The idea behind this was to make them foreigners in South Africa.

Further measures were taken to prevent black South Africans from living in cities or areas which the government considered should be 'white only'. These 'white only' areas had better housing and facilities than the places where blacks were allowed to live. During the 1960s over 1.5 million black South Africans were moved against their will into the overcrowded Bantustans. These changes were strengthened in 1968 by the creation of a new state security organisation, the Bureau of State Security (BOSS). Its role was to torture and terrorise the enemies of apartheid.

Police were given increased powers to arrest black people, and black people were banned from writing or broadcasting material. They were also banned from leaving their homes at certain times of the day.

Mounting pressure to change

By the 1970s, continued resistance both inside and outside South Africa meant that the apartheid regime in South Africa came under pressure to change. There were a number of reasons for this pressure.

- An international boycott (ban) of links with South Africa, both economic and sporting, began to damage the country's economy. International companies, for example, Pepsi Cola, IBM and Peugeot, closed down factories and offices in South Africa. Many others withdrew investments.

- A new 'Black Consciousness' movement was set up under Steve Biko. This movement stood for the idea that black people in South Africa should stop thinking of themselves as second-class citizens. The state feared organisations like this so much that Biko was arrested in 1977. He was tortured by the police and as a result of this died in police custody.

- The oil price rise of 1973 led to world-wide inflation. This inflation meant that the price of food and other basics increased. The result was that black workers demanded better pay. When employers refused, strikes spread across the country.

- In 1976 a revolt by students in Soweto, a township outside Johannesburg, against the educational system resulted in the death of many people and led to a country-wide boycott of schools.

- Outside South Africa, countries with black governments such as Mozambique, Zambia and Botswana now surrounded the apartheid state. They were sympathetic to the cause of black freedom and some allowed anti-apartheid fighters to be trained in their countries.

- International awareness about the unfairness of apartheid was raised by human rights groups like Amnesty International.

Digging deeper

Soweto 1976

On 16 June 1976 a protest of schoolchildren took place in the township of Soweto. By the time the protest had ended (three days later), 575 people, most of them black South African schoolchildren, had been killed, and more than 2000 injured. The incident in Soweto sparked unrest across South Africa that lasted a year.

SOURCE B

In 1959 the apartheid government issued a new set of instructions for all schools in South Africa. Only the English and Afrikaans could be used in secondary schools. From now on, lessons taught in an African language could only be taught in primary schools. This change was a direct insult to the black South African communities, especially because the Afrikaans language was hated as the language of apartheid. In 1974 the government went further and insisted that the following subjects were taught in Afrikaans: Mathematics, Social Studies, Geography and History. As a result the schoolchildren began to boycott lessons to be taught in Afrikaans. In May 1976 the students at Orlando West Junior Secondary School walked out of school in protest. This led to similar walk-outs in a number of schools across the country.

An historian writing in 2000.

SOURCE C

Brothers and Sisters, I appeal to you to keep calm and cool. We have just received a report that the police are coming. Don't taunt them, don't do anything to them. Be cool and calm. We are not fighting.

A student, Tietsi Mashinini, addressing the crowd outside Soweto police station at 9.00am on the morning of 16 September 1976.

SOURCE D

Unrest in Soweto still continues. The children of Soweto are well trained. The students have established student councils. The basic danger is a growing black consciousness and the inability to prevent incidents, what with the military precision with which they act. The minister proposes that this movement must be broken and thinks that police should perhaps act a bit more drastically and heavy-handedly which will entail more deaths. Approved.

From notes made by the Minister of Police, Jimmy Kruger, at the South African cabinet meeting, 10 August 1976.

SOURCE E

A dying schoolboy, thirteen-year-old Hector Petersen, in Soweto in 1976. For many people this image has come to represent the black struggle against apartheid in South Africa.

SOURCE F

Despite the tense atmosphere the students remained calm and well ordered. Suddenly a white policeman lobbed a tear gas canister into the front of the crowd. People ran out of the smoke, dazed and coughing. The crowd retreated slightly but remained facing the police, waving placards and singing. A white policeman drew his revolver. Black journalists standing by the police heard a shot: 'Look at him. He's going to shoot at the kids'. A single shot rang out. There was a split second's silence and pandemonium broke out. Children screamed. More shots were fired. At least four students fell and others ran screaming in all directions.

From Whirlwind Before the Storm *(1980) by Alan Brooks and Jeremy Brickhill.*

SOURCE G

The killing of children led to violence throughout the country. The world-wide flood of sympathy strengthened the campaign against apartheid. The government dropped the idea of lessons being taught in Afrikaans and many white South Africans became really aware of the demands of the black South Africans. A new democratic South Africa grew from the ashes of those terrible days.

By an historian writing in 1997.

Question time

Use the information in Sources B to G to write an account of events in Soweto, 1976. Include sections on the following:

- the causes of the uprising
- the uprising itself
- the consequences of the uprising.

From apartheid to democracy

By the early 1980s it was clear to South Africa's rulers that they had to win the support of some parts of the black community. They recognised that without this support they had little chance of holding on to power in the long term.

In 1978 P.W. Botha became leader of South Africa. He tried to introduce limited change in order to avoid demands for more extensive change. In 1983, he set up a new parliamentary system which included coloured and Indian representatives but no black Africans. However, this did little to end calls for further political change. In the mid-1980s the laws against mixed marriages and passbooks (see page 208) were abolished.

In February 1990, more pressure from inside and outside South Africa led to the decision of Botha's successor, President F.W. de Klerk, to free Nelson Mandela after 27 years in jail. Difficult negotiations between all parties about the future of South Africa were held at the Convention for a Democratic South Africa in February 1990. These meetings took place against the background of increasing frustration and violence between police and black South Africans, and between rival groups of black South Africans. However, an agreement was reached in 1992 between Mandela and de Klerk. The main points were:

- a new constitution was to be drawn up

- a new government would oversee the move to democracy

- political prisoners would be released

- there would be attempts to end the violence in the country.

The first democratic election was held in April 1994. The ANC won the greatest number of seats in the new National Assembly. In 1995, Nelson Mandela was chosen by the National Assembly to be president of South Africa.

As part of creating a new country that could look forward rather than back, in 1995 the South African Parliament set up the Truth and Reconciliation Commission with Archbishop Desmond Tutu as chairman. The committee invited torturers to give evidence to the commission in front of those they had tortured, and murderers to explain their actions in front of the families and friends of those they had murdered.

In return those who had committed such crimes were granted an amnesty. This meant that they would not be charged automatically for their crimes. The committee would then recommend awarding payments in compensation to those who had suffered. There was much pain and anguish as the violence of both sides was revealed in public.

Digging deeper

Nelson Mandela : From rebel to president

Nelson Rolihlahla Mandela was born in the Transkei on the 18 July 1918. After receiving a good education, Mandela trained to be a lawyer. Whilst training he joined the ANC in 1942 and was soon involved in changing the tactics of the movement. With other young African nationalists such as Oliver Tambo, Mandela attempted to widen the ANC's appeal and change its tactics from sending petitions to the government to strikes, boycotts and mass demonstrations. When the apartheid laws were introduced in the 1950s, he travelled round South Africa organising black opposition.

SOURCE H

Nelson Mandela on his release in February 1990.

In 1955 Mandela played a key role in making popular the Freedom Charter drawn up by groups who opposed apartheid. During this time, he worked tirelessly as a campaigner against the separate education system. This came to the attention of the authorities. Mandela was arrested as an opponent of the state and imprisoned on a number of occasions. He and other leaders of the ANC, such as Albert Luthuli, were charged with treason.

In late 1961 Mandela became leader of MK. He travelled abroad trying to raise support for the ending of apartheid. The following year Mandela was arrested, convicted and sentenced to five years in prison on charges of leaving the country illegally and trying to persuade workers to go on strike. While in prison he was charged with sabotage and tried at Rivona in 1963–4. At the trial Mandela attacked the basis of apartheid (Source I).

Mandela was found guilty, sentenced to life imprisonment and sent to Robben Island Prison, a maximum security prison on a small island near Cape Town. On Robben Island, Mandela had to endure a brutal regime with years of work in a lime quarry.

Over the next twenty years, the political situation in South Africa gradually changed. In the 1980s Mandela was transferred from Robben Island to Pollsmoor Prison in Cape Town, and in December 1988 he was sent to Victor Verster Prison near Paarl.

Eventually pressure from the outside world and within South Africa itself forced the government of P.W. Botha to release Mandela. On 11 February 1990, he walked out of Victor Verster Prison a free man. He then threw himself into the task of negotiating an end to apartheid and the introduction of democracy. In 1994 he became president of South Africa and set about rebuilding a country based on the principles of forgiveness and tolerance.

Question time

1 Discuss the following point in groups or pairs.

In 1985 few people would have predicted that, in 1994, Nelson Mandela would be President of South Africa. What are the reasons why apartheid collapsed?

Now put your reasons in order of importance. Report back to the class, explaining your choice.

2 In your book put the title 'The fall of apartheid'. After hearing the views of other groups, make a final choice about your *three* most important factors that led to the collapse of apartheid. Explain these three choices carefully in your book.

The Middle East 1919–96

The Middle East is the birthplace of Judaism, Islam and Christianity, but it is also a region that has experienced bitter conflict and violence.

Reasons for conflict

There are a number of reasons for violence in the Middle East. Some of them go back over hundreds of years.

- The land of Israel has been central to Jews since biblical times, when Judaism teaches that it was promised to Jews by God, and there has always been a Jewish presence there. In AD 66–70 the Jews in Judea carried out an unsuccessful revolt against the Romans, who had governed the land for many years. At this time, not all Jews lived in Judea. For almost 500 years Jews had also lived in other countries following their exile by the Babylonians, but all the while continued to pray towards Jerusalem and believed that one day they would return. Over the next 1800 years, Jewish people suffered from periods of persecution. During the nineteenth century in particular Jews living in eastern Europe experienced terrible persecution and poverty, and many of them fled to the USA. Some decided to move to what was then called

Palestine, and in 1897 the first Zionist Congress was set up with the aim of creating a Jewish homeland there.

- Most of the Middle East is populated by Arabs. Palestine was taken over by the Arabs in the seventh century as the Islamic religion spread through the Middle East. The Palestinian people, many of whose families have lived in Palestine for around 1500 years, consider it their homeland. The Dome of the Rock in Jerusalem is as important a religious site to Muslims as the Western Wall is to Jews. It is built where the prophet Muhammad was taken up to heaven.

- One of the main reasons for conflict is that both Palestinian Arabs and Jews claim that Palestine, or Israel as it is now known, is their rightful home.

The background to the conflict

Before the First World War most of the Middle East was part of the Ottoman Empire. During the war, the Ottomans were driven out by the British, French and their Arab allies.

During the First World War, the British were desperate to gain support for their campaign to defeat the Ottoman Empire. As a result they made promises to Arabs and Jews about the shape of a post-war Middle East. In return for Arab support, they promised independence when the war was over. Throughout the war the British encouraged the Arabs to rise up and defeat the Ottomans. This rebellion was supported by people like T.E. Lawrence (Lawrence of Arabia), an officer in the British army who commanded an Arab force in the fight against the Turks.

The Middle East as it is today, showing the disputed borders.

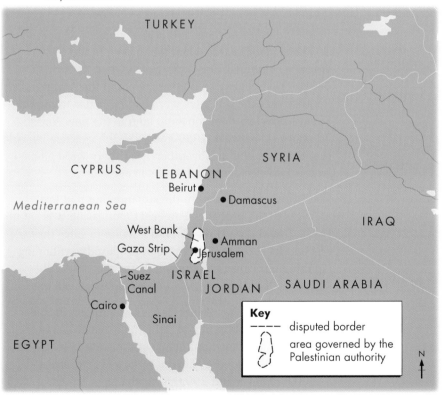

Britain was also very keen to get the support of the Jewish people across Europe for the war effort. In 1917, the British foreign secretary, Arthur Balfour, wrote a letter to a leading Zionist that became known as the Balfour Declaration. In it he said that the British government favoured the establishment in Palestine of a national home for the Jewish people (see Source A).

His Majesty's government views with favour the establishment in Palestine of a national home for the Jewish people, and will use their best endeavours to facilitate the achievement of this object, it being clearly understood that nothing shall be done which may prejudice the civil and religious rights of existing non-Jewish communities in Palestine, or the rights and political status enjoyed by Jews in any other country.

An extract from the Balfour Declaration, 1917.

At the end of the war only Saudi Arabia was given its independence. The rest of the Middle East was placed under the control of Britain and France. The Arabs in Palestine felt very let down and angry.

As the twentieth century progressed, it became clear that there were huge oil reserves in the Middle East. As the economies across the world became increasingly dependent on oil as a source of fuel, so the Middle East took on a new importance.

Britain controls Palestine

In 1920 the League of Nations (which was set up after the First World War to try to ensure peace in the world) placed the control of Palestine in the hands of Britain. This was called giving Britain a mandate (an order) to rule the country. The mandate was to last until 1948. The British took over control of Palestine in a difficult situation. In 1922, around 11 per cent of the population of Palestine was Jewish. Over the next ten years the British allowed Jewish immigration into Palestine, so that by 1932 the Jewish population had doubled to 180,000. By 1937 the number had risen to 400,000, many of whom were Jews fleeing persecution in Nazi Germany (see Chapter 6).

In 1937 the Peel Commission proposed partitioning Palestine between the Arabs and Jews.

In 1929 the first serious outburst of violence against the Jewish settlers in Jerusalem took place. In the 1930s violence continued. The Jews rioted when the British decided to limit Jewish immigration and the Arabs rioted because they felt the Jews were getting better treatment. Some Arabs lost their jobs and land to the new Jewish immigrants. Between 1936 and 1939 the violence became more serious and in November 1937 there were pitched battles between Jews and Arabs in Jerusalem.

The British struggled with the situation but had few answers to the problem. The Peel Commission was set up by the British government in an attempt to solve the dispute. In 1937, the commission proposed partitioning (splitting up) Palestine between Arabs and Jews. They suggested that the new partition would work like this:

- The Jewish state of Israel was to be mainly in the north of the state. It was to include coastal territory from the northern boundary of the state to just south of the town of Jaffa. This new state would include 300,000 Jews and 290,000 Arabs.

- An Arab state in the south would be united with Jordan.

- In between the Jewish and Arab states the British proposed a British-controlled strip of land which included Jerusalem.

The Arabs rejected the Peel Commission's proposal and violence broke out, leading to attacks on homes, synagogues and Jews. Some Jews accepted the Peel Commission's proposals as it gave the Jews a chance to control a state of their own.

Campaign of terror

The Holocaust and the murder of six million Jews by the Nazis (see Chapter 6) strengthened support for Zionists and a Jewish state, especially in the USA where there was a very large Jewish community. Trouble began to flare up when Britain refused a number of ships, such as the *Exodus*, carrying Jews escaping persecution into Palestine. This was because they feared upsetting Arab opinion. A number of Jews in Palestine joined terrorist groups including Irgun and the Stern Gang in an attempt to get rid of the British. From 1945–8 they waged a campaign of terror against the British authorities. Their most spectacular action was in July 1946 when they blew up the British army headquarters in Jerusalem, the King David Hotel, with the loss of 91 lives.

Having failed to find a solution to the problems in the Middle East the British handed the problem over to the United Nations in April 1947. In May 1947 a UN Committee toured the Middle East to gather information about the best possible solution to the problems in the Middle East. It finally proposed a plan in November 1947 for the partition of Palestine into Jewish and Arab states.

Digging deeper

The British in Palestine 1946–7

In the 1920s and 1930s there were a number of attacks by Arabs on the Jews who had settled in Palestine. In one attack in 1929 around 150 Jews were killed. In 1936 there was an Arab uprising against Jewish settlement in Palestine. In the light of this violence and the events of the Holocaust (see Chapter 6) some Jews decided to turn to violence as the means of getting a Jewish state.

The following extracts are adapted from articles printed in the *Daily Telegraph* newspaper, 1946–7.

SOURCE B

Jewish terrorists are condemned to death

Leaders of Irgun, the Jewish terrorist organisation, have promised that the three Britons that they hold as hostages will be killed, if death sentences passed on two of their number are carried out.

27 June 1946.

SOURCE C

British ban Jews from Palestine

Today two more ships are expected to join the flotilla [fleet of small ships] of misery outside the port of Haifa. The ships, carrying 1500 Jewish refugees from Europe to Palestine, are stranded there by a blockade of British warships and have become floating slums.

11 August 1946.

SOURCE D

Let more Jews into Palestine, urges US

President Truman of the United States of America has sparked a diplomatic war with Britain over the future of Palestine. He backed the Jewish plan for the creation of a Jewish state in an 'adequate' area in Palestine. He repeated an earlier demand for Britain to admit 100,000 European Jews into Palestine immediately.

4 October 1946.

SOURCE E

Death toll rises as Jews and Arabs clash

Just a week ago an Arab force of about 600 crossed the border from Syria, where they had been training, and attacked three Jewish settlements. On this occasion the Jews joined with the British to repulse the Arab attacks.

16 January, 1948.

SOURCE F

Jewish terrorists kill eight British troops

Eight British servicemen were killed in Jerusalem today, as Jewish terrorists launched a wave of bombings and shootings. Eleven other members of the security forces were badly hurt.

Four died in what was one of the worst outrages yet, when a mine was detonated underneath a truck carrying the men from a cinema to their billets.

17 November 1946.

SOURCE G

Barracks blown up by Jews in Tel Aviv

Four British policemen were killed and six others injured in a massive explosion at the police barracks at Sarona, east of Tel Aviv today. Hundreds of windows in the town were shattered by the blast, which was heard thirty miles away. The bombs are thought to have been planted by the Jewish Stern gang.

24 April 1947.

Activity time

Study Sources B to G.

Write a report from a British official in Palestine to the British foreign minister. In your report you must:

- advise on the situation in the country
- make proposals as to what the British should do next.

The creation of Israel in 1948

The proposed new Jewish state was three times the size of the Palestinian one, although the uninhabited Negev desert made up almost half of the area. After the UN accepted the partition plan, violence erupted and thousands of Palestinians fled to neighbouring countries. Full scale war broke out in April 1948, and on 14 May the state of Israel was proclaimed. The surrounding Arab nations of Syria, Egypt, Jordan, Iraq and Lebanon invaded Israel, and the combined Arab forces outnumbered the Jewish army. At the start of the war the Arab forces were better equipped than the Jewish forces, but the Jews gradually acquired better weapons from countries such as Czechoslovakia.

The Arab armies, which were relatively inexperienced and divided amongst themselves, were defeated and the Palestinians lost land to the new Israeli state. Some 160,000 Palestinians remained in the state of Israel and eventually become citizens of the new state. The Palestinians were left with just the Gaza Strip and the West Bank. The U.N. estimate states that about 5–600,000 Palestinians fled their homes or were forced out in the course of the hostilities. Many were housed in refugee camps in Jordan, Syria, Lebanon (see page 223) and Egypt where they were to stay for generations. These camps became a breeding ground for those who wanted revenge and the destruction of the new Jewish state.

Israel at war 1956–91

For the next 25 years no peace treaties were signed and the state of Israel fought a series of wars against its neighbours.

The Suez Crisis 1956

In 1952, a colonel in the Egyptian army, Gamal Nasser, seized power in Egypt. He bought weapons from the Soviet Union and in 1956 took control of the Suez Canal which was owned by Britain and France. Nasser made it clear that the canal now belonged to Egypt. This was a blow to the pride of Britain and France and a threat to their economic security. The Suez Canal was vital for the transport of oil from the oil fields of the Middle East to Europe and beyond. But Nasser was not just interested in the issue of oil or control of the canal. He also wanted to lead the Arab world in its fight against Israel and had armed Palestinian groups willing to attack their enemy.

Britain, France and Israel made a secret agreement and invaded Egypt. The Israelis captured the Sinai desert but Britain and France failed to reach their objectives. Both the USA and the Soviet Union were angry at what had happened. They believed that Britain and France were no longer the important colonial powers they had been and that they had no right to send troops to the Middle East. Eventually the British and French withdrew in what was a humiliation.

The Israelis managed to destroy Palestinian bases in Egypt but did not end Palestinian resistance. In the following years the Palestinian Liberation Organisation (PLO) was formed and a number of attacks were made on Israel's borders. The Sinai desert which the Israelis had captured during the war was policed by a United Nations Force.

Israeli gains in the Six Day War, 1967

The Six Day War 1967

Border attacks on Israel continued and Syria began bombing Israel from the Golan Heights. In 1967 Nasser closed access to the port of Aqaba and told the United Nations forces to leave Sinai. It was clear that the Arab states were planning another attack on Israel.

Israel did not wait for any attack. On 5 April 1967 it attacked Arab airfields wiping out their air forces on the ground. They then launched tank attacks into Sinai and seized the Gaza Strip. In the north they captured the Golan Heights from Syria. The Jordanian army collapsed and the West Bank fell into Israeli hands. The Israeli army lost just 750 men, the Egyptians over 40,000.

The threat to Israel from its neighbours was therefore greatly reduced, but the war led to a change in Palestinian tactics. The PLO and the Popular Front for the Liberation of Palestine (PLEP) turned to terror as their means of attacking the Israeli state. The most shocking incident took place at the Munich Olympics in 1972 when a number of Israeli athletes were taken hostage by members of the Palestinian terrorist group, Black September, and were killed. On 10 June there was a ceasefire but permanent peace was not achieved. The Arab states still refused to recognise Israel, demanding that territories occupied during the war were returned. Israel, on the other hand, was determined to keep these territories to ensure secure and defensible borders.

The Yom Kippur War 1973

In 1970, Nasser was replaced by Anwar Sadat as president of Egypt. Sadat was determined to gain revenge for the defeat in 1967 and prepared Egypt more effectively for war. The Syrians also wanted revenge and made a secret pact with Egypt to attack Israel on the most sacred day in the Jewish calendar, Yom Kippur. They hoped that the Israelis would not be ready to fight on this day.

Initially the Israeli army was stunned by the attacks. The Syrian army pushed into the Golan Heights. A week later the Israelis counter-attacked and defeated the Syrian army quickly. Victory over the Egyptians was not to be as easy for Israel as it had been in 1967. The Egyptians were well armed with surface to air missiles (SAM) bought from the Soviet Union. However, their success did not last long; the Israelis attacked and crossed the Suez Canal. At that point the USA and the Soviet Union pressurised both sides into a ceasefire.

Throughout the war, the USA had supported Israel. The Arab countries were angry and decided to strike back at the USA and the economics of the western world. In 1973 the oil-producing Arab nations, known as OPEC, increased their prices by 70 per cent, which made oil much more

The coffins of Israeli soldiers killed in the Yom Kippur War, 1973.

expensive. Petrol and oil prices rose rapidly across the western world. It also meant that oil was now an even more important issue.

The war also changed attitudes. Just under 3000 Israeli soldiers were killed in the conflict, which was a far greater number than during the Six Day War. As a result Israel was prepared to talk to its neighbours about peace. In addition, Arab states (which had refused to talk to Israel about peace between 1967 and 1973) accepted the 1973 U.N. resolution which included the principle of negotiation.

Question time

What were the most important consequences for Israel of the following wars:

- the Suez War 1956
- the Six Day War 1967
- the Yom Kippur War 1973?

Choose your top *three* points and explain them in detail.

In the last quarter of the twentieth century a number of people searched for a settlement in the Middle East. However, the peace they looked for was not to be found.

The Camp David Agreement 1978

After the Yom Kippur War, Israel and Egypt spent a lot of money on more weapons. Neither country could really afford this spending – the money was needed for better hospitals and schools in their countries. Slowly they realised that talking would be better than war. Following the peace conference in 1973, Israel and Egypt agreed to the disengagement of their forces along the Suez Canal and in 1975 the canal was re-opened to shipping. In 1977–8, the Egyptian President, Anwar Sadat visited Israel. In return, the Israeli Prime Minister, Menachem Begin, visited Egypt. On these visits discussions took place about making peace.

In 1978 both sides travelled to Camp David in the USA, the holiday home of the US President Jimmy Carter. There an agreement was reached:

- Israel would withdraw from the Sinai desert over a period of three years and Jewish settlers in the Sinai would have to leave

- Egypt recognised the right of Israel to exist.

The reaction of other Arab countries was one of horror. There was nothing in the agreement for the Palestinians. In 1981, Sadat was assassinated by those who opposed this peace.

War in Lebanon

After the Camp David Agreement 1978, the PLO set up bases in Lebanon where many Palestinians had lived since 1948. From here it launched attacks on Israel. In 1978 and in 1982, Israel launched invasions of Lebanon to wipe out the PLO. In 1982, the Lebanese capital Beirut was heavily bombed.

In one of the worst incidents of the war, Palestinian refugees were massacred at refugee camps at Sabra and Chatila by Lebanese allies of Israel. Israel was accused of failing to intervene and stop the massacre. The PLO leader, Yasser Arafat, was forced to leave Lebanon with his 12,000 men. Within three years many had returned to Lebanon and started attacking Israel once again.

SOURCE 1

Beirut under attack in 1982.

Digging deeper

Massacre at Sabra and Chatila

In 1982 the Israeli government ordered its troops to invade Lebanon in order to destroy the PLO, who were attacking Israel from across the border. Israel had already done so in 1978 but the United Nations had intervened to stop them. In Lebanon a number of armed groups were attempting to seize control of the country which was in a state of civil war. One such group of Lebanese Christians was called the Phalangists. The Phalangists, like the Israelis, wanted the Palestinians out of Lebanon. In the summer of 1982 the PLO agreed to leave Lebanon and set up in other Arab states as part of a deal arranged by the international community. However the fighters of the PLO had to leave their families behind in refugee camps in the capital city Beirut.

In West Beirut there were two large refugee camps called Sabra and Chatila. These camps were packed with Palestinian women and children who had not been evacuated with the fighters of the PLO. They were an easy target for the Phalangists who had fought against the Palestinians and were their sworn enemies. The Phalangists were keen for revenge because, only two days before, their leader Bashir Gemayel had been assassinated. At 5.00pm on 16 September, the Phalangists entered the camps and began the massacre of the innocent civilians that lasted a day and a half. After the massacre the Phalangists used bulldozers to bury the dead. As they retreated, foreign journalists were allowed into the camps.

The estimates of the number of dead in the camps varied. The Lebanese police argued that 460 died, while Israeli intelligence put the figure at 700–800. The International Committee of the Red Cross put an initial figure of 1500 dead. Palestinian sources believed that the number of victims was between 3000 and 3500. All figures are estimates as so many bodies had been buried in mass graves. Whatever the figure, the massacres provoked outrage across the world. On 16 December 1982 the United Nations General Assembly condemned the massacre and declared it to be an act of genocide.

SOURCE J

The scene at the Chatila camp, when foreign observers entered on Saturday morning, was like a nightmare. Women wailed over the deaths of loved ones, bodies began to swell under the hot sun, and the streets were littered with thousands of spent cartridges. Houses had been dynamited and bulldozed into rubble, many with the inhabitants still inside. Groups of bodies lay before bullet-pocked walls where they appeared to have been executed. Others were strewn in alleys and streets, apparently shot as they tried to escape. Each little dirt alley through the deserted buildings, where Palestinians have lived since fleeing Palestine when Israel was created in 1948, told its own horror story.

An American journalist, Loren Jenkins, writing on 23 September 1982.

SOURCE K

When we entered Sabra and Chatila on Saturday 18 September 1982, the final day of the killing, we saw bodies everywhere. We photographed victims that had been mutilated with axes and knives. Only a few of the people we photographed had been machine-gunned. Others had their heads smashed, their eyes removed, their throats cut, skin was stripped from their bodies, limbs were severed, some people were eviscerated [their insides cut out]. The terrorists also found time to plunder Palestinian property as well as books, manuscripts and other cultural material from the Palestinian Research Centre in Beirut.

By American journalists Ralph Schoenman and Mya Shone, who were eyewittnesses to the aftermath of the massacre in 1982.

The Intifada

By the late 1980s, a generation of Palestinians had grown up knowing nothing but life in refugee camps. In 1988, an uprising of young Arabs in the West Bank and Gaza Strip took the form of rock throwing and demonstrations against Israeli occupation. What made this demonstration different was the involvement of so many women and children for the first time. Pictures were shown around the world of young rock throwers being fired at by Israeli soldiers. The Intifada (which means uprising) was a propaganda victory for the Palestinians.

The Gulf War 1991

Throughout the 1980s, Iran and Iraq had fought a horrific war against each other which cost millions of lives. The war had been started by the Iraqi leader Saddam Hussein who invaded Iran in the hope of gaining control of the country. Hussein had built up a large arsenal of missiles bought from the Soviet Union. He also needed money to pay for the war against Iran. In August 1990, Saddam Hussein ordered Iraqi armies to invade the small oil-rich country of Kuwait. The response of the USA, Britain and France was to send armies to expel Saddam from Kuwait in January 1991. Israel was bombed during the war by Iraqi rockets but it did not retaliate.

The Gulf War brought new possibilities for peace in the Middle East. In October 1991, the presidents of the USA and the Soviet Union met the leaders of Israel, Lebanon, Jordan and Syria, together with Palestinian leaders, in Madrid, with the aim of exploring ways to create a lasting peace. The introduction of western troops into the Middle East pleased those whom they protected. It offended others, especially extremist Muslims who felt that the presence of non-Muslim soldiers was an insult to their religion.

Attempts at peace 1992–6

In 1992, Yitzak Rabin was elected Israeli prime minister. Rabin believed that some kind of compromise with the Palestinians was needed if there was to be peace in Israel and the Middle East. The leader of the PLO,

SOURCE L

The signing of the Middle East Peace Accord in Washington in 1995. Yasser Arafat (right) and Yitzak Rabin (left) are joined by the President of the USA, Bill Clinton.

Yassar Arafat, also believed that there had to be compromise in order to achieve peace. Secret talks started between the two sides. These talks were held in Norway, far away from the tension of the Middle East. A number of agreements were signed between the two sides. The climax of the negotiations was the signing by Prime Minister Rabin and PLO Chairman Arafat of the Middle East Peace Accord in Washington in September 1995. By this agreement:

- the PLO recognised the state of Israel

- Israel agreed to Palestinian self-government in the Gaza Strip and West Bank.

Jewish reactions to the peace accord

The reactions to the peace accord were mixed. Many in Israel supported the peace process and hoped that the new Palestinian authority in the West Bank and Gaza Strip would mark the beginning of peace. However, some Israelis with extreme views opposed the peace plan. They believed that Yitzak Rabin had signed away land promised to the Jews by God. In particular the deal would mean that some Jewish people who had settled on the West Bank would now be in Palestinian-governed territory. On 4 November 1995, an Israeli opponent of the peace accord, Yigal Amir, assassinated Yitzak Rabin. For the next year the Israeli government remained committed to the peace process although with less enthusiasm than before.

Palestinian reactions to the peace accord

Many Palestinians hoped that the peace accord marked the beginning of a Palestinian state. Other Arabs were less positive. Two extremist Islamic groups, Hamas and Hezbollah, continued to attack Israel in a number of ways. For a while they maintained attacks from Lebanon, but in early 1996 they used a new tactic – suicide bombers. These people would blow themselves up in a place where they could cause maximum terror to the Israeli population: on buses, in shops and restaurants.

Negotiations continued between Israeli and Palestinian officials about finding a final peace settlement. The main point of disagreement was over who should control Jerusalem. This most historic of cities was of emotional and religious importance to both sides and contains monuments central to Judaism and Islam.

- Judaism's most sacred shrine, the Western Wall on Temple Mount, was the last remaining part of the ancient Holy Temple of the Jews. It was destroyed by the Romans in AD 70.

- Haram-al-Sharif is sacred to Muslims as it is from there that the prophet Muhammad is believed to have ascended into heaven. The site is home to al Aqsa Mosque and the Dome of the Rock. The traditions of the Muslim faith say that one prayer at the al Aqsa Mosque is worth 500 elsewhere.

However all attempts to come to an agreement about the control of Jerusalem have failed, and fighting continues to this day.

Question time

Why were the Jews able to gain their independence?

Work together in groups when dealing with this question. Each group should focus on one or two of the following issues:

- Jewish immigration
- the impact of the Second World War
- Arab division
- Jewish terror
- the role of the U.N.

For each issue you should do the following:

- describe what happened
- explain how these events helped lead to Jewish independence.

Ireland 1914–98

From the twelfth century, the English attempted to rule Ireland. For a considerable time they failed to control much beyond 'the Pale' – the area surrounding Dublin. In the sixteenth and seventeenth centuries, Europe became divided by religion during the Reformation. In Ireland the vast majority of people remained Catholic. In England and Scotland the majority became Protestants.

It became clear that the best way for the English to control Ireland was to forcibly take the land away from the Irish and give it to English and Scottish settlers. The seventeenth century was a period in which a large number of farmers from England and Scotland were given land in Ireland. The Scots were mainly strict Protestants known as Presbyterians, who had a deep hatred of Catholicism. They were mostly settled in an event which became known as the Plantation of Ulster.

Causes of conflict

For the next 200 years a series of events took place that strengthened the hatred between the settlers and the native population of Ireland.

- In 1641, a massacre of Protestants in Ulster by Catholics increased the sense of the Protestant community that it was under attack.

- In 1649–50, the English ruler, Oliver Cromwell, attacked a number of Irish towns, including Drogheda and Wexford, in which thousands were massacred, English and Irish alike. The majority of those massacred were Catholics. At the end of his campaign, Cromwell took large areas of land and handed it out to his officers. The Irish Catholic view that the English were violent and repressive invaders was strengthened.

- In 1688, the Protestant city of Londonderry held out against a siege laid by the Catholic forces of James II. The Protestant cry of 'No Surrender' (to the Catholics) was first heard.

- In 1690 at the Battle of the Boyne, the new English Protestant King, William III, defeated the Catholic forces of James II whom he had deposed. A long period of the Protestants dominating Ireland, known as the Protestant Ascendancy, began.

- In 1801, Britain closed the Irish Parliament. Ireland was to be ruled from London.

- In the 1840s, Ireland suffered a terrible famine because of the failure of the potato crop. Over 1 million died and 1.5 million emigrated. Many Irish people blamed the British for their misfortune.

- The industrialisation and increased prosperity in Britain in the nineteenth century spread to Ireland but only to Ulster. The rest of Ireland was still overwhelmingly agricultural. This division of industrial and agricultural reinforced the sense of division between north and south (Protestant and Catholic).

Ireland during the First World War

By 1914, there were a number of groups in Ireland with different views of what should happen to the country.

Nationalists

Irish Nationalists can be divided into:

- **Constitutional Nationalists** They believed in Home Rule – an Irish Parliament to run Irish affairs. In 1912 the British Parliament finally passed a Home Rule Act for Ireland that came into force in 1914.

- **Revolutionary Nationalists** They believed in winning independence from Britain through the use of force and violence. In the nineteenth century, this strand was represented by the Fenians.

In 1905, a journalist called Arthur Griffith founded a new political party, Sinn Fein. He believed that violence was not the answer but that Irish Nationalists should simply ignore the British Parliament and set up their own government in Dublin. However, events moved on and by 1913 there were some who believed that force was the only answer to the question of Irish independence. In 1913 an armed force, the Irish Volunteers, was formed.

Unionists

The Unionists believed in keeping links with Britain. They were mainly Protestants and increasingly based in the north of the country. In 1912, 400,000 Unionists had signed a Solemn League and Covenant protesting against Home Rule. They hated the idea of being ruled by an Irish Parliament dominated by Catholics. Their leader was Sir Edward Carson who set up a private army 100,000-strong called the Ulster Volunteers. Their cause was supported by the Conservative Party in Britain.

The outbreak of the First World War against Germany in 1914 meant that the introduction of Home Rule was postponed. It also meant that a likely civil war between Unionists and Nationalists was avoided. Around 170,000 Irishmen from both sides volunteered to fight for Britain against the Germans.

The Constitutional Nationalists believed that if they fought for Britain, then the British government would look favourably on their cause at the end of the war. The Unionists felt that by fighting for Britain they might get their way. If they couldn't prevent Home Rule then they would ask for Ireland to be partitioned (divided) into a Protestant North that would stay part of Britain and a Catholic South with its own Parliament.

In April 1916 a group of Revolutionary Nationalists known as the Irish Republican Brotherhood launched an armed uprising in Dublin and proclaimed an Irish Republic. They seized the General Post Office and fought a vicious battle for five days. Eventually the leaders of what became known as the Easter Uprising, Padraic Pearse and James Connolly, surrendered and were executed in May 1916. Their casualties had been high and it was clear that they had no chance of defeating the British forces.

Digging deeper

The execution of the leaders of the uprising in 1916

The British army commander in Ireland believed that the leaders of the rebellion should be shot. Consequently, fourteen of the leaders of the uprising were executed in Dublin.

SOURCE A

I never knew such a transformation of opinion as that caused by the executions ... They [the British] have lost the hearts of the people beyond all hope of retrieving their mistakes ... Pearse has achieved his objectives better than he must have thought he would.

Adapted from a letter from Tim Healy, an Irish politician, to his brother, June 1916.

SOURCE C

Within a week of Connolly's execution, the British ambassador in Washington had reported an anti-British shift in US opinion. This may have played a part in securing the setting aside of the death sentence passed on Eamon de Valéra, who, because of his American birth, could claim US citizenship.

By historian John Ranelagh. Eamon de Valéra became leader of Sinn Fein and led the campaign for Irish independence from Britain.

SOURCE B

A prisoner's painting of the execution of one of the Easter Uprising leaders, at Kilmainham Jail, May 1916.

Colonisation and Conflict 1750–1990

SOURCE D

You are washing out our whole life's work in a sea of blood. Thousands of people, who ten days ago were bitterly opposed to the whole Sinn Fein movement and to the rebellion, are now becoming angry with the government because of these executions.

Adapted from a speech by John Dillon (a Constitutional Nationalist) to the House of Commons in May 1916.

Question time

Try to understand the viewpoint of *a* a British general and *b* a Constitutional Nationalist in 1916 in Dublin.

- What would be your attitude towards the rebels?

- In role, write *two* short speeches showing the likely attitudes of first one and then the other.

As the talk of the uprising continued, the British prepared for their offensive on the Somme (see pages 122–4). Thousands of Ulster Volunteers had been formed into the 36th Ulster Division. On the first day of the Battle of the Somme, on 1 July 1916, they were opposite the German positions at Thiepval. Ignoring instructions to walk, the Ulstermen left their trenches early and charged the German lines. Although they were initially successful, those around them had been cut to ribbons and the Ulster Division was forced to fall back. In a few days in July, the Division suffered over 5500 casualties. The sacrifice of the men of Ulster on the battlefields of France was to become an important bargaining chip when the future of Ireland was decided after the war.

In the wake of 1916, public opinion amongst those who wanted an independent Ireland swung behind Sinn Fein, led by Eamon de Valéra, because they had sympathy with Valéra's cause after the executions in May 1916. Such was the support for Sinn Fein that in the November 1918 elections to the British Parliament they won a resounding victory. Of 107 seats, Sinn Fein won 73, the Constitutional Nationalists 6 and the Unionists 26. The Sinn Fein MPs decided that, instead of going to Parliament in Westminster, they would set up their own Parliament in Dublin, the Dáil Eireann.

The War of Independence 1919–21

The Dáil Eireann faced many problems. It had set up its own courts and police but was short of money and was not recognised by Unionists or the British government. So began two years of violence which shaped the development of Ireland for the next eighty years.

- The Irish Republican Army (IRA) was set up in 1919 by Michael Collins to wage a war of terror against the British, the police and anybody who supported them.

- This campaign of terror was matched by the brutality of the British forces sent to help the Irish police, the Black and Tans. Manned by many ex-servicemen, the Black and Tans (so named because of the colour of their clothes) launched reprisals for IRA attacks.

- The British army was sent to Ireland in 1921 to restore order. It was much more effective against the IRA than the Black and Tans. In May 1921, it defeated an IRA attack on the Dublin Customs House.

Key
- Northern Ireland
- Irish Free State

N ↑

NORTHERN IRELAND

Londonderry
ANTRIM
LONDONDERRY
DONEGAL
● Larne
TYRONE
Dungannon ● Belfast
FERMANAGH ● Portadown
Armagh DOWN
SLIGO ARMAGH
MONAGHAN ● Newry
MAYO LEITRIM CAVAN LOUTH
ROSCOMMON
LONGFORD ● Drogheda
MEATH
GALWAY DUBLIN
Galway ● WESTMEATH ● Dublin
OFFALY
KILDARE
CLARE LAOIS WICKLOW
CARLOW
Limerick ●
TIPPERARY
LIMERICK KILKENNY
WEXFORD
KERRY
CORK WATERFORD
● Cork

IRISH FREE STATE

0 ——— 100 km
——— 60 miles

The division of Ireland in 1922.

Despite the effectiveness of the British army, the British Prime Minister, David Lloyd George, believed that some kind of settlement must be agreed. However, for there to be peace, all of the main groups needed to be satisfied with the settlement. This was unlikely considering that the War of Independence had hardened attitudes, especially amongst the Unionists in the North. In 1920, the Government of Ireland Act separated the six counties of Ulster, four of which had a Protestant majority, from the rest of Ireland. A large minority of Catholics was included in this new state.

The IRA and Sinn Fein were opposed to the partition of Ireland. In October 1921, discussions began between the Nationalists, led by Arthur Griffiths and Michael Collins, and the British government. The discussions ended in compromise, and the Treaty of London was signed in December 1921.

- Ireland was to be partitioned between a six county Northern Ireland and a twenty-six county Irish Free State.

- The Free State was to have considerable say over its own affairs. However, it was to stay in the British Empire and an oath was still to be sworn to the king.

- A boundary commission would review the border between Northern Ireland and the Free State.

For many Nationalists the fact that Ireland was still in the British Empire and now divided was a source of bitter disappointment. In Belfast, the IRA fought battles with the police. In the south, the Dáil accepted the treaty but by only seven votes. The Irish people also accepted the treaty in a vote in June 1922. However the Nationalists were divided. A bitter civil war broke out between those for and against the treaty. Those in favour won but not before one of their leaders, Michael Collins, was assassinated.

Question time

1 Why did the British partition Ireland?

2 What was the result of partition?

Ireland 1922–69: North and South

In this period little happened to bring the communities of Ireland together. In fact the two communities seemed to drift further apart.

The South

In 1932, Eamon de Valéra was elected into power. He stayed in power, with a couple of short breaks, until 1959. De Valéra's policies had an important influence on relations with the Protestants in the North.

- The Irish constitution of 1937 stated that the South did not accept partition or the existence of Northern Ireland.

- A special place in Irish life was given to the Catholic Church.

- Ireland was to have an Irish head of state, not a British monarch.

These measures pleased many Nationalists but strengthened the view of many Protestants in the North that there should never be a united Ireland. In 1949, Ireland was declared a republic and left the British Commonwealth.

The North

Poor living conditions for a Catholic family, Londonderry, 1960

In Northern Ireland, power was held exclusively by the Protestants. They had little intention of sharing power with the Catholics. They believed that only the people living in the north should decide the destiny of Northern Ireland. The Nationalists believed that the people in the whole of Ireland should decide the future of the North.

The Catholics in Northern Ireland were discriminated against. They were given the worst jobs, the worst housing and poor education. The police force in Northern Ireland was exclusively Protestant. This force was known as the 'B Specials' and was feared by Catholics for its occasional brutality.

In the 1960s, a new Protestant prime minister of Northern Ireland, Terence O'Neill, recognised that the Catholics were being treated as second-class citizens and he promised to introduce reform which would help them. However, many Catholics became impatient and founded the Civil Rights Association in 1967 to campaign for equal rights for Catholics.

The demonstrations of the Civil Rights Association provoked a violent reaction from Protestants, led by people such as the Reverend Ian Paisley, who opposed giving in to Catholic demands. By mid-1969 Northern Ireland had descended into chaos. Catholic families were terrorised out of their homes by Protestant gangs and many families fled over the border into the Irish Republic in fear of their lives.

The British army was called out to restore order. The period from 1969 to the late 1990s has been called 'The Troubles'. During that time, the violence between the two communities claimed the lives of over 3000 people.

Nationalism

The introduction of the British army onto the streets of Northern Ireland in 1969 failed to restore order. A number of Nationalists broke away from the IRA to form the Provisional IRA. They believed that the time was now right to remove the British from Ireland with a campaign of terror. A number of other Nationalist groups such as the Irish National Liberation Army (INLA) also resorted to violence, attacking Protestants, members of the Royal Ulster Constabulary, the army and even people within their own community. The examples of terror are many but some of the worst are shown in the box below.

Many Nationalists did not support the violence of the IRA and INLA and hoped that they could bring about change by peaceful means. In 1970 the Social Democratic Party (SDLP) was formed under the leadership of Gerry Fitt to campaign for change by peaceful means. They had to cope with attacks from Unionists and also from Nationalists who believed violence was the only way to achieve their aims. In the 1980s, John Hume took over from Gerry Fitt. He was to play a very important role in moving Ireland towards peace.

Attacks by Irish Nationalist terrorists during the Troubles

February 1978 An IRA bomb attack on a hotel in County Down killed twelve people.

August 1980 Lord Mountbatten, the uncle of the Prince of Wales, was killed by an IRA bomb on his boat off the coast of County Donegal in the Irish Republic. At virtually the same time an IRA bomb exploded under an army bus at Warrenpoint. As the survivors staggered off the bus they were caught by the explosion of a second bomb. Eighteen soldiers and one civilian died.

October 1984 An IRA bomb exploded at the Grand Hotel in Brighton during the Conservative Party conference. Five were killed and thirty injured. The Prime Minister, Margaret Thatcher, had a narrow escape.

November, 1987 Eleven people were killed by an IRA bomb which exploded during a Remembrance Service in Enniskillen, County Fermanagh.

January 1992 Eight building workers were killed by the IRA at Teebane for working for the army.

March 1993 Two children, aged three and twelve, were killed by an IRA bomb planted in a rubbish bin in the centre of Warrington, Cheshire.

October 1993 An IRA bomb killed ten Protestants in a butcher's shop on the Shankhill Road, the heart of the Unionist area of Belfast.

August 1998 The extremist Nationalist group, the Real IRA, planted a bomb in the centre of the town of Omagh in County Tyrone. Twenty-nine people were killed and hundreds were injured.

Unionism

During The Troubles the Unionist movement in Northern Ireland developed along similar lines to the Nationalists. Some Unionists turned to organised violence as the means of achieving their goals. In the 1970s the Ulster Volunteer Force (UVF) and the Ulster Defence Association (UDA) were formed. They began to use terror against the Catholic population with a campaign of shootings and bombings. These groups called themselves 'loyal' to the British crown and are therefore also known as Loyalists. The Loyalist Volunteer Force (LVF) proved to be one of the most violent of these organisations.

Attacks by Unionist terrorists during the Troubles

December 1971 The UVF killed fifteen people in an attack on a Belfast pub.

October 1975 The UVF launched a series of attacks on the Catholic population, leaving twelve dead.

May 1974 Bombs were planted in Dublin by Loyalist terrorists, killing 22 people.

March 1988 A lone Loyalist gunman, Michael Stone, opened fire on a crowd at the funeral of IRA members shot in Gibraltar by British forces. Three people were killed.

February 1992 Five Catholics were killed by Loyalist gunmen in a betting shop.

October 1993 In one of the worst attacks during the Troubles, Loyalist gunmen broke into the Rising Sun bar in Greysteel, shouted 'trick or treat' and opened fire on the customers. Seven died in this attack.

November 1993 Three Catholics were killed by Loyalist gunmen in a betting shop.

As with the Nationalist community, most Unionists reject violence. Most Unionists supported either the Ulster Unionist Party (UUP) or the Democratic Unionist Party (DUP). Both parties rejected any idea that the Irish government would have a role in the government of Northern Ireland. The DUP was led by Ian Paisley who never changed his mind on these matters. The UUP slowly accepted the need for discussions with Nationalists over the future of Northern Ireland.

Digging deeper

The Peace People Movement

It is wrong to see all of the people of Northern Ireland as being divided into two warring tribes. The majority of people in Northern Ireland want peace. However it takes tremendous courage and bravery to stand up to people of violence. In 1976 that is what happened.

On 10 August a woman called Anne Maguire was out for a walk with her three children, Andrew, a six week old baby, John, aged 2 and Joanna, aged 8. As she was walking along she heard a bang. A British army patrol had shot at an IRA man who was driving a car. The soldiers hit the driver and the car sped off the road, hitting the

Maguire family. The three children were crushed to death.

Anne Maguire's sister, Mairead Corrigan, was shocked by the killings and spoke out against IRA violence on television. After the children's funeral she joined forces with Betty Williams and founded the Peace People Movement. At their first rally a crowd of over 30,000 appeared.

Soon rallies and demonstrations for peace took place across Britain and Ireland. The message of Williams and Corrigan was clear – whatever the problem, the solution must be non-violent.

The two women were awarded a number of prizes in recognition of their work, including the 1976 Nobel Peace Prize. However, they became a target for abuse and intimidation from both sides of the divide in Northern Ireland. After they had won international prizes the media began to lose interest in their cause. The violence they tried to stop continued and members of the Peace People Movement began to quarrel between themselves.

Williams eventually moved to the USA and their movement collapsed. Their legacy was that they showed the world that it was possible to speak out against terrorism. They also highlighted that there was support for another way forward in Ireland, that of peace.

Mairead Corrigan and Betty Williams, December 1984.

The response of British and Irish governments

From 1969, such was the violence in Northern Ireland that the British government passed a law which allowed them to round up and imprison suspected terrorists without trial. Known as internment, the policy failed and the violence continued. By 1972 it was clear that the situation in Northern Ireland was out of control. The British government decided that Northern Ireland's Parliament should be closed and the province should be ruled from London. In 1974 the British government tried to introduce power sharing between Protestants and Catholics. Many Protestants objected to such a move and a strike of Protestant workers against power sharing led to its collapse.

The British government refused to recognise captured terrorists as political prisoners. In 1981 Bobby Sands and other IRA members went on hunger strike and Sands died. To many Catholics he was a martyr. His death and that of nine others raised tension considerably, but the British government refused to change its policy towards the prisoners.

Most politicians in the Irish Republic hoped for a united Ireland. In the 1980s, the governments of Britain and Ireland began to co-operate more closely over Ireland. Until that time relations between the two had often been tense.

In 1985, the British Prime Minister Mrs Thatcher and the Taoiseach Garret Fitzgerald, signed the Anglo-Irish Agreement which allowed the Irish Republic influence in the running of Northern Ireland. The Unionists opposed the move and thousands turned out in Belfast to hear Ian Paisley repeat the words of Edward Carson that there would be 'No Surrender'.

Question time

Imagine you are a journalist writing an article for a magazine in the late 1980s. Your article has the title 'Time For Peace'. You are to use the information in this section to explain the following:

- why do you think that it is time for peace in Northern Ireland
- what are barriers to peace?

From ceasefire to peace?

Before there could be peace in Ireland, as in South Africa, a number of changes had to take place. In August 1994, the IRA called a ceasefire. The leader of Sinn Fein, Gerry Adams, had been persuaded by John Hume of the SDLP that the IRA (the terrorist wing of Sinn Fein) should look for ways of moving forward peacefully. The IRA ceasefire led to a Loyalist ceasefire. However the IRA ceasefire did not last long and series of attacks in 1996–7 showed how many in the IRA wanted to continue to use terrorism. By mid-1997 the IRA had called another ceasefire.

With Sinn Fein again committed to a ceasefire, talks took place in October 1997 between Unionists and Republicans over the future of Ireland. In April 1998, the Good Friday Agreement was made and welcomed by British and Irish governments, the Official Ulster Unionists, the SDLP and Sinn Fein.

The Good Friday Agreement included certain proposals:

- The creation of a Northern Ireland Assembly. Ministers would be chosen from all parties represented in the Assembly. All must agree to non-violence.

- The creation of a North-South Council with powers to improve co-operation between Northern Ireland and the Republic.

- All terrorists were to hand in their weapons by May 2000 if they wanted their political representatives to sit in the Assembly.

- The RUC (Royal Ulster Constabulary) was to be made more representative of both communities.

- Prisoners imprisoned for terrorist offences should be released within two years.

Although the agreement did not lead to immediate peace, it laid the foundations for peaceful negotiations.

7 Assessment section

In this chapter there are three case studies of how conflict has been dealt with in various parts of the world.

- In South Africa there is some violence in the country but the conflict over apartheid has been resolved.

- In Ireland both sides have gone a long way down the road to peace although peace is still insecure.

- In the Middle East the problems have not been resolved.

In groups of three, choose one of the following questions. You should try, as a group, to discuss these questions together. Then you need to answer the questions individually on paper. When finished, you should report your ideas back to your group.

- Why did the conflict end in South Africa?

- Why has there been progress in Northern Ireland to end the conflict?

- Why hasn't there been a solution to the conflict in the Middle East?

Extended writing

Choose one of the three countries you have studied in this chapter. Describe the conflict in that country since 1945 and suggest the way forward for a peaceful outcome.

Research activity

Collect as much news as you can about a conflict which is currently taking place in the world. You can collect information from the following places:

- newspapers

- television

- magazines

- the Internet.

Present your work as a wall display or as a project in a folder.

Further reading

Nelson Mandela *Long Walk to Freedom* (Abacus, 1995)

Sean Sheehan *Lives in Crisis: South Africa since Apartheid* (Hodder Wayland, 2002)

The post-1900 changing world

Looking back to 1900 we see a very different world from today. Britain and France had empires that stretched around the world. The German, Austrian and Russian empires dominated Europe. However, the world was on the verge of a conflict, the First World War, that was to tear the world apart and change it forever.

Many people who lived in countries that were colonies wanted to rule themselves. As the twentieth century progressed, so the demands for independence grew. The Second World War was an important turning point. The defeat of European armies by the Japanese showed that the Europeans were not invincible. The war also weakened the economies of the colonial powers. This meant that they could not afford the cost of defending their empires. The process of decolonisation – giving independence to countries that had been colonies – was about to begin.

The twentieth century also saw the rise and fall of governments dominated by ideology – beliefs and ideas shaped into a political system. One of the most powerful ideologies was communism which, by 1950, dominated the governments of half the world's population. By the end of the century, the communist system of government had collapsed virtually everywhere.

The end of empire

In 1900, Britain, France and other European powers controlled much of the world's trade through a system of empires (see Chapter 1). The process of dismantling these empires was peaceful in some countries but provoked bitter violence in others.

There are many reasons why the European empires in Africa and Asia collapsed. In most colonies, there were organisations formed to promote the cause of independence.

India

In India the Indian National Congress was founded in 1885 with the aim of ending British rule. By the 1920s, the leader of the Indian National Congress, Mahatma Gandhi, had developed the strategy of *satygraha* (non-violent resistance) as a means of uniting Indians against the British. The cause of independence became even more popular in many colonies in the 1930s. One reason for this was that India, like many colonies, suffered economically during the global depression in the 1930s. It had been forced by Britain to base its economies on the production of raw materials such as sugar for export to Britain. In the depression, the price of raw materials and the market for them collapsed.

NORTH KOREA
1945

PAKISTAN
1947

TUNISIA
1956

LEBANON
1946

EAST PAKISTAN
1947

BURMA
1948

MOROCCO
1956

MALTA
1964

CYPRUS
1960

UNITED ARAB
EMIRATES
1971

LAOS
1954

WESTERN SAHARA
1975

ALGERIA
1962

LIBYA
1951

SYRIA
1946

VIETNAM
1954

SOUTH KOREA
1948

MAURITANIA
1960

ERITREA
1962

KUWAIT
1961

INDIA
1947

SENEGAL
1960

MALI
1960

NIGER
1960

CHAD
1960

SUDAN
1956

YEMEN
1967

PHILIP
19

GAMBIA
1965

VOLTA
1960

NIGERIA
1960

DJIBOUTI
1977

CAMBODIA
1953

GUINEA
BASSAU
1974

CENTRAL
AFRICA
1960

ETHIOPIA
1941

SOMALIA
1960

MALAYSIA
1957

GUINEA
1958

CAMEROON
1960

PAPUA NE
19

SIERRA LEONE
1961

TOGO
1960

UGANDA
1962

KENYA
1963

CEYLON
1948

IVORY
COAST
1960

DAHOMEY
1960

CONGO
1960

RWANDA
1962

BURUNDI
1962

MALDIVES
1965

GHANA
1957

EQUATORIAL
GUINEA
1968

ANGOLA
1975

ZAMBIA
1964

TANZANIA
1964

MOZAMBIQUE
1975

INDONESIA
1948

GABON
1960

MADAGASCAR
1960

RHODESIA
1965

MALAWI
1964

MAURITIUS
1968

SWAZILAND
1968

BOTSWANA
1966

LESOTHO
1966

Colonies of European countries and their dates of independence.

Colonisation and Conflict 1750–1990

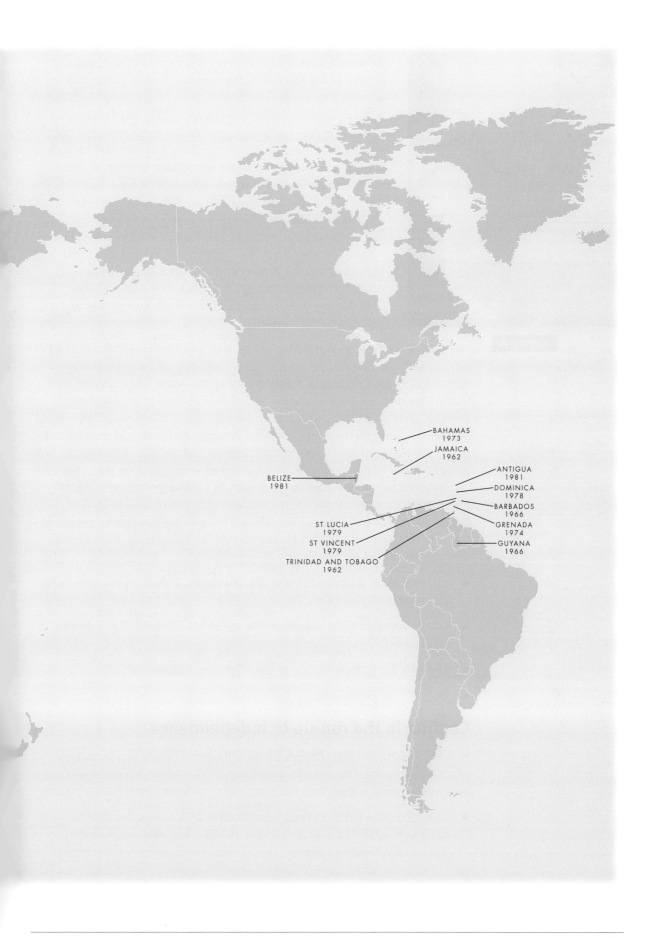

BAHAMAS
1973

JAMAICA
1962

ANTIGUA
1981

DOMINICA
1978

BARBADOS
1966

GRENADA
1974

GUYANA
1966

BELIZE
1981

ST LUCIA
1979

ST VINCENT
1979

TRINIDAD AND TOBAGO
1962

Subhas Chandra Bose.

During the First and Second World Wars (see Chapters 4 and 5), most colonies agreed to fight alongside their European rulers. At the start of the Second World War, the British Governor-General, Lord Linlithgow, declared war on behalf of India against Germany without consulting any Indians. However, many Indians supported the British in their fight against the Japanese in the Far East, and 180,000 Indians became casualties during the war. Other Indians, such as Subhas Chandra Bose (Source A), fought for the Japanese in the hope that the British would be defeated. Japanese success in beating the European powers destroyed the myth of European superiority. In February 1942 the British were forced to surrender to the Japanese at Singapore. The defeat of France and the Netherlands by Germany in 1940 weakened them in the eyes of those they ruled. These humiliations were noted by all those who wanted to end European colonialisation.

The end of the Second World War left all European nations militarily and economically exhausted. As a result they could not afford to keep their empires. The new dominant superpowers in the world, the USA and the Soviet Union, were keen to see the end of the empires of the European powers. They wanted to extend their own influence over areas of the world previously dominated by countries like Britain and France. In the colonial powers, such as Britain, some people argued that the time was right to give independence to their colonies because it was wrong to deny other people the freedom to rule themselves. In Britain, a Labour government led by Clement Attlee came to power in 1945 and was determined to give independence to a number of countries. This was because many people in the Labour Party belived that having an empire was wrong. They argued that people should be free to rule themselves.

- In 1947 India was divided into two countries, India and Pakistan, and given its independence.

- In 1948 Britain gave independence to Ceylon (Sri Lanka) and Burma (Myanmar).

- In 1946 the French withdrew from Syria and Lebanon.

- In 1948 the Dutch gave up Indonesia.

Conflict in the run-up to independence

In many countries in the British Empire the move to independence was generally peaceful. However, in a number of places independence was not achieved without a fight.

- In Cyprus, the Greek Cypriot organisation EOKA waged a violent campaign against the British in the 1950s. They also attacked the Turkish Cypriot community.

Digging deeper

Mahatma Gandhi (1869–1948)

SOURCE B

Mahatma Gandhi.

One of the most famous campaigners against the British Empire was Mahatma Gandhi. For much of his early adult life, Gandhi lived in South Africa and worked as a lawyer. In 1914 he returned home to India. During the First World War, Gandhi spoke in favour of the British Empire. However, he was to turn against it in the wake of the massacre at Amritsar in 1919. During the war the British government had passed a law saying that those who spoke against the British could be put into prison without trial. After the war, the law was not revoked (cancelled). In Amritsar 10,000 Indians demonstrating for peace were faced by a force led by Brigadier-General Dyer. Without warning, Dyer ordered his troops to open fire on the crowd. In 10 minutes 379 people were killed and 1208 were injured. The massacre changed Gandhi's attitude towards the British Empire. He told his followers, 'co-operation in any shape or form with this satanic (evil) government is sinful'.

Gandhi understood that he and the Indian National Congress he came to lead could not defeat the British by using force. Instead he and his movement opposed British rule by using the non-violent method of *satygraha* or 'soul force'. Gandhi argued that everything British should be boycotted. Not only would British goods be left unsold but Indians should ignore the courts, schools and every institution created by the British. Gandhi was supported by a number of well-educated Indians such as Jawaharlal Nehru who became President of Congress in 1930.

As a sign of his rejection of European values, Gandhi dressed in a dhoti, the simple clothes of the Indian peasant. He also took part in a number of actions of passive (peaceful) resistance that raised the profile of the campaign. In 1930, he walked 250 miles in 24 days, raising support for a campaign of peaceful protest that ended with 60,000 Indians being imprisoned. In 1933, he campaigned against British plans for India by holding a hunger strike in prison and refusing all food.

In the 1930s, Gandhi made his home in Sevagram in the centre of India, living without electricity or running water. Here he discussed the issues of how to make India independent. In 1942 he issued his call for Britain to 'Quit India'. He was imprisoned until after the end of the Second World War in 1945.

Gandhi was also concerned about the religious divisions within India and the violence it was producing. Whilst others negotiated Indian independence, Gandhi travelled around the country attempting to end the violence.

In Calcutta fierce fighting was stopped at his request in what became known as the 'miracle of Calcutta'. After independence in 1947, around one million Indians died in the violence between Hindus and Muslims. In the city of Delhi, Gandhi went on a hunger strike which he only ended when Muslims and Hindus signed an agreement that they would end the violence. However, there were some who resented Gandhi's determination to protect Muslims. In 1948, he was shot by assassin, Nathuram Godse.

- In Kenya, there were around 30,000 European settlers who owned the best land in the country. In the 1950s, a group fighting for independence and land for black Kenyans, the Mau Mau, attacked and murdered thousands of European settlers and black Kenyans who worked for them. This violence was only to end in 1963 with Kenyan independence.

- In Malaysia, a bitter war was fought between the British and Malaysian communists. By 1957, the communists had been defeated and the newly-independent state of Malaysia was created as a non-communist state.

Question time

In the year 2000 a number of votes were taken across the world to select the 'Most Admired Person of the Twentieth Century'. In many of these polls the person who came out top was Mahatma Gandhi.

Using the information on page 241, write a speech which explains why Gandhi should be considered one of the most important people of the twentieth century.

It wasn't just the British who encountered difficulties in ending their empires. The French were less willing to let their colonies have independence. In south-east Asia, the French army fought a bitter war in Vietnam against the Vietminh led by Ho Chi Minh. At Dien Bien Phu in 1954, the French suffered a humiliating defeat when their forces were surrounded and forced to surrender. This surrender was to have serious consequences because it led to US involvement in the region.

Even more serious for the French was the problem they faced in Algeria. In 1954 the Algerian organisation, the FLN, launched a campaign against the European settlers and French forces. A bitter struggle followed and divided France as some French people felt that Algeria should be given independence, whilst many others felt that France should keep Algeria at all costs. In the end, the French leader General de Gaulle decided that Algeria should join its North African neighbours, Tunisia and Morocco, as independent states. In 1962, the French withdrew and Algeria became independent.

Digging deeper

Vietnam

Before the Second World War, Vietnam in south-east Asia was a French colony. During the war the Japanese army occupied the country. Vietnamese communists (called Vietminh) led by Ho Chi Minh fought a war of resistance against the Japanese invasion. After 1945 the French returned to rule Vietnam but the Vietminh were unwilling to accept their rule. For nine years a costly war was fought, ending with French defeat at Dien Bien Phu in 1954. The country was divided between a communist North Vietnam and a capitalist South Vietnam.

The USA had supported the French in their fight against the communist Vietminh. The US President Truman believed in the 'domino effect' – that if Vietnam fell to the communists, other countries in the region (such as Cambodia or Thailand) might also fall. In 1955 a new President of South Vietnam, Ngo Dinh Diem, was chosen. He was given full military and financial support from the USA because he was anti-communist. Some South Vietnamese, known as the Vietcong and supported by Ho Chi Minh in the North, opposed Diem because they felt that his rule was too harsh. However US President J.F. Kennedy and his successor in 1963, L.B. Johnson were clear in their desire to protect the capitalist South.

In 1963 North Vietnamese gunboats in the Gulf of Tonkin attacked US ships. The USA responded by increasing military activity. In February 1965 US bombers launched huge raids on North Vietnam and Vietcong supply routes from North to South. The response of the Vietcong was to build a series of tunnels, 30,000 miles long. The supplies continued. Soon large numbers of US troops were sent to fight in Vietnam. By 1967 half a million troops were in the country. Many of these troops were young, often under the age of twenty, and many had been chosen by a system known as the draft. By this system young people in the USA were expected to register for the armed services and were called up when they were needed.

This system became unpopular and some Americans refused to register for the draft, including the boxer, Muhammad Ali.

In Vietnam, the US soldiers found it difficult to defeat the Vietcong. Many peasants in the countryside sheltered Vietcong fighters who would disappear into the jungle when the US troops attempted to find them. Many US troops were disturbed by the brutality of the war. Some took part in massacres such as the murder of 350 peasants in the village of Mai Lai in 1968. When the Vietcong attacked, as in the Tet Offensive of 1968, the Americans defeated them. However images on the television in the USA of young Americans being killed made the war increasingly unpopular. The USA used over 8 million tons of bombs in Vietnam. They also dropped chemicals such as 'Agent Orange' which were designed to kill the rainforest and so expose the Vietcong.

By 1973 the USA had withdrawn all of their troops from Vietnam and two years later the communist Vietcong had conquered South Vietnam. The war had resulted in defeat for the USA, the deaths of over 2 million Vietnamese people and 58,000 US soldiers. For the USA the attempt to contain the spread of communism in south-east Asia had failed. Not only did Vietnam become communist, so too did neighbouring Laos and Cambodia.

Coming to terms with the end

By 1960 it was clear that the days of European empires were numbered and this was recognised by most European politicians. In 1960, the British Prime Minister Harold Macmillan visited South Africa. In a speech to South African politicians he indicated that the days of empire were over (Source C).

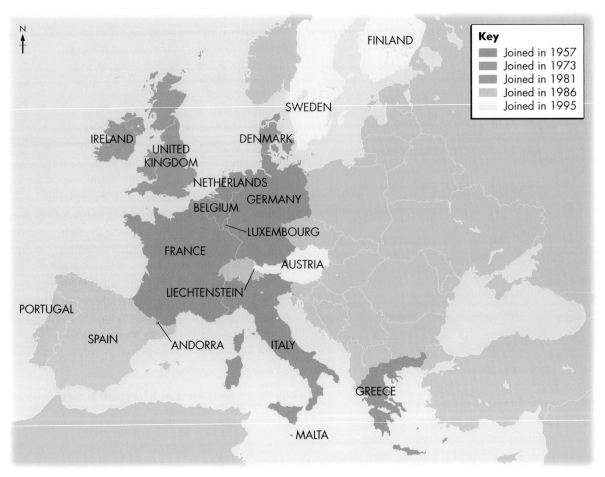

N
↑

FINLAND

Key
- Joined in 1957
- Joined in 1973
- Joined in 1981
- Joined in 1986
- Joined in 1995

SWEDEN

IRELAND
DENMARK
UNITED
KINGDOM
NETHERLANDS
BELGIUM   GERMANY
LUXEMBOURG
FRANCE
AUSTRIA
LIECHTENSTEIN
PORTUGAL
SPAIN   ANDORRA   ITALY
GREECE
MALTA

The European Union, initially set up in 1957 under the Treaty of Rome.

It took time for Britain, France and the other European colonial powers to come to terms with the loss of their empires. Britain attempted to keep a certain amount of influence by founding the British Commonwealth, an organisation comprising most of the states of the old British Empire. In 1956 Britain and France attempted to regain control of the Suez Canal in Egypt by force but were humiliated. It was clear that the time when they could act as they wished was over.

By the end of the twentieth century, the European powers had turned away from the idea of having an empire. In 1957, the Treaty of Rome was signed that set up the European Economic Community (EEC). This organisation aimed to promote greater European understanding, better trade links and the prevention of another war like those of 1914–18 and 1939–45. The original members included France and the Netherlands who had been colonial powers but now looked to European co-operation for their future. Britain did not join the EEC until 1973 and found the change from empire to Europe difficult. In 1993 the EEC became the European Community (EC), forming the basis for the European Union (EU). Its aim was for even greater political and economic union between European countries.

Independence from an empire

There are a number of different views on the idea of an empire. Those countries that suffered as a result of being ruled by another country have a very different view of their struggle for freedom from that of their colonial powers. Your task is to try to see if you can find different opinions about the same event.

Use an encyclopedia or the Internet to find as much information as you can about the people, event or group you want to research. Here are some examples:

- Subhas Chandra Bose
- the Amritsar massacre
- the militant Kenyan group, the Mau Mau.

The rise and fall of communism

As the European empires declined, other countries stepped in to try to influence how parts of Africa and Asia were run. After 1945 the two most powerful countries to emerge were the USA and the Soviet Union. These countries were run in very different ways.

- The USA was capitalist. In a capatalist country, people are free to make money as they wish. Businesses are owned privately.

- The Soviet Union was communist. Communism is the belief that property and business should be owned by the state on behalf of the people. It comes from the ideas of the nineteenth-century German writer and philosopher, Karl Marx. Marx believed that, because it was the workers who produced wealth through their hard work, then they ought to own the factories, and miners the mines. He believed that the only way this could come about would be through violent revolution.

In 1900, few people believed in communism and fewer would have guessed that by 1950 a large proportion of the world's people would live in countries with communist governments. The communists wanted to destroy the economic system of capitalism. Those countries that had a system of capitalism, such as the USA or Britain, were to become the strongest enemies of the Soviet Union.

The Russian Revolution of 1917

From 1914 the Russians were at war with the German and Austrian Empires (see Chapter 4). By 1917, life in Russian cities was very hard. There was a lack of bread and other basic foodstuffs. In 1917 there were two revolutions in Russia. In February a revolution broke out which ended with the overthrow of the Russian tsar (emperor), Nicholas II. A provisional government took over and promised that they would try to improve the situation, but Russia did not withdraw from the First World War and the problems remained.

Lenin and the Bolsheviks

At this time the Communist Party in Russia was called the Bolshevik Party and was led by Vladimir Lenin. He believed that the Bolsheviks should seize power by force. Although they were a small party, the Bolsheviks had the support of many workers in the main cities, and of soldiers and sailors who wanted an end to the war. These groups had their own organisations called Soviets.

In October 1917, Lenin persuaded other leading Bolsheviks that the time was right to take power. The Bolsheviks had control of the Soviets and the support of a large number of armed workers and soldiers. They seized the Winter Palace in the then Russian capital, Petrograd, and also the telephone exchange. Members of the government fled or were arrested. The revolution had succeeded and the Bolsheviks had taken power.

Once the Bolsheviks were in power they undertook the following policies in order to maintain their control:

- They had promised to end the war, and in April 1918 they signed the Treaty of Brest-Litovsk with Germany. Although they lost a large amount of land to the Germans, peace was achieved.

- They had promised to give the peasants land and the workers control of the factories. However, Lenin believed that this would happen in time. In the short term, he argued that the state should own and run factories on behalf of the people.

SOURCE A

The storming of the Winter Palace in Petrograd in 1917.

The governments of other states were frightened that a communist revolution would take place in their own countries. Lenin hoped that this might be the case because communist Russia had few friends abroad. However, revolutions failed in Germany and Hungary and Lenin's Russia became dangerously isolated.

In 1918 civil war broke out in Russia with the opponents of the communists, the Whites, being supported by non-communist countries such as Britain, the USA and Japan. Despite this foreign aid, the Whites were defeated. One of the Bolshevik leaders, Leon Trotsky, was put in charge of the communist army, the Red Army, and he turned it into an effective fighting force.

Lenin set up a secret police force, the Cheka, that was to unleash a reign of terror, known as the Red Terror, on all opponents of communism in Russia. By 1921, the communists (who had now changed their name from Bolsheviks) were more secure and the Whites and their allies were defeated.

Stalin and the Soviet Union

Following communist success in the civil war, areas that were captured became socialist republics. In 1924 these socialist republics joined together to form the Union of Soviet Socialist Republics (USSR), or Soviet Union. Lenin died in 1924 and was succeeded by Joseph Stalin. Stalin believed that all opposition to a communist government should be silenced. Up to 20 million Russians died in the 1930s in what became known as 'the purges' as Stalin tried to gain complete control over society. Stalin believed that all farms should be owned by the state and all farmers become workers on what were known as collective farms. Anyone who opposed this move was arrested.

He also believed that the Soviet Union needed to build up its industry. From 1928 huge projects were undertaken such as the Dneiper Dam, and the country's coal, iron, oil and electricity industries grew rapidly. However, the growth seen in the 1930s was at the expense of the country's population which worked hard for little reward or even as near slave labour in labour camps.

The Second World War

In 1939, Stalin signed a pact with Nazi Germany (see Chapter 5). The aim behind this was to buy time for the Soviet Union in the face of Nazi expansion. However, in June 1941 Germany invaded the Soviet Union in what became a desperate battle between the ideologies of Nazism and communism. By fighting the Nazis, the Russians became the allies of its ideological enemies, capitalist Britain and (from when it joined the war in December 1941) the USA. Ideological differences were set aside in the cause of defeating the Nazis. From 1943 the tide of war turned and it was clear that the Nazis would eventually be beaten. Soviet troops slowly pushed the German army back and by 1944 had started to liberate the countries of eastern Europe from Nazi rule.

The thoughts of the Allies then turned to the shape of post-war Europe. In February 1945, Britain, the USA and the Soviet Union met at Yalta in the Soviet Union to discuss a number of issues including the future of Poland. Britain and the USA wanted a democratically-elected government in Poland. However, the communists believed that only communists should stand as candidates. Arguments about the future of Europe were sharper at the Potsdam Conference in July/August 1945. By then Soviet troops were in Berlin and had occupied much of eastern Europe.

The spread of communism and the Cold War

Having worked together as Allies against Nazi Germany, differences and hostility began to develop between the two ideologies of capitalism (the USA, Britain and France) and communism (the Soviet Union). Stalin believed that the Soviet Union would be secure only if it turned the countries of eastern Europe into communist states, to act as 'buffer zones' between it and the capitalist countries of the west. Between 1945 and 1948 politicians in Poland, Czechoslovakia, Romania, Bulgaria and Hungary who opposed communism were arrested and disappeared. Elections were held but were fixed in favour of the communists. By 1948 these countries had 'puppet' governments under the control of the communist Soviet Union. In Germany the Soviets controlled the eastern half of the country including part of the capital Berlin which was deep inside the Soviet zone. In a speech made in 1946 Churchill referred to this (Source B), saying that an 'iron curtain' had come down across the continent of Europe, dividing the communist countries of eastern Europe from the west. In 1947 there was much support for communism in France and Italy, and in Greece communists attempted to take over. The US President Truman was so worried about the spread of communism that he developed the idea of containment – that the USA and the non-communist world should try to contain communism and prevent it from spreading.

The struggle between communism and capitalism for influence around the world became known as the Cold War.

Soviet control of eastern Europe in 1945.

Key
- Countries under influence of Soviet Union
- Other communist countries
- Non-communist countries
- — Iron curtain
- 1945 Date when communist government was established

From Stettin in the Baltic to Trieste in the Adriatic, an iron curtain has descended across the continent. The communist parties, which were very small in all of these eastern states, are seeking everywhere to obtain control.

Extract from a speech by Winston Churchill in 1946.

Stalin wanted to make sure that communism was secure in eastern Europe at all costs. Increasingly tension grew between the Soviets and the USA and their allies. This was focused in Berlin which had been divided into four zones in 1945. The USA decided that the best way to prevent countries in western Europe becoming communist was to help their economies recover. In 1947 the USA introduced the Marshall Plan by which the USA gave US$13,000 million to western European countries including the western part of Germany.

The communists could not compete with this kind of generosity. Stalin felt threatened and in June 1948 he cut all road and rail links to the Allied-controlled West Berlin. The western powers responded by setting up an airlift to fly supplies to the citizens of West Berlin. By spring 1949, 8000 tonnes of supplies were being flown in every day. The airlift lasted until May 1949, when Stalin called off the blockade. Stalin had seen that the West would not give in but the blockade had ended any chance of Berlin being united.

The Berlin Wall

Berlin remained a source of tension throughout the Cold War. In 1953 Stalin died and was replaced by Nikita Khrushchev as Soviet leader. Khrushchev stated that he wanted to live in peaceful co-existence with the West, but he was not prepared to see communism undermined. An attempt by the Hungarians to have greater freedom from the Soviet Union was crushed by tanks in 1956. Khrushchev also believed that the western powers should withdraw their troops from Berlin. Large numbers of Germans living in communist East Germany were using Berlin to escape to the West – over two million people escaped up to 1961. Many of these were skilled workers that East Germany could ill afford to lose. Khrushchev's reaction was to encourage the East German government to build a barrier in Berlin to divide the east and west sectors of the city. On 13 August 1961 the East Germans erected a barbed wire border, which three days later became a 45-kilometre concrete wall. The flow of people escaping to the West was stopped.

The nuclear threat

This division between East and West was to be made far more serious by the existence of the atom bomb. In 1945, the USA exploded two nuclear bombs in Japan at Hiroshima and Nagasaki to end the war (see Chapter 5). Communist spies in the USA were able to smuggle the secrets of how the bomb worked into the Soviet Union, and in 1949 the Soviet Union tested their first atom bomb.

The non-communist countries of Europe and North America feared Soviet military power and in 1949 formed the North Atlantic Treaty Organisation (NATO). The communists responded in 1953 by setting up their own organisation, the Warsaw Pact. The two sides had formed into two military blocks. Over the next 35 years, an arms race developed between the two sides, each attempting to produce bigger and more deadly weapons than the other. Rockets, which were used at the end of the Second World War, were developed to carry nuclear warheads. Both sides invested huge amounts of money into developing the next generation of nuclear weapons.

Supremacy in space

As part of the struggle for supremacy, both sides took the first steps in attempting to explore space. At first the Soviets were more successful in their programme. In October 1957, they launched the first satellite into space, called Sputnik. US attempts to follow suit failed. In 1961, the Russian, Yuri Gagarin was the first man in space. It seemed that the communist world had surpassed the USA in technology and science. In 1961, the new US President J. F. Kennedy, promised that the USA would put a man on the moon. Sure enough, in 1969, the Apollo 11 mission successfully landed there and Neil Armstrong was the first human being to walk on the moon.

The fall of communism

By the late 1960s, it was clear that the US economy was much stronger than that of the Soviet Union. The system created by Stalin in the 1930s was not capable of producing the consumer goods which were available in the west. The system needed reforming. However, from 1964–85 there was very little change in the Soviet Union. It was felt that if the communist system underwent reform, it might collapse. For a time in the 1970s, the two countries attempted to improve relations with what was known as *détente* (which means 'loosening' or 'relaxing').

By the 1980s, the Soviet Union was unable to compete with the USA. By 1980 the Soviet Union was spending 12 per cent of its national budget on defence, which amounted to more than double that of the USA. In 1980, Ronald Reagan became President of the USA with the promise that the United States would spend even more money on weapons and technology. As part of this programme, Reagan proposed the Strategic Defence Initiative (SDI), known as Star Wars. He wanted to spend billions of dollars on developing a defence system that could destroy Soviet nuclear missiles in space. The Soviets simply could not compete.

Gorbachev: perestroika and glasnot

By 1980 the communist system was under pressure in eastern Europe. In Poland a non-communist trade union called Solidarity, led by an electrician called Lech Walesa, demanded that the country's communist government allow greater political freedom. Solidarity was attacked by the communist government and many of its leaders were imprisoned. However, it showed again that the communist system was in need of reform.

In 1985 Mikhail Gorbachev became leader of the Soviet Union. He believed that it was time to try to reform the communist system. His economic restructuring was called 'perestroika'. He believed that the Soviet Union could survive only if its economy was rebuilt. Since the days of Lenin, people in communist countries had been denied the right to speak out freely. Gorbachev believed that this damaged communism, and he insisted on greater openness or 'glasnost' in Soviet life. The arms race was destroying the Soviet economy and Gorbachev made it a priority to negotiate a reduction in nuclear arms with the USA. This he did successfully in 1987.

The problem for Gorbachev was that reform did undermine the communist system. People wanted to see the benefits of reform much more quickly than it was happening and Gorbachev came under attack. In addition, in December 1988 he made it clear that the Soviet Union would no longer send tanks into eastern European countries to enforce communism. Once this became clear, events moved fast.

- In May 1989 the Hungarian government opened its border with non-communist Austria. This was the first breach in the iron curtain.

- In May 1989 the communists were defeated in elections in Poland. Solidarity formed the first non-communist government in the country since 1945. It was clear that communism in eastern Europe was under threat.

- In November 1989 the Berlin Wall was pulled down. The communists were thrown out of power in Czechoslovakia in what was known as the Velvet Revolution, as the move to democracy happened peacefully and with no violence.

Demands for the end of communist control then spread to the Soviet Union itself. After the Second World War Stalin had insisted that independent countries such as Latvia, Lithuania and Estonia were made part of the Soviet Union. They now demanded their independence. Boris Yeltsin challenged Gorbachev's rule. Yeltsin had been a communist but he now stood against those who tried to restore communism. In August 1991 the communists who wished to see a return to the old days tried to seize power. Yeltsin personally took control of the forces in Moscow who were against the attempted take-over. The plot failed and by the end of the year the Soviet Union had begun to break up. By the end of 1991 the Soviet Union fell apart when communism collapsed.

Lech Walesa addressing a Solidarity meeting.

Digging deeper

Communism in China

It was not just in Europe that communism spread. From 1927 Chinese communists led by Mao Zedong challenged the government led by Chiang Kai-shek. A long guerrilla war ended in 1949 with the communists taking control of the country.

Although they were both communist states, the Soviet Union and China did not get on. Mao introduced reforms similar to those of Stalin. In 1958, collective farms were set up and industries were built in what was known as the Great Leap Forward. Just as Stalin had destroyed all opposition in the 1930s, so Mao removed all potential enemies during 1966–9 in what became known as the Cultural Revolution.

The non-communist world was very concerned at the development of a communist China. Between 1950 and 1953, the USA and its allies fought a war in Korea to prevent the spread of communism. They were opposed by communist Koreans and their Chinese backers.

After Mao's death in 1976, the new leader Deng Xiaoping moved away from the ideas of a communist economy and encouraged the introduction of an economy in which the state took less of a role and private property was allowed. However, the Chinese authorities did not change their attitudes to human rights, such as freedom of speech. On 3 June 1989 a large group of protesters demanding democracy met in Tiananmen Square in the Chinese capital Beijing. Their demonstration was crushed by government tanks. Communism in China had changed but had not collapsed.

Digging deeper

The fall of the Berlin Wall

For 28 years the Berlin Wall was the clearest symbol of the divisions between East and West. It cut the city in two where the two ideologies of communism and capitalism met. Some East Germans had attempted to climb the wall and even dug underneath it. However, if caught escaping they were liable to be shot, and around 200 Germans died in this way.

In May 1989 it was clear that the borders of eastern Europe were opening up. Thousands of East Germans travelled to Hungary in the hope of being able to cross the border into Austria, but only 4500 were allowed through. Across East Germany the voices were beginning to be heard of those who wanted an end to the communist system. In Leipzig thousands held peaceful demonstrations demanding the freedom to speak, write, travel, dissent, discuss and vote.

Such was the weight of demonstrations that the East German government buckled under the pressure. On 9 November 1989, East German television announced that East Germans could travel to the West without any restrictions. The border was open. Thousands made their way through the checkpoints of the Berlin Wall to be met by thousands of joyful West Berliners. The West German government announced that every citizen from the East would be given DM 100 (around £35) to spend because the East German currency was virtually worthless. The shops of West Berlin were crammed as thousands of East Berliners bought items that were difficult to buy in the East.

At the centre of Berlin stands the Brandenburg Gate, a symbol of past Prussian and German might. For nearly 20 years it had sat in no man's land between East and West. Crowds began to climb on the wall in front of the gate, chipping away with hammers, chisels and anything they could find. It seemed that the Berliners would tear down the wall on their own.

On the evening of 11 November the wall began to be demolished mechanically, the city government pulling away the first concrete slab to the cheer of thousands of onlookers. As Christmas approached, so families divided by the wall could be re-united.

In celebration of the fall of the wall, the Berlin Philharmonic Orchestra, conducted by the famous German-American composer Leonard Bernstein, held a concert which included the playing of Beethoven's Ninth Symphony *Ode to Joy*. The words of the chorus were changed on this special occasion to include the word *freiheit* – freedom.

Activity time

From the text you have read so far try to organise the events of the period 1945–91 into the following categories:

- the Soviet conquest of eastern Europe by the end of the Second World War
- the arms race in the 1980s
- repression
- the demands of east Europeans for freedom
- successful revolutions.

Which events relate to the rise of communism, and which to its fall?

SOURCE D

The Berlin Wall being dismantled, November 1989.

8 Assessment section

In this chapter we have looked at two important developments in the twentieth century:

- the collapse of the empires built up by European powers in the nineteenth and early twentieth centuries

- the rise and fall of communism.

A turning point is a moment when history changes. In this chapter a number of turning points are explained. Your task is to identify those turning points that you think are most important.

- Choose *six* turning points (at least one concerning each of the developments above).

- Explain each turning point and say why you feel that it is important.

Project work: Then and Now

Many of the countries mentioned in the chapter have changed since the end of empire and the fall of communism. The aim of the project is for you to research the history of the country or countries of your choice *then* and *now*.

Choose your country or countries from this list:

- India

- Kenya

- Cyprus

- Germany

- Russia/Soviet Union.

To find information for your project, use this chapter, books in the local or school library or the Internet. Look for information about the country's history and some of its main features today. This might include its population size, the main cities and provinces, its rulers, its main industries and the crops grown in the country. You should also look at the culture of the country – what do people eat? What is the country famous for? Present your work as outlined below.

Section A – Then

Explain the history of the country over the past 100 years. This can be done by researching what you think are ten important events in your country's recent history.

Put the events you have chosen onto a timeline.

Explain the events you have chosen – what happened and what was the importance of that event.

Section B – Now

Explain what the country is like now. You can do this in a number of ways.

- Present your information as a factfile, with the information you have discovered neatly laid out.

- You might wish to write an article about the country of your choice which includes all the information you have researched.

Further reading

Boris Pasternack *Dr Zhivago* (Harvill Press, 1996)

Aleksandr Solzhenitsyn *A Day in the Life of Ivan Denisovich* (Penguin, 2000)

Index